To Effie, Mort, and
Jody, with love,

Don

9/3/85

COMPUTER LITERACY
with an introduction to BASIC programming

Neal Golden

HBJ **Harcourt Brace Jovanovich, Publishers**
Orlando   New York   Chicago   San Diego   Atlanta   Dallas

ABOUT THE AUTHOR

BROTHER NEAL GOLDEN, S.C.
Chairman, Department of Mathematics
and Computer Science
Brother Martin High School
New Orleans, Louisiana

CONSULTANT

DR. ANTONIO M. LOPEZ, JR.
Chairman, Mathematical Sciences
Department
Loyola University
New Orleans, Louisiana

EDITORIAL ADVISORS

R. LAWRENCE LISS
Manager of Student Information
Palm Beach County School District
West Palm Beach, Florida

BETTY VANDENBOSCH SHAW
Coordinator of Mathematics
Flint Community Schools
Flint, Michigan

MARY ANN NORTON
Program Director of Mathematics
Spring ISD
Houston, Texas

MURIEL THATCHER
Mathematics Supervisor/Computer
Specialist K–12
Scotch Plains-Fanwood Public Schools
Scotch Plains, New Jersey

APPLE is a registered trademark of Apple Computer, Inc.
ATARI is a registered trademark of Atari, Inc.
BANK STREET WRITER is a registered trademark of Broderbund Software, Inc.
COMMODORE is a registered trademark of Commodore Business Machines.
IBM is a registered trademark of International Business Machines Corporation.
SCRIPSIT and TRS-80 are registered trademarks of Tandy Corporation.

Printed in the United States of America

ISBN 0-15-359122-6

CONTENTS

Chapter 5:   Flowcharts and Programs 233

Flowcharts

Flowcharts to Programs

v

1

INTRODUCTION TO COMPUTERS

LESSONS

FEATURES

Universal Product Code

Computers and the Home

Binary System

1-1 WHAT IS A COMPUTER?

OBJECTIVE: **To list and explain the four functions of a computer**

IS IT A "SUPERBRAIN"?

Stories in books and movies and on television have given many people false ideas about computers. Some think of computers as "superbrains" that can think, walk, and talk. Actually, a computer has no mind of its own. It simply does what humans tell it to do. Any knowledge in a computer was put there by a person.

ARE THEY EXPENSIVE?

Computers seem to be everywhere today. In the 1950's and 1960's, a computer cost millions of dollars and filled an entire room. Only government agencies, corporations, and universities could afford them. But today's computers are quite small and inexpensive.

ARE THEY REALLY EVERYWHERE?

Your school probably has at least one **microcomputer** which can easily fit on a desk. Some computers are small enough to fit in your hand! These tiny computers are found in digital watches, television sets, microwave ovens, video game machines, automobiles, and many other devices. For example, the computer in a microwave oven lets you set the oven to cook for a certain time at a specific temper-

ature. The computer in a video game tells the machine what to show on the screen, how to interpret a player's moves, how to keep score, when the game is over, and so on. It is safe to say that every person comes in contact with a computer almost every day.

WHAT IS A PROGRAM?

A television set or a microwave oven does only one job. However, a computer can do many things—play music, solve mathematics problems, write letters, monitor a patient's heart, and play chess. But when you switch on a computer, it will do nothing until you tell it what to do. A computer cannot "think" for itself. However, given a set of instructions to follow, a computer can calculate at lightning speed and make decisions based on those calculations. The set of instructions is called a **program.** Any computer must perform four functions.

a. Storage   b. Input   c. Processing   d. Output

Storage is listed first because any computer must have a built-in **memory.** Otherwise, any information you put into the computer will be lost. Using the first letter of each word, these four functions can be abbreviated as **SIPO.** Because even the smallest computer must have SIPO, we often talk of a "computer system" rather than of just a "computer."

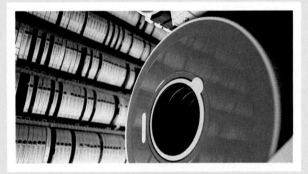

Programs are stored on tapes.

HOW DOES A COMPUTER WORK?

The way a computer works can be compared to the way a person solves a problem. Suppose you want to multiply 9 times 7. Your ears hear the problem or your eyes see it. This is the **input.** One part of your brain, the memory, remembers the numbers. This is the **storage.** Another part of your brain handles the job of multiplying the numbers. This is the **processing.** Your mouth speaks the answer or your hand writes it. This is the **output.**

WHAT IS A COMPUTER SYSTEM?

Now let's compare this with a **computer system.** The diagram below will help you follow what a microcomputer does. You first type the instructions (the *program*) on a keyboard. This is the input. The "joy sticks" or "game paddles" that are used with video games are another method of input.

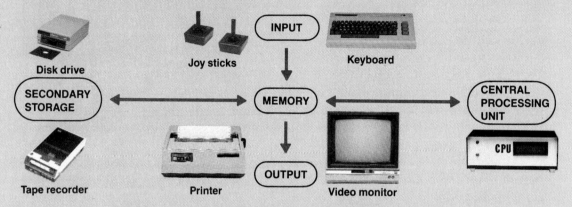

Disk drive

SECONDARY STORAGE

Tape recorder

Joy sticks

INPUT

Keyboard

MEMORY

Printer

OUTPUT

Video monitor

CENTRAL PROCESSING UNIT

CPU

What you type automatically goes into the computer's memory. The computer's memory is the storage. What you put into the computer will be lost, however, when the computer is turned off. Because of this, some systems can record what was placed in memory on a **magnetic tape** or a **diskette (disk).** This is referred to as **secondary storage.** This allows you to save programs and data outside the computer.

HOW LARGE IS THE MEMORY?

The size or capacity of the memory in a computer is described as being "8K," "16K," "32K," "64K," and so on. The **K** (from "kilo-") means a factor of about 1000. Thus a "16K" computer has about 16,000 positions of memory. Each memory location can hold a digit or a letter or any one symbol that you type.

WHAT IS A MICROCOPROCESSOR?

Once a program is in memory, the **central processing unit (CPU)** can carry out (execute) what the program says to do. In today's computers, the CPU is a **microprocessor.** This is a tiny chip that can fit on your thumb.

The CPU can do millions of computations in one second. Although shown to one side in the diagram above, the CPU is actually the logical center of any computer. It tells all the other parts of the system what to do.

WHAT IS A CRT?

The output from a program is shown on a display screen, which is formally known as a **cathode ray tube (CRT).** If the computer has a printer, then the output can be printed.

WRITTEN EXERCISES

Classify each part of a computer system as **A** *(input),* **B** *(storage),* **C** *(processing), or* **D** *(output). Some items may belong in more than one category.*

1. keyboard   **2.** joy stick   **3.** memory   **4.** magnetic tape

5. microprocessor   **6.** disks   **7.** printer   **8.** cathode ray tube

Complete each statement in Exercises 9-18.

9. A computer cannot think for itself but instead must have a __?__ to follow.

10. Anything typed on the keyboard will go into the computer's __?__ .

11. What you put in a computer's __?__ is lost when the machine is turned off.

12. "K" refers to the size of a computer's __?__ .

13. "K" comes from the prefix __?__ and stands for a factor of about __?__ .

14. The logical center of any computer is the __?__ .

15. "CPU" stands for __?__ .

16. A program is executed by the __?__ of the computer.

17. The CPU is a __?__ , a tiny integrated circuit chip.

18. A TV screen is formally known as a __?__ .

19. Where do computers get their knowledge?

20. List four devices that usually contain computers.

21. State a basic difference between the work done by a computer and the work done by a television set or a microwave oven.

22. Compare the way a person computes 9×7 with the four functions of a computer.

23. How can you save a program from being lost when a computer is turned off?

COMPUTER LAB ACTIVITIES

Learning About Your Computer

Because there are different kinds of microcomputers, it is important for you to learn how the computer you are using works. The following exercises will help you to learn this.

1. **a.** Find the CRT (or monitor) for your computer. Does it have a separate on–off (power) switch? If so, where is it?

   b. If the monitor is not already turned on, turn it on.

2. **a.** Find your computer's on–off switch. Where is it located?

   b. If the computer is not on, turn it on. If it is on, turn it off and then on again.

   c. When you turn your computer on, is there a light that indicates that the computer is on? If so, where is the light? Does the light stay on as long as the computer is on?

   d. When the computer is turned on, how long does it take before something appears on the screen? What does appear on the screen?

3. **a.** Is there a disk drive connected to your computer? If so, does the disk-drive have a separate on–off switch? If it does, where is it located?

   b. If the disk drive is not on, turn it on. (A small red or green light may come on to show that the disk drive is in operation.)

   c. Is there a second disk drive connected to the computer? If so, does it have its own power switch? If it does, where is it located?

   d. If the second disk drive is not turned on, turn it on.

4. **a.** Is there a printer connected to your computer? If so, where is its power switch located?

   b. If the printer is not on, turn it on. Does a light appear to show that the printer is receiving power?

5. If your computer has any other parts, such as a cassette recorder, turn each of them on until all parts of the system are receiving power.

6. Turn off all of the computer parts you have turned on.

1-2 HARDWARE AND SOFTWARE

OBJECTIVES:

To state the basic differences mainframes, minicomputers, and microcomputers

To state how storage, input, processing, and output relate to a program

Computer hardware comes in three basic sizes.

MAINFRAME

A **mainframe** is a very large computer. This type fills an entire room and costs hundreds of thousands of dollars. A mainframe is like an octopus because many machines are connected to it. Some of these machines are terminals. Information can be fed into the one large mainframe through each terminal. These terminals may be in another room, another building, another city, or on another continent. Mainframes are found at universities, banks, and government agencies. Airlines keep track of flight reservations by means of terminals in many cities that are connected to a mainframe computer.

MINICOMPUTERS

Minicomputers came into use in the early 1970's. These computers were about the size of an office desk. Since these systems cost $15,000 or less, many more businesses could afford computers. A minicomputer cannot store as much information as a mainframe. However, a minicomputer may have terminals connected to it. Thus, a minicomputer is simply a small mainframe.

MICROCOMPUTERS

In 1975, the first **microcomputer** was developed. These computers are small enough to fit *on* a desk. Since microcomputers could be purchased for less than $1,000 and today, for less than $100, individuals and families could afford computers. Thus, the terms **personal computer** and **home computer** have come to mean the same as "microcomputer."

SOFTWARE

So far the discussion has centered on <u>hardware</u>, the electronic units themselves: keyboards, CRT's, CPU's, printers, and so on. But hardware is useless without <u>software</u>. **Software** refers to the programs which tell the computer what to do. As one writer stated: "A microcomputer without software is like a record player without records."

PROGRAMS

Computers do not yet understand English. To "talk" to a computer you must speak its language. The most common language for microcomputers is **BASIC** (Beginners' All-purpose Symbolic Instruction Code). This is the language that will be taught in this course. A **program** is a list of commands to a computer to solve a problem. To illustrate a computer language, here is a short program in BASIC. This program will find the sum of any three numbers.

```
10 INPUT A, B, C
20 LET S = A + B + C
30 PRINT "SUM = ";S
40 END
```

Even this short program uses the four parts of any computer system (**SIPO**). The program consists of four **statements** (commands). Each statement is numbered. In Chapter 2, you will learn why the statement numbers are multiples of 10.

INPUT AND STORAGE

The first statement, **INPUT A, B, C**, tells the computer to accept any three numbers that are typed on the keyboard and to remember them. NOTE: Any letters could be chosen to represent the three numbers.

PROCESSING

The next statement, **LET S = A + B + C**, is the processing step. This tells the computer to add the three numbers and to call the answer S.

OUTPUT

Statement 30, **PRINT "SUM = "; S**, produces the output. It will display the answer on the CRT screen. If the computer has a printer, it can print the value calculated for S.

Statement 40, **END**, tells the computer to stop.

After writing this program on paper, you would sit at the keyboard and type it exactly as it appears at the right.

```
10 INPUT A, B, C
20 LET S = A + B + C
30 PRINT "SUM = "; S
40 END
```

Once entered, the program might produce these results.

RUN   ←——— **Type RUN to tell the computer to execute the program that is stored in its memory.**

?. 7.5,6.3,1.4 ←——— **The computer will now show a ?. You type the numbers.**

SUM = 15.2 ←——— **The computer will display the answer.**

]   ←——— **This symbol means that the computer is ready for another command.**

NOTE: Some computers print **READY, OK, >**, or some other symbol that means the same as].

OPERATING SYSTEM

One special program is the oper-ating system. This is the "master" program that must be in the computer to make it function when you turn it on. The **operating system** controls the way parts of the computer system communicate with each other. Without the operating system, the computer cannot accept and run any programs.

Depending on the computer, the operating system may already be in memory when you turn on the machine or it may be on a **diskette** ("floppy disk"). In this second case the operating system is called a **disk operating system (DOS)**.

BOOTING

To "boot" a computer means to load its operating system. To boot some machines, all you need do is turn them on. Other computers load the system from a disk.

MEMORY

The memory of a a microcomputer is divided into RAM and ROM. **RAM** stands for **random-access memory.** ROM means **read-only memory.** ROM contains information that stays in memory even when the computer is turned off. The operating system may be in ROM, along with the BASIC inter-preter. (The BASIC **interpreter** is the program that accepts and carries out BASIC commands.) Since it contains information the computer must have to work, ROM is "off–limits" to the user. The user's programs and data go into RAM, which is empty when the machine is turned on. The program and data are erased when the computer is turned off. When a computer is described as "16K" or "48K," that usually refers to the amount of RAM.

Computer tapes are stored in a library.

WRITTEN EXERCISES

Match each of Exercises 1–8 with one of the following.

a. Mainframe **b.** Minicomputer **c.** Microcomputer

1. Size of a desk **2.** Fills a room

3. Can fit on a desk **4.** First developed in 1975

5. Personal computer **6.** Costs over $100,000

7. Airline reservation system **8.** Home computer

Complete each statement.

9. The most common programming language for microcomputers is ___?___ .

10. A list of commands to a computer to solve a problem is a ___?___ .

11. The electronic units of a computer system are known as ___?___ .

12. Computer programs are referred to as ___?___ .

13. The ''master'' program that controls the computer is the ___?___ , which is either in memory when you turn on the computer or on a ___?___ that you put into the machine.

14. DOS stands for ___?___ .

15. Getting a computer ready to work is called ___?___ the computer.

16. ''RAM'' stands for ___?___ .

17. ''ROM'' stands for ___?___ .

For Exercises 18–20, tell whether each statement refers to RAM or ROM.

18. Holds information that stays in memory even when the computer is turned off

19. Is off-limits to the user

20. Contains information that is erased when the machine is turned off

21. Classify each of the first three statements of this **BASIC** program as input, storage, processing, or output. A statement may fit into more than one category.

```
10 INPUT X, Y
20 LET Z = X - Y
30 PRINT "ANSWER IS ";Z
40 END
```

COMPUTER LAB ACTIVITIES

Your Computer Keyboard

1. Turn on your computer and its monitor.

2. When a computer is ready to receive commands in the **BASIC** language, it displays a special symbol such as] or › or the word **READY**. What is the ''ready'' symbol on your machine?

3. A computer also uses a symbol called a **cursor**. This is usually an underline (___) or a solid block (■). The cursor marks your place as you type on the screen.

  a. What is the cursor symbol on your computer?

  b. Does the cursor flash on and off?

4. Type **NEW** on your computer keyboard. Do the letters appear as capital letters or as small letters?

> NOTE: If your answer is ''small letters'', go on to Exercise **5**.
> If your answer is ''capital letters,'' omit Exercise **5** and go on to Exercise **6**.

5. a. Look for a key marked **SHIFT LOCK**. Press the key. Then look for a key marked **DEL** (meaning **DEL**ete). Press this key three times. The cursor should move to the left and erase the letters you typed in Exercise **4**.

b. If there is no **DEL** key, look for a key marked with a **left arrow** (◄—). Press the key three times to move the cursor back to the beginning of the line. Type the word **NEW** again. Are the letters N, E, W capital letters? If they are, go on to Exercise **6**. If they are not, go on to Exercise **5c**.

c. If the letters in Exercise 5b are not capital letters, use the **DEL** or ◄— key to move back to the beginning of the line. Hold down the **SHIFT** key and type **NEW**. Does **NEW** now print in capital letters?

6. a. Look at the right end of the keyboard. Is there a key labeled **RETURN**? If so, press the key. What happens on the screen? If the keyboard has a **RETURN** key, you must press it at the end of <u>each</u> line you type.

> NOTE: If your computer does *not* have a **RETURN** key, go on to Exercise **6b**. If your computer has a **RETURN** key, you have now completed this set of exercises.

b. If your computer has no **RETURN** key, look for a key labeled **ENTER**. Press the key. What happens on the screen? If the keyboard has an **ENTER** key, you must press it at the end of <u>each</u> line you type.

> NOTE: If your computer does *not* have an **ENTER** key, go on to Exercise **6c.** If your computer has an **ENTER** key, you have now completed this set of exercises.

c. If your computer has neither a **RETURN** nor an **ENTER** key, look for a key that is labeled something like this: ◄—┘ Press the key. What happens on the screen? If your computer has such a key, you must press it at the end of <u>each</u> line you type.

1-3 HISTORY OF COMPUTER HARDWARE

OBJECTIVE: **To have a basic understanding of the history of the development of computer hardware**

ABACUS

Throughout history people have worked with numbers. The oldest known calculating device is the **abacus**. It was used by the Chinese as early as 2600 B.C. At the age of 19, **Blaise Pascal** (1623–1662) built the first mechanical adding machine. In 1671, **Gottfried Leibniz** (1646–1716) developed a machine that could multiply and divide as well as add and subtract.

PUNCHED CARDS

In 1801, **Joseph Jacquard** (1752–1834) used a roll of **punched cards** to feed instructions to a textile loom to weave designs. He used the cards to communicate with the machine. The language consisted of two "words": *hole* and *no hole*. This approach is still the basis of our communication with computer equipment.

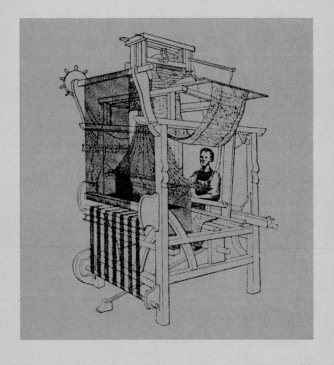

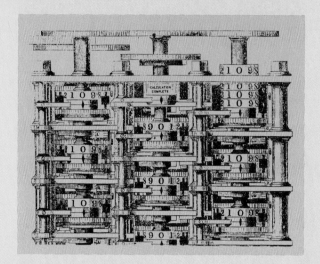

ANALYTICAL ENGINE

A person far ahead of his time was **Charles Babbage** (1791–1871). He had the idea of a computer that would solve equations. He spent his life trying to build this machine which he called the **analytical engine**. Unfortunately, his computer was never finished because the electronic and mechanical knowledge that was needed to build the computer had not been invented.

STATISTICAL MACHINES

In 1887, the U. S. Census Bureau finally completed the 1880 census. Because of the rapid growth of the population, it was feared that the 1890 census might not be finished within the required ten years. Fortunately, **Herman Hollerith** (1860–1929) invented the first statistical machines using punched cards. With his devices, the U. S. Census Bureau finished the 1890 census in one-fourth the time needed for the 1880 census even though the population in 1890 was 25% more than the population in 1880.

Herman Hollerith started a company which eventually (1924) became <u>International Business Machines Corporation (IBM)</u>. From 1900 to 1940, punched card equipment spread to more and more offices around the world. However, except for Babbage's dream, actual computers did not enter the picture until World War II.

MARK I

In 1944, a team of scientists at Harvard University led by **Howard Aiken** completed an electromechanical computer named **MARK I**. Aiken based its design on Babbage's plans. The five-ton machine contained 760,000 parts and about 500 miles of wire!

ENIAC

Meanwhile, another group was at work at the University of Pennsylvania on a truly electronic computer named **ENIAC** (Electronic Numerical Integrator And Calculator). Led by **John W. Mauchly** (1907–1980) and **J. Presper Eckert** (1919–) this team finished ENIAC in 1945 and delivered it to the U.S. Army. ENIAC was 1000 times faster than MARK I. Costing $500,000 and weighing 30 tons, ENIAC filled a basement. It was so large you could walk inside it. It could multiply two ten-digit numbers in 0.002 second. Yet this is not even as fast as today's pocket calculators!

STORED PROGRAMS

One member of the ENIAC team was **John von Neumann** (1903–1957). ENIAC had to be rewired after every program. John von Neumann's idea was to feed the program into the computer and to keep the program in memory with the data. This is known as the **stored program concept**.

UNIVAC I

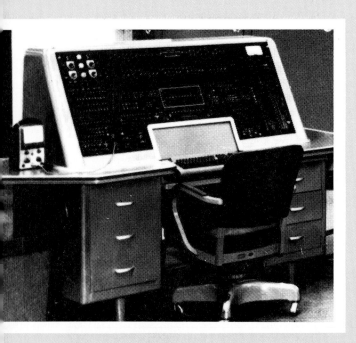

John Mauchly and J. Presper Eckert went to work for *Remington Rand* (now called *Sperry-Rand*), where they developed **UNIVAC I** (**UNIV**ersal Automatic Computer). This was the first computer made by a private company. In 1951, the first UNIVAC was delivered to the Census Bureau. Three years later, General Electric's Louisville plant became the first business installation to buy a computer. "Experts" predicted that as many as 50 companies would install computers.

TIME–SHARING

By the 1960's, computers were fast enough to make **time–sharing** possible. (See the diagram at the top of the next page.) In a time-sharing setup, terminals are connected by telephone lines to a central computer that can execute dozens of programs at the same time. Each customer shares the cost of the computer by paying only for the time the customer uses. Before microcomputers (1975), time–sharing gave many schools access to computers.

COMPUTER GENERATIONS

Computer scientists speak of four generations of electronic computers.

Generation	Starting Date	Principal Component	Timing Unit
First	1945	vacuum tube	millisecond (thousandth of a second)
Second	1958	transistor	microsecond (millionth of a second)
Third	1964	large-scale integrated circuits (LSI)	nanosecond (billionth of a second)
Fourth	1975	very large-scale integrated circuits (VLSI)	picosecond (trillionth of a second)

FIFTH GENERATION

It is generally agreed that the present microcomputers are the fourth generation. It is also agreed that the fifth generation computers will understand spoken language and be as simple to use as a telephone. In 1981, the Japanese Information Processing Development Center announced a plan for the development of a fifth generation computer. This project is expected to take ten years. Some experts say that such a computer is 25 years away. The United States government and large corporations are also working at the present time to build a fifth generation computer.

WRITTEN EXERCISES

Match each name on the left with the invention on the right.

1. Blaise Pascal
2. Howard Aiken
3. Charles Babbage
4. Herman Hollerith
5. Gottfried Leibniz
6. John W. Mauchly
7. J. Presper Eckert
8. Joseph Jacquard
9. John von Neumann

a. ENIAC
b. abacus
c. MARK I
d. analytical engine
e. loom operated by punched cards
f. first mechanical adding machine
g. first machine to multiply and divide
h. first statistical machines using punched cards
i. stored program concept

Complete each statement.

10. The oldest known calculating device is the __?__ used by the __?__ as early as 2600 B.C.
11. Hollerith's machines were first used at the U.S. __?__ .
12. Hollerith started a company which in 1924 became __?__ .
13. MARK I was completed in the year __?__ at __?__ University by a team led by __?__ .
14. The design of MARK I was based on the plans of __?__ from the previous century.
15. ENIAC was finished in the year __?__ at the University of __?__ .
16. When finished, ENIAC was delivered to the __?__ .
17. The first computer made by a private company was __?__ , which was short for __?__ and which was made by __?__ Company.
18. In a __?__ set-up, many users with terminals connect by telephone lines to a large computer.
19. The largest computer manufacturer is __?__
20. The principal electronic component of first generation computers was the __?__ .
21. The principal component of second generation computers was the __?__ .
22. The third generation of computers began in the year __?__ . The principal electronic component was the __?__ .
23. The fourth generation of computers began in the year __?__ .

Copy and complete this time–line. The time–line refers to the history of the development of computer hardware.

Year	Event
24. 2600 B.C.	Chinese invent the __?__.
25. 1642 A.D.	__?__
26. 1671	__?__
27. __?__	Jacquard programs a textile loom using punched cards.
28. 1871	__?__
29. 1887	__?__
30. 1924	__?__
31. 1944	__?__
32. __?__	First electronic computer, ENIAC, is completed.
33. 1951	__?__
34. 1958	__?__
35. __?__	First third generation computers are built.
36. 1975	__?__
37. 1981	__?__

38. What ''language'' did Jacquard use to communicate with his loom?

39. What is the advantage of a time–sharing system?

40. What two features will fifth–generation computers have?

What part of a second is each of the following?

41. microsecond   **42.** nanosecond   **43.** picosecond

MORE CHALLENGING EXERCISES

Briefly give the contributions of these individuals to the development of computer science. Research will be necessary.

44. Lee DeForest   **45.** John Atanasoff

46. Maurice Wilkes   **47.** Vannevar Bush

48. Thomas J. Watson, Sr.   **49.** James Powers

50. Alessandro Volta   **51.** Jack Kilby

52. John Bardeen, Walter Brattain, and William Shockley

Your Computer Keyboard

A **program** *is a set of instructions for a computer. Although you have not learned the meaning of the terms used in the program shown below, the following exercises will help you to become familiar with the keyboard on your computer.*

This **BASIC** program will find the sum of three whole numbers. Follow these instructions.

```
10 INPUT A, B, C
20 LET S = A + B + C
30 PRINT "SUM = ";S
40 END
```

1. a. Type lines 10–40 exactly as they appear.

   b. Remember to press **RETURN, ENTER,** or ◄─┘ after you enter each line. Each line will appear on the screen. Each zero will probably appear on the screen with a slash through it (∅).

     i. The large key across the bottom of the keyboard is called a **space bar.** When you press it, the **cursor** moves one space to the right.

     ii. If you type a letter or symbol incorrectly, look for a key marked **DEL** (for **DEL**ete). If there is such a key, press it. The cursor should move left one space and it will "erase" the symbol that was there.

       If there is no **DEL** key, look for a key marked ◄─. If there is one, press it. The cursor should move left one space. The previous symbol may not be erased but you can now type over the symbol.

2. a. When you have typed the lines of the program, type **RUN.** Press **RETURN** (or **ENTER,** or ◄─┘). A ? (question mark) should appear under the word **RUN.**

   b. Type 7, 6, 5 (including the commas) and press **RETURN.** The computer should print **SUM = 18** and then display its "ready" symbol. If it does, you have entered and **RUN** your first program of this course!

3. Type **RUN** again. When the question mark appears, type 7.5,6.3,1.4 (including the commas) and press **RETURN.** The computer should display **SUM = 15.2** followed by its "ready" symbol.

4. a. Type **NEW** (and press **RETURN** or **ENTER** or ◄─┘).

   b. Enter the program shown on the right. Type **RUN** and press **RETURN.** When the ? appears, type 1987, 888. Then press **RE-TURN.**

```
10 INPUT X, Y
20 LET Z = X - Y
30 PRINT "ANSWER IS ";Z
40 END
```

COMPUTERS AND THE HOME

In time the computer will become a standard part of the home, just as the telephone, radio, and television set have become.

Doing Homework

Laurie Wilson is writing a report on the fishing industry in Maine. To obtain information, she uses the microcomputer in her room which is connected to a nationwide **telecomputing** service. From a list of choices on the screen, she selects the encyclopedia **database**. She then types **FISHING IN MAINE**. A portion of an encyclopedia article on Maine appears on the screen. Instead of copying this information, she presses a key and obtains a printout. To get additional information, she selects a **knowledge-index program**. This program produces a list of titles of books and magazine articles on the topic.

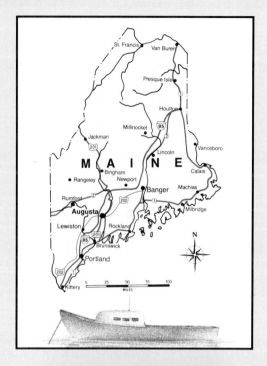

Shopping at Home

Harry Carlton's home computer is tied in with a major department store. With this service, he is able to see a complete catalog of the items that the store carries. After selecting a category, he views the products on the computer screen, decides what he wants, and presses the appropriate button. The items he choses will be delivered to his home. When he presses the button, a "chip" inside his computer identifies him from the millions of other credit-card holders who use this service. Thus, the cost is automatically charged to his credit-card.

PROJECTS

1. Obtain the names and addresses of at least two telecomputing services available in your area. Make a list of the services that each provides.

2. List the advantages and disadvantages of a computer-based shopping at home service.

1-4 COMPUTER LANGUAGES

OBJECTIVE: To be aware of the different languages that are used by computers

Ada Lovelace (1815–1852), a friend of Charles Babbage, was the first computer programmer. She wrote an explanation of how his analytical engine could be programmed to solve problems in mathematics. The programming language developed in 1979 for the U. S. Defense Department was named **Ada** in her honor.

MACHINE LANGUAGE

The first computers, like **ENIAC** and **UNIVAC I**, had to be programmed in "machine language." This language consists only of numbers and differs from machine to machine. An example of a short program in machine language is shown below.

NOTE: This program will work only on machines with a 6502 micro-processor. Also, you <u>cannot</u> enter this program or the other programs in this lesson into a BASIC–speaking computer and run them.

Machine Language	**Assembly Language**
20FDE3	CRLF=$E9F0
8500	RBYTE=$E3FD
20F0E9	NUMA=$EA46
20FDE3	JSR RBYTE
F8	STA 00
18	JSR CRLF
6500	JSR RBYTE
8501	SED
20F0E9	CLC
A501	ADC 00
2046EA	STA 01
18	JSR CRLF
90FD	LDA 01
	JSR NUMA
	LOOP
	CLC
	BCC LOOP

ASSEMBLY LANGUAGE

In the early 1950's, **Grace Hopper** (1906-   ) developed a program for the UNIVAC to translate from letter abbreviations to machine language. For example, **REA** could be used for **read, PRT** for print, and **STA** for **store the accumulator.** Her work started a trend that has made programming less technical.

Grace Hopper at work on a manual tape punch.

FORTRAN

At IBM in 1954, the first "high–level" programming language called **FORTRAN** (**FOR**mula **TRAN**slator) was developed. With FORTRAN, engineers and other scientists could write programs without being machine language specialists. A high-level language contains some English words but they must be used in a precise way. It was only a short step from machine language to assembly language, but it was a long step from assembly language to FORTRAN.

```
      INTEGER F,S,R
      READ (5,10) F
      READ (5,10) S
10    FORMAT (I2)
      R = F + S
      WRITE (6,20) R
20    FORMAT(' THE ANSWER IS ',I3)
      END
```

COBOL

In 1960, a committee organized by the Defense Department produced a computer language for business called **COBOL** (**CO**mmon **B**usiness-**O**riented **L**anguage). Grace Hopper was a member of this committee. COBOL programs have sentences and paragraphs. Here is a short COBOL program.

```
01   PROGRAM-VARIABLES.
     05   FIRST-NUMBER          PIC 99.
     05   SECOND-NUMBER         PIC 99.
     05   RESULT-OF-ADDITION    PIC 999.
PROCEDURE DIVISION.
MAIN-PARAGRAPH.
     ACCEPT FIRST-NUMBER.
     ACCEPT SECOND-NUMBER.
     ADD FIRST-NUMBER TO SECOND-NUMBER GIVING
RESULT-OF-ADDITION.
     DISPLAY 'THE ANSWER  IS ' RESULT-OF-ADDITION.
     STOP RUN.
```

BASIC

BASIC was created in 1965 at Dartmouth College. It has been the primary language for time–sharing and for microcomputers. (You saw a **BASIC** program on page 8.) The main advantage of a high-level language like **BASIC** is that most computers will understand it. After learning to program in **BASIC,** you can run your programs, with little or no change, on almost any microcomputer.

PASCAL

In 1971, the **Pascal** language (named for the great mathematician mentioned on page 13) was developed in Switzerland. It has become popular in the United States, especially in college computer science departments. Here is a short Pascal program.

```
PROGRAM ADDEM;
VAR F, S, R : INTEGER;
BEGIN
   READ (F);
   READ (S);
   R := F + S;
   WRITELN (' THE ANSWER IS ', R)
END.
```

LOGO

In the early 1970's, **LOGO** was developed at the Massachusetts Institute of Technology (MIT) by a group led by Seymour Papert. This language is used mainly in elementary schools. It features

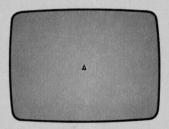

"turtle graphics," named after a symbol called a "turtle" that the programmer can move around the screen.

TRANSLATION

Each computer still has its own **numerical language.** You might think that languages like **BASIC** and Pascal have removed any need for machine language programming. However, many video game programs are written in machine language because the computer can execute such programs faster. This is because the program is already in the language that the machine understands. Each command of a **BASIC** program must be translated by another program called an **interpreter** before the machine can execute it. The interpreter is in the computer's ROM or loaded from a disk. This **translation** step adds to the time the computer takes to run the program.

You do not have to know a programming language in order to use computers. A person without any knowledge of programming or the inner workings of computers can run software written by someone else.

ALL THAT A COMPUTER USER MUST LEARN

1. How to turn on the computer.
2. How to load and run a program from a tape or a disk.
3. How to give the program any information it needs.

However, it is important for you to learn a programming language. First, programming in any language trains you to think logically and precisely. Secondly, if you can write programs yourself, you will not always have to depend on others to program for you. That is why, starting in Chapter 2, you will learn how to program in **BASIC**.

WRITTEN EXERCISES

Match each item on the left with a programming language on the right.

1. Developed in 1954 at IBM
2. Consists of numbers only
3. Produced in 1960 for business use
4. Named for the first programmer
5. The first "high–level" language
6. Created in 1971 in Switzerland
7. Born at Dartmouth College in 1965
8. One step above machine language
9. Developed at MIT in the early 1970's
10. Needs no translation for the computer to understand it
11. Primary language for microcomputers
12. The only language of ENIAC
13. Features "turtle" graphics

a. Machine language
b. FORTRAN
c. COBOL
d. BASIC
e. Pascal
f. Ada
g. Assembly language
h. LOGO

State what each of these stands for.

14. COBOL   15. FORTRAN   16. BASIC

Complete each statement.

17. An explanation of how Babbage's analytical engine could be programmed was written by __?__ .

18. **COBOL** was produced by a committee organized by the __?__ .

19. An important member of the **COBOL** committee was __?__ .

20. A **BASIC** program must be translated by a program called an __?__ .

21. A person can use computers without knowing how to __?__ .

22. A group led by Seymour Papert developed the language __?__ .

Copy and complete this "time–line." The time–line refers to the history of the development of computer software.

Year	Event
23. __?__	Ada Lovelace, the first computer programmer, is born.
24. 1951	__?__
25. 1954	__?__
26. __?__	**COBOL** is produced.
27. 1965	__?__
28. 1971	__?__
29. 1979	__?__

30. What trend was started by the work of Grace Hopper in the early 1950s?

31. What are two advantages of a "high–level" programming language?

32. Why is machine language still used for some programs?

33. List two reasons why it is important for a person to learn to program.

34. List three tasks that a computer user must know how to do.

MORE CHALLENGING EXERCISES

35. Give the names of three programming languages not mentioned in the lesson. If the name is an abbreviation, also give the complete name.

Go to a library or some other source to find out the name of the programming language invented by these individuals.

36. John Backus   37. John Kemeny and Thomas Kurtz   38. Niklaus Wirth

COMPUTER LAB ACTIVITIES

How Fast is Your Computer?

EXPLORE

*Although you have not learned the meaning of the terms used in the program shown below, the exercises will help you to understand how fast your computer can perform computations. Remember! After you type in a line of instructions, press the **RETURN**, **ENTER**, or ⬅ key. Each line will appear on the screen. Each zero will probably appear on the screen with a slash through it (∅).*

1. The **BASIC** program at the right adds the whole numbers from 1 to 50. Enter (type) this program into your computer exactly as it is listed here. (If necessary, see page 20.)

```
10 LET S = 0
20 FOR I=1 TO 50
30 LET S = S + I
40 NEXT I
50 PRINT "SUM IS ";S
60 END
```

2. Before typing **RUN**, guess how many seconds it will take the computer to add the 50 numbers.

3. Type **RUN**. About how many seconds does it take the computer to add the 50 numbers?

4. Change the program so that it adds the whole numbers from 1 to 100. To do this, type **20 FOR I = 1 TO 100**. Then type **RUN** again. About how many seconds does it take for the computer to add the 100 numbers?

5. Experiment by having the computer add the first 150 numbers, the first 300 numbers, the first 500 numbers, the first 1000 numbers, and so on. (See Exercise 4). Now complete this sentence.

   It takes the computer about 2 seconds to add the first __?__ numbers.

Did You Know?

The **Universal Product Code (UPC)**, or "bar code," is a pattern of black and white bars found on cereal boxes, paperback books, and other items sold in stores.
The checkout clerk passes the UPC over a **laser scanner**. The scanner "reads" the bar codes and sends them to a computer. The computer <u>translates</u> the code into an item description and looks up the price. This information then appears on a view screen where the customer can see it. The information is also printed on the cash register tape that the customer receives.

BINARY SYSTEM

Computers store numbers in a form that corresponds to the **on** and **off** states of electronic circuits. Because the method that is used is based on the two digits 0 and 1, it is called the **binary system**.

Imagine four lights side-by-side as in the diagram below.

8　　　　4　　　　2　　　　1

Each light can be turned on independently of the others. When a light is on, it represents the number listed under it. Any whole number from zero through fifteen can be coded by using combinations of the four lights.

EXAMPLE 1　Which lights should be turned on to represent 9?

Solution:　**9 = 8 + 1**. So turn on the "**8**" and "**1**" lights.

8　　　　4　　　　2　　　　1

What the lights above show can be translated into a binary code by using the digits 0 and 1.

1: Light is **on**.
0: Light is **off**.
Thus, in Example 1, the binary code for
ON OFF OFF ON　is
1 0 0 1.

	Light Position			
	8	4	2	1
On/Off	ON	OFF	OFF	ON
Code	1	0	0	1

EXAMPLE 2 Write the binary code for 13.

Solution: $13 = 8 + 4 + 0 + 1$
So the binary code is **1 1 0 1**.

	Light Position			
	8	4	2	1
On/Off	ON	ON	OFF	ON
Code	1	1	0	1

EXAMPLE 3 For what number is 1 0 1 1 the binary code?

Solution: 1   0   1   1
$8 + 0 + 2 + 1 = $ **11**

	Light Position			
	8	4	2	1
Code	1	0	1	1
Number	8	+0	+2	+1

Each time you type a number on a computer keyboard, the circuits translate the number into binary form and store it in memory. Since letters and special characters such as =, ?, or + must also be stored, more than four binary positions (**bits**) are needed. The common micro-computer code is **ASCII** (American Standard Code for Information Interchange). Here are the ASCII versions of some characters.

Character	ASCII code	Character	ASCII code
A	0 1 0 0 0 0 0 1	F	0 1 0 0 0 1 1 0
M	0 1 0 0 1 1 0 1	T	0 1 0 1 0 1 0 0
(	0 0 1 0 1 0 0 0	+	0 0 1 0 1 0 1 1

PROJECTS

1. Write the binary code for each whole number from 0 to 31. (Hint: Five bits will be needed. The value of the fifth binary position from the right is 2^4, or 16.)

2. Find the meaning of the word "byte."

3. Does your computer use the ASCII code? If not, what code does it use? Give some examples of how characters are stored in that code.

4. Find information about the octal system. Write the octal code for each whole number from 0 to 31.

5. Find information about the hexadecimal system. Write the hexadecimal code for each whole number from 0 to 31.

1-5 COMPUTERS IN DAILY LIFE

OBJECTIVES:

> To be aware of career areas that are computer-related
>
> To be aware of the types of tasks that are appropriate and those that are not appropriate for computers

Computers can do some things better than humans. There are other jobs that computers cannot do as well as humans. For the present, these tables summarize what computers can and cannot do well.

Computers are good at jobs that involve:	Examples
Repeating the same actions	Painting cars
Large amounts of calculation	Keeping a spacecraft on course
Storing large amounts of data	Storing income tax records

Computers are NOT good at jobs that require:	Examples
Judgment	Choosing a new dress
Creativity	Producing a new recipe
Handling unforeseen situations	Refereeing a hockey game

Suppose that you owned a business.

Jobs you would use a computer for:	Jobs you would NOT use a computer for:
Compute and print the paychecks of your employees	Decide which employees to hire or promote
Keep your inventory; that is, how many of each item you sell are on hand	Make the final decision on a site for your new store
Print bills to your customers and record their payments	Compose a jingle for a radio commercial

Computers have made some jobs <u>easier</u>. If there were no computers:

- The telephone company could not keep track of all the long distance calls that are made.

- Air traffic controllers could not safely direct all the take–offs and landings at airports.

- Banks could not handle all the checks that are written.

Air Traffic Control Center

Computers have made some jobs <u>possible</u>. If there were no computers:

- Doctors could not do three-dimensional brain scans or install artificial hearts.

- Spacecraft could not have sent pictures from Mars and Jupiter back to Earth.

- The United States could not have put men on the moon.

Photo of Mars from Viking 2

Do computers take jobs from humans? The best answer is "yes and no." Computers do eliminate some jobs. Many low-level tasks are now done by computers. Operating an assembly–line and monitoring intensive care equipment in hospitals are examples of these jobs. Many companies have reduced the number of secretaries because word processors allow fewer people to produce more work.

Computers have created new jobs. For example, more people now design, build, program, sell, service, and operate computers. Generally, these jobs require more education than those eliminated by computers. Here are some of these new jobs.

Year	Number of Computer–Related Jobs
1970	765,000
1978	1,158,000
1990	2,140,000

Electrical engineers design computers and related equipment. They have college degrees in engineering.

Computer technicians assemble, test, and repair computer equipment. They have electronics training but not college degrees.

Programmers create computer software. They usually have a degree in computer science.

Systems analysts advise businesses on which computer system to buy and what programs will be needed to solve that company's data processing problems. Systems analysts often start as programmers and have college degrees in computer science, accounting, business, or some related field.

Computer salespersons sell computers in computer stores or through visits to businesses. Such persons do not need the technical schooling of engineers or programmers. They are usually trained by their company.

Computers provide job opportunities for the handicapped. Here mouthstick is used to punch computer terminal keys.

Computer operators run mainframes and minicomputers. They load programs and data from cards, tapes, or disks and make sure that all parts of the system are running smoothly. They are not programmers and generally do not need a college degree. Usually, they are trained by their company.

Data entry clerks punch programs and data into cards or onto tapes or disks for input to computers. They must be good typists, but special knowledge of computers is not required.

Many times you hear someone complain that "the computer made a mistake." Actually, when a bill or report card from a computer is wrong, it is usually because a human made a mistake. The error could be either of two types.

1. Incorrect data was entered into the computer. For example, a charge of $10.78 was typed as $107.80.
2. The program contains a mistake (**bug**). For example, a long distance call on Sunday costs less than a weekday call, but the programmer did not tell the computer this.

WRITTEN EXERCISES

1. List three types of jobs that computers do well. Give an example of each type.
2. List three types of jobs that computers do <u>not</u> do well. Give an example of each type.
3. List three jobs that the head of a business would use a computer to do.
4. List three jobs that the head of a business would not use a computer to do.
5. List three jobs that computers have made easier.
6. List three achievements that would have been impossible without computers.
7. What is the best answer to this question. "Do computers take jobs from humans?" Explain.
8. Give two examples of jobs that have been eliminated by computers.

Briefly explain how each of the following careers involves computers.

9. Electrical engineer
10. Computer technician
11. Programmer
12. Systems analyst
13. Computer salesperson
14. Computer operator
15. Data entry clerk

16. Which occupations in Exercises 9–15 usually require a college degree?
17. When someone claims that "the computer made a mistake," who or what usually made the error?
18. What are two types of errors humans make that cause wrong output from computers?

Which of these jobs would computers do relatively well?

19. Predict the weather
20. Control traffic lights
21. Judge an art contest
22. Direct a play
23. Track stolen vehicles
24. Store recipes
25. Design other computers
26. Diagnose illnesses
27. Compose music
28. Play music
29. Tell time
30. Make speeches
31. Play chess
32. Teach you how to play chess
33. Control the air–conditioning in a hotel
34. Produce the checkout bills in a supermarket

COMPUTER LAB ACTIVITIES

Loading Your Computer

EXPLORE: SAVING PROGRAMS

If your computer has a disk drive, start at Exercise 1.
If your computer does not have a disk drive, start at Exercise 5.

1. If your computer has a disk drive attached to it, obtain a disk from your teacher that contains one or more **BASIC** programs. Usually, each machine has some kind of **LOAD** command that tells the computer's operating system to copy a program from the disk and place it in memory. Ask your teacher how to use the necessary commands to load and **RUN** one of the programs on the disk.

2. To learn how to save a program on a disk, follow this procedure.

   a. Enter the program at the right.

   b. **RUN** the program. The output should be the whole numbers from 1 to 10. (Running the program is a check on whether it has been entered correctly.)

   ```
   10 FOR I=1 TO 10
   20 PRINT I
   30 NEXT I
   40 END
   ```

   c. If the output is correct, obtain a disk from your teacher that can be used to save the program.

      Usually, each computer has some command such as **SAVE** for copying a program from the computer's memory onto the disk. After deciding on a "file name" for the program, ask your teacher how to save the program onto the disk.

3. Each disk operating system has a command such as **CATALOG** or **DIR** (for **DIR**ectory) for obtaining a listing of the names of the files stored on the disk. With the help of your teacher, obtain a directory of the files on the disk. Check that the program you just saved is listed in the directory.

4. When the program is on the disk, use the commands from Exercise 1 above to load the program. **RUN** the program again.

5. If your computer has a tape recorder attached to it, obtain a tape from your teacher that contains one or more **BASIC** programs. Then apply the steps of Exercises 1–4 above to load a program from the tape, **RUN** the program, and save a program to tape.

Chapter Summary

Section 1–1

1. The earliest computers were large and expensive. Today computers are small and inexpensive.

2. A computer cannot think for itself. It can only follow the instructions given in a program.

3. Even the smallest computer is a **system** that consists of four components: **storage, input, processing, output.** The major forms of input are keyboards, magnetic tapes, diskettes and joy sticks. The major methods of output are **CRT screens** and **printers.** Storage is divided into main (memory) and secondary.

Section 1–2

4. Computers come in three sizes: **mainframes, minicomputers,** and **microcomputers.** Computer hardware is useless without software.

5. A **program** is a list of commands a computer can follow to achieve a goal. To function, a computer must have a master program called the **operating system.**

Section 1–3

6. The major people who influenced the pre–20th century history of computing are Blaise Pascal, Gottfried Leibniz, Joseph Jacquard, Charles Babbage, and Herman Hollerith. The major figures in 20th–century computing are Howard Aiken, Ada Lovelace, John Mauchly, J. Presper Eckert, Grace Hopper, and John von Neumann.

7. There have been four generations of computers.

Section 1–4

8. The major high–level computer languages are **FORTRAN, COBOL, BASIC, Pascal,** and **LOGO.**

Section 1–5

9. Computers are ideal for jobs that involve repetition, considerable calculation, or handling large amounts of data.

10. Computers have made some jobs easier. They have made other tasks possible. Computers have eliminated some jobs, but computers have also created new jobs.

11. Major careers involving computers include electrical engineer, computer technician, programmer, systems analyst, computer salesperson, computer operator, and data entry clerk.

Chapter Review

Complete each of Exercises 1–18 with the correct term or terms from the following list.

Ada	Hollerith	machine	software
Babbage	Hopper	mainframe	Sperry Rand
BASIC	IBM	memory	storage
billionth	input	millionth	thousandth
circuits	integrated	operating	time-sharing
COBOL	language	output	transistor
ENIAC	Leibniz	Pascal	tube
FORTRAN	Lovelace	processing	vacuum

1. The four functions that any computer must perform are __?__ .
2. A large computer system is called a __?__ .
3. A computer's main storage area is called __?__ .
4. The person who planned the analytical engine was __?__ .
5. The U.S. Census of 1890 was completed in record time due to machines invented by __?__ .
6. A programming language that was created in Europe but is now popular in the United States is __?__ .
7. Before microcomputers, __?__ gave many schools access to computers.
8. Grace Hopper helped create a language for business programming called __?__ .
9. A language developed at IBM in 1954 was __?__ .
10. LET P = A + B + C is a statement of the programming language __?__ .
11. The programs that tell computer hardware what to do are classified as __?__ .
12. The principal electronic component of the first generation of computers was the __?__ .
13. The principal component of second generation computers was the __?__ .
14. A nanosecond is one– __?__ (what fraction) of a second.
15. Third generation computers featured __?__ as their main component.
16. The first computer programmer who had a programming language named for her was __?__ .
17. The only language a computer can understand without translation is its __?__ .
18. Developed at the University of Pennsylvania, the first electronic computer was __?__ .

Give the meaning of each of these.

19. CRT   **20.** RAM   **21.** IBM

22. COBOL   **23.** FORTRAN   **24.** BASIC

Match each item on the left with its corresponding date on the right.

25. MARK I		**a.** 1642
26. UNIVAC I		**b.** 1671
27. Pascal's adding machine		**c.** 1801
28. Jacquard's loom		**d.** 1887
29. Hollerith's tabulating machines		**e.** 1924
30. FORTRAN		**f.** 1944
31. ENIAC		**g.** 1945
32. BASIC		**h.** 1951
33. COBOL		**i.** 1954
34. Leibniz's calculator		**j.** 1960
35. First microcomputer		**k.** 1965
36. Pascal language		**l.** 1971
37. IBM formed		**m.** 1975

Which of these jobs do computers do relatively well?

38. Store student records   **39.** Compute missile paths

40. Grade essays   **41.** Record long–distance calls

42. Correct multiple-choice tests   **43.** Carve statues

Briefly explain what a person in each of these occupations does.

44. Computer technician   **45.** Systems analyst

Chapter Test

For Exercises 1–18, match each item with the corresponding name or term in **a–y.**

1. A programming language invented at MIT

2. The part of memory where a user may store programs

3. The name for about 1000 memory positions

4. One-millionth of a second

5. One step higher than machine language

a. Herman Hollerith

b. COBOL

c. Ada Lovelace

d. time-sharing

e. LOGO

6. The first computer programmer

7. A programming language developed for business in 1960

8. The abbreviation for a computer video screen

9. A system that allows many people to use the same computer at the same time

10. The oldest high–level programming language

11. A programming language named for the inventor of an adding machine

12. The woman who made assembly language possible

13. The master program that must be in the computer when it is turned on

14. Any very large computer

15. A person who advises businesses concerning which hardware and software to purchase

16. The electromechanical computer built at Harvard by a team led by Howard Aiken

17. The Census Bureau employee who invented the first statistical machines using punched cards

18. The inventor of the stored program concept

f. CPU

g. John von Neumann

h. nanosecond

i. MARK I

j. Grace Hopper

k. assembly language

l. BASIC

m. ENIAC

n. mainframe

o. systems analyst

p. RAM

q. operating system

r. ROM

s. CRT

t. minicomputer

u. microsecond

v. Jacquard

w. 1K

x. FORTRAN

y. Pascal

For Exercises 19–21, give the meaning of each of these.

19. DOS   20. CPU   21. ROM

22. List the four functions that any computer system must perform.

23. Give two examples of jobs that computers do well.

24. Give two examples of jobs that computers do *not* do well.

25. Explain the difference between computer hardware and software.

26. Explain briefly how electrical engineers are involved with computers.

27. Why is machine language still used for some programs, especially for game programs?

28. Explain how a person with no knowledge of programming can use a computer.

29. Name two kinds of errors made by computer users that can cause incorrect output from the computer.

30. Why has the number of computer–related jobs increased over the last few years?

FEATURES

Synthesizer
Mouse
Digital Watch
Word Processing
Computers and Typing

LESSONS

2-1 DIRECT COMMANDS

OBJECTIVE:

To use PRINT statements as direct commands

To "talk" to a computer, you type on its keyboard. The computer "talks" to you on its screen. When a computer is ready to "listen" to you, it displays a special word or symbol. Some computers print]; others show a >. Some print **READY**. In any case, the symbol or word is called the "ready prompt." It prompts or cues you to enter a new command or program.

NOTE: Some computers skip a line before printing the ready prompt.

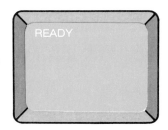

As you type on a computer keyboard, a special symbol called a **cursor** marks your place on the screen. The cursor is usually an underline (_) or a solid block (■). On many machines, the cursor flashes on and off.

Suppose that you type **PRINT "HI"** and stop. The computer does nothing. It is waiting for you to finish your sentence. To do this, you do not type a period. Instead you press a special key. This key is usually near the right end of the keyboard. On most machines, this key is labeled **RETURN**. On others, it is labeled **ENTER**. On some machines, there is a broken arrow (↵) on the **RETURN** key.

Suppose that you type **PRINT "HI"** and press the **RETURN** (or **ENTER**) key. The computer immediately carries out this command and displays **HI** on the screen right below what you typed. **PRINT "HI"** is a **direct command** which the machine executes immediately.

A **BASIC** direct command has these properties.

1. It has no number in front of it.

2. The computer forgets a direct command as soon as it has executed it. If you want the machine to "say" **HI** again, you must type **PRINT "HI"** and press **RETURN** another time.

3. If a program (or part of a program) has been entered into the memory of the computer but is not presently being **RUN**, the machine can carry out most direct commands without harming the program. An exception to this is the command **NEW** which will be explained later in this chapter.

When you type a command, you must type the exact words. If you do not, the computer will not understand the statement and will print **?SYNTAX ERROR** or some such message. **Syntax** refers to the **rules** of a language. If you type a command that contains a syntax error, you do not "hurt" the computer. It simply prints **?SYNTAX ERROR** or a similar message and its ready prompt. Then it waits for your next instruction. You can then type the command correctly and see whether it is executed correctly.

```
"PRINT GO!"
?SYNTAX ERROR
READY
```

EXAMPLE 1 Which commands are correct and contain no syntax errors?
Give a reason for each answer.

	Command	Correct?	Reason
a.	PRENT "YES"	No	**PRINT** is misspelled.
b.	PRINT "YES INDEAD"	Yes	Although **INDEAD** is misspelled, it is inside the quotation marks. The computer will print the words **YES INDEAD** as typed.
c.	"PRINT ?????"	No	**PRINT** must be outside the quotation marks.
d.	PRINT "HELLO	Probably	Many computers will assume that the other " is at the end of the line.

The computer prints whatever is typed inside quotation marks after the word **PRINT**. It does <u>not print</u> the quotation marks.

NOTE: On computer keyboards there is no difference between the open quotation mark and the closed quotation mark. Both are typed with the same key.

EXAMPLE 2 Write the exact output of each command.

Command	Output
a. PRINT "LET'S GO!"	LET'S GO!
b. PRINT "$123.50"	$123.50
c. PRINT "S P A C E S"	S P A C E S
d. PRINT "SPELLED RONG"	SPELLED RONG

NOTE: To produce the output shown in Example 2, you must end each command by pressing the **RETURN** (or **ENTER**) key.

The computer will pay attention to any blanks inside quotation marks in a **PRINT** command. However, blanks between **PRINT** and the quotation marks usually make no difference. On most machines, **PRINT"START"** will have the same effect as **PRINT "START"** or **PRINT "START**. However, **P R I N T "START"** usually is a syntax error. That is, do not put spaces <u>within</u> the BASIC word **PRINT**.

WRITTEN EXERCISES

Complete each statement.

1. The special symbol or word a computer displays to indicate it is waiting for you is called its __?__ .

2. As you type on a computer keyboard, your place on the screen is marked by a symbol called the __?__ .

3. Each line you type on a computer keyboard must be ended by pressing the __?__ key.

4. A statement such as **PRINT "HELLO"** (without a number in front of it) is called a __?__ .

5. The rules of a language are called its __?__ .

6. In a **PRINT** command, the computer will pay attention to any blanks __?__ quotation marks.

For Exercises 7–18, state which commands are correct and contain no syntax errors. Give a reason for each answer.

7. PRINT "MONDAY

8. PRINT "TUSDAY"

9. PRINT "I LOVE BASIC".

10. PRIMT "FINISHED"

11. PRINT "READY"?

12. "PRINT AUGUST"

13. PRINT "PRINT"

14. PRINT"E.T. CALL HOME"

15. "PRINT "I'M TIRED"

16. PRINT"HELLO THERE!"

17. PRINT "YOU RANG?"

18. P R I N T "YES"

For Exercises 19–24, write the exact output of each command.

19. PRINT "OK"

20. PRINT"OK, BOSS?"

21. PRINT "I'M A COMPTER"

22. PRINT " SPLENDID!"

23. PRINT "★★★★★ "

24. PRINT "?/%&"

Did You Know?

Commands

Answer these questions for the computer you are using.

1. What is the computer's ready prompt?

2. Does the computer skip a line before printing its ready prompt?

3. Does the computer keyboard have a **RETURN** key? If so, where is it?

4. Does the computer keyboard have an **ENTER** key? If so, where is it?

5. Where is the quotation mark key on the keyboard? Do you have to hold down the **SHIFT** key in order to type the quotation mark?

6. Exactly what does the computer print when a command contains a syntax error?

*Enter into a computer the commands of Example 1 on page 41. Remember to press the **RETURN** or **ENTER** key after each command.*

7. For commands **a** and **c** of Example 1, does your computer print

   ?SYNTAX ERROR

   or some such message?

8. Does your computer execute commands **b** and **d** of Example 1?

9. Enter into a computer the commands of Example 2 on page 42. Is the output for each command the same as the output shown in Example 2?

10. Enter into a computer the commands of Exercises 7–18 on page 43. Did you correctly predict which commands would contain syntax errors?

EXPLORE: VARIATIONS IN PRINT COMMANDS

11. The BASIC "spoken" by one computer model is not exactly the same as the BASIC spoken by another type of computer. For example, many computers allow a ? in place of the word **PRINT**. Instead of typing **PRINT "HELLO"**, enter ? **"HELLO"** into a computer. Does the computer accept the substitution?

*For Exercises 12–17, type each command into a computer. For which statements does the computer print **?SYNTAX ERROR** or a similar message?*

12. PRINT HELLO

13. PRINT "HELLO

14. PRINT HELLO"

15. PRINT"HELLO"

16. P RINT "HELLO"

17. PRINT "HELLO""

2-2 FIRST PROGRAMS

OBJECTIVE:

> **To write the output of programs containing PRINT and END statements**

After the computer executes a direct command, that command is no longer in memory. To keep commands in memory, you must put them into a program. To do this, you use a <u>statement number</u>.

```
10 PRINT "START THE PROGRAM."
```

After you type this line and press **RETURN** (or **ENTER**), nothing happens on the screen. However, the computer has put statement 10 into its memory. To prove this, type the direct command **LIST**. The computer will print back any lines of the program you have entered. To complete this short program, type **20 END**.

To make the computer execute the program, type the direct command **RUN**. Now you will receive the output **START THE PROGRAM**. Each **PRINT** command or statement normally produces one line of output. When the computer reaches statement **20 (END)**, it prints its ready prompt and waits for your next command.

EXAMPLE 1   Write the output of each program.

Program	Output

a. 10 PRINT "THIS IS A"
   20 PRINT "SHORT PROGRAM."
   30 END
	THIS IS A
	SHORT PROGRAM.

b. 10 PRINT "* * * * *"
   15 PRINT "   *   "
   20 PRINT "   *   "
   25 PRINT "   *   "
   30 END
	* * * * *
	    *
	    *
	    *

NOTE: You can use counting numbers to number the statements of a program. Usually 99999 is the largest statement number allowed.

In each program of Example 1, the output is followed by the computer's ready prompt. That prompt is different for each type of machine. It is not actually produced by the program itself. For these reasons, it will not be included in any output shown in this book.

As with direct commands, the statements of a program must be typed exactly as shown. Otherwise, the computer will stop and print

?SYNTAX ERROR IN 10

(meaning statement 10) or some similar message when the program is **RUN**.

EXAMPLE 2   Correct any errors in the given program.

```
10 PRINT I SPEAK BASIC TO
20PRINT "MY COMPUTER AND"
30 PRINT  "SOMETIMES IT
40  PRINT "UNDERTANDS ME"!
50 END
```

Statement	Correction

`10 PRINT I SPEAK BASIC TO`
`20PRINT "MY COMPUTER AND"`
`30 PRINT  "SOMETIMES IT`
`40  PRINT "UNDERTANDS ME"!`
`50 END`
	10 PRINT "I SPEAK BASIC TO"
	None needed on most machines.
	None needed on most machines.
	40 PRINT "UNDERSTANDS ME!"
	None needed.

Here are some additional comments on the program of Example 2.

Statement	Comment
10	**I SPEAK BASIC TO** must be placed inside quotation marks.
20	Most computers will automatically add a space between 20 and **PRINT**.
30	Most computers will assume that there is another '' after IT.
40	Statement 40 contains two errors. **1.** The ! outside quotation marks is a syntax error. It would be caught by the computer. **2.** Misspelling **UNDERSTANDS** is not a syntax error, since the word is inside quotation marks. However, misspelling a word is an error to the programmer and should be corrected. NOTE: On most machines, the double space between 40 and **PRINT** will cause no problem.

EXAMPLE 3 Write a program to produce the output shown.

```
            X
        X       X
      X           X
    X               X
```

Program
```
10 PRINT "          X"
20 PRINT "      X       X"
30 PRINT "    X           X"
40 PRINT "X                 X"
50 END
```

NOTE: Most forms of **BASIC** allow you to omit the **END** statement. However, it is good programming practice to include it as the last statement of every program.

WRITTEN EXERCISES

Complete each statement.

1. To keep commands in memory, you must put them into a __?__ .
2. In **10 PRINT "LET'S GO!"**, 10 is the __?__ .
3. To make the computer display the program in its memory, type __?__ .
4. To make the computer execute the program in its memory, type __?__ .
5. The last statement of every program should be __?__ .

For Exercises 6–11, which statements are direct commands?

6. LIST   **7.** PRINT "READY?"   **8.** 60 END

9. 20 PRINT "* * *"   **10.** RUN   **11.** 15 PRINT "YES"

For Exercises 12–17, write the output of each program.

12.
```
10 PRINT "I LOVE WEEKENDS,"
20 PRINT "DON'T YOU?"
30 END
```

13.
```
100 PRINT "ARE YOU"
200 PRINT "HAPPY?"
300 END
```

14.
```
10 PRINT "COM-"
20 PRINT "PUTERS"
30 PRINT "ARE"
40 PRINT "FUN."
50 END
```

15.
```
1 PRINT "SAN"
2 PRINT "FRANCISCO,"
3 PRINT "CALIFORNIA"
4 END
```

```
16. 10  PRINT  "  *  "
    20  PRINT  " * * "
    30  PRINT  "*   *"
    40  PRINT  " * * "
    50  PRINT  "  *  "
    60  END
```

```
17. 5   PRINT  "X       X"
    10  PRINT  " X     X"
    15  PRINT  "  X X"
    20  PRINT  "       X"
    25  END
```

Correct any errors in each program.

```
18. 10  PRINT  "* * * *"
    20  PRINT   * * * *
    30 PRINT   "* * * *
    40    PRINT * * * *"
    50 PRINT"* * * "*
    60  END
```

```
19. 10PRINT"GOOD MORNING!"
    15  PRINT "WHAT IS
    20    PRINT "YOUR NAME"?
    25  PRINT HOW ARE YOU
    PRINT   TODAY?"
    35  END
```

For Exercises 20–23, write a program to produce the output shown.

20. MY COMPUTER LOVES ME

21. HAIL TO THE CHIEF!

22. DON'T YOU LIKE
ICE CREAM?

23. GO,
TEAM,
GO!

MORE CHALLENGING EXERCISES

For Exercises 24–27, write a program to produce the output shown.

```
24. HELLO        25. H            26. ZZZZZ       27. # # # # # #
    E                I                Z               # # # # #
    L                  M              Z                # # # #
    L                    O            Z                 # # #
    O                M               Z                   # #
                                     ZZZZZ                #
```

*For Exercises 28–30, write a program as indicated. If you have access to a computer, **RUN** each program.*

28. Write a program that prints your initials in large block letters (like the Z in Exercise 26) across the screen or printer.

29. Write a program that prints a circle, or as close to a circle as can be produced, on your screen.

30. Write a program that prints a large X with the two "arms" crossing at about the middle of the screen or printer page.

COMPUTER LAB ACTIVITIES

First Programs

1. a. Enter this program into a computer. Remember to press **RETURN** or **EN-TER** at the end of each line.

```
10 PRINT "THIS IS A"
20 PRINT "SHORT PROGRAM."
30 END
```

b. When you have typed the three lines of the program, type **LIST**.

c. If a statement is incorrect, retype it correctly starting with the same statement number. Then **LIST** the program again.

d. When the program is correct, type **RUN**. The computer should display the output shown in Example 1a on page 45.

2. To erase the program of Exercise 1 from memory type **NEW** (or **SCRATCH** on some machines).

3. Type **NEW**. Then enter this program. **RUN** the program. Does it produce the required output?

```
10 PRINT "       X"
20 PRINT "    X    X"
30 PRINT "  X        X"
40 PRINT "X            X"
50 END
```

For Exercises 4–9:
*a. Enter and **RUN** the program of each exercise as indicated.*
b. State whether you predicted the output of each program correctly.

4. Exercise 12, page 47   **5.** Exercise 13, page 47   **6.** Exercise 14, page 47

7. Exercise 15, page 47   **8.** Exercise 16, page 48   **9.** Exercise 17, page 48

For Exercises 10–12:
*a. Enter and **RUN** each program you wrote.*
b. If necessary, make changes until the desired output is produced.

10. Exercise 20, page 48   **11.** Exercise 22, page 48   **12.** Exercise 23, page 48

EXPLORE: ? FOR PRINT

*In the EXPLORE on page 44, you learned whether your computer accepts ? in place of **PRINT** in direct commands. Now test whether the machine accepts ? for **PRINT** in a program.*

13. Type **NEW**. Then enter the program of Exercise 1 above. Type statement 10 as: **10 ? "THIS IS A"**. After all the statements have been entered, **RUN** the program. Did the computer accept the substitution?

14. Many computers that accept a question mark (?) for **PRINT** substitute the word **PRINT** when listing a program. **LIST** the program you revised in Exercise 13. What did the computer do?

2-3 EDITING PROGRAMS

OBJECTIVES:

> **To change, add, and delete statements of a program**
> **To use the system commands NEW, LIST, and RUN**

This is the program of Example 1a on page 45.

```
10 PRINT "THIS IS A"
20 PRINT "SHORT PROGRAM."
30 END
```

The statement numbers allow you to make changes in a program. For example, suppose you wanted to change the output as follows.

```
THIS IS A VERY
SHORT PROGRAM.
```

Simply type   **10 PRINT "THIS IS A VERY"**   . In the computer's memory, the new statement 10 now replaces the old 10. A program can contain only one statement 10.

If you type **LIST**, the computer will show the program with the new statement 10.

```
10 PRINT "THIS IS A VERY"
20 PRINT "SHORT PROGRAM."
30 END
```

If you wish to see only one statement of a program, type **LIST** followed by the number of that statement. For example, **LIST 20** causes the computer to display the current statement 20.

Another way to use statement numbers is in correcting a statement. Suppose that you accidentally type **30 EMD**. To correct the error, all you need to do is retype statement 30. In memory, the computer will replace the old statement 30 with the new one. Each computer usually has additional methods for changing lines (such as special keys like **DELETE** or **◄──**). But retyping the statement with the same line number will work on every system.

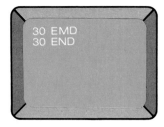

A statement could be added to the program on page 50 by typing **15 PRINT**. This "dummy" **PRINT** statement would cause the output to be double-spaced with a blank line between **THIS IS A VERY** and **SHORT PROGRAM**. Program statements, to start with, should be numbered by 10's so that space is left to add statements later. Typing **LIST** now would cause this output.

```
10 PRINT "THIS IS A VERY"
15 PRINT
20 PRINT "SHORT PROGRAM."
30 END
```

NOTE: Statement 15 has been stored between statements 10 and 20 in the computer's memory.

A statement can be erased from a program by typing its number and pressing **RETURN** (or **ENTER**). To erase statement 15 above, type 15. Typing **LIST** now would produce these results.

```
10 PRINT "THIS IS A VERY"         Statement 15 is no longer
20 PRINT "SHORT PROGRAM."    ◄───  in the program.
30 END
```

> In memory, the computer always saves your statements **in increasing order of statement numbers,** regardless of the order in which the statements were entered.

EXAMPLE 1 What would the listing of this program look like?

```
10 PRINT "THIS IS YOUR"
20 PRINT FRIENDLY COMPUTER."
30 PRINT
40 PRINT "I SPEAK"
30
20 PRINT "FRIENDLY COMPUTER."
50 PRINT "BASIC.   DO YOU?"
60 END
5  PRINT "HI!"
```

Listing
```
5  PRINT "HI!"
10 PRINT "THIS IS YOUR"
20 PRINT "FRIENDLY COMPUTER."
40 PRINT "I SPEAK"
50 PRINT "BASIC.   DO YOU?"
60 END
```

EXAMPLE 2 What must be typed to correct any syntax errors, to remove line 20, and to end the output with the words **END OF PROGRAM**?

```
10 PRINT "THE CAPITAL OF MISSOURI"
20 PRINT
30 PRINT IS JEFFERSON CITY."
40 END
```

Solution Type these lines in any order.

```
20                                    ◄── Removes line 20 from the program.
30 PRINT "IS JEFFERSON CITY." ◄── Corrects the error in line 30.
35 PRINT "END OF PROGRAM."    ◄── Adds a new line to the program.
```

Another useful direct command is **NEW**. On most machines, typing **NEW** erases the current program from memory. Although the old program may still be on the screen, it has been erased from memory.

SUMMARY OF EDITING METHODS

1. To change a statement of a program, retype the statement using the same statement number.

2. To add a statement to a program, type the statement with a number that will put it in the proper place in the program.

3. To erase a statement from a program, type the number of the statement and press **RETURN** or **ENTER**.

4. To see all statements of a program in memory, type **LIST**.

5. To see a particular statement of a program, type **LIST** followed by the number of that statement.

6. To clear a program from memory, type **NEW**.

WRITTEN EXERCISES

Complete each statement.

1. In memory, the computer stores the statements of a program in __?__ order of statement numbers.

2. To see all the statements of a program in memory, type __?__ .

3. To erase a program from memory, type __?__ .

4. To start, program statements should be numbered in multiples of __?__ .

5. To see just statement 50 of a program, type __?__ .

For Exercises 6–9, suppose that a student enters the lines shown and then types **LIST**. *What would the listing look like?*

6.
```
60 END
50 PRINT "TOMORROW"
40 PRINT "TODAY"
30 PRINT "YESTERDAY"
20 PRINT
```

7.
```
10 PRNT "X"
20 PRINT " X"
30 END
25 PRINT "  X"
10 PRINT "X"
```

8.
```
10 PRINT "*    *"
20 PRINT "*    *"
30 PRINT "******"
20
5  PRINT
40 PRINT "*    *"
50 END
```

9.
```
100 PRINT "------"
110 PRINT
105 PRINT CENTER
105 PRINT "CENTER"
120 PRINT "------"
130 PRINT
140 END
```

Suppose that a student has written the program at the right. The student types this program into the computer, makes mistakes, and tries to correct the errors.

```
10 PRINT "THIS IS"
20 PRINT "MY FIRST"
30 PRINT "PROGRAM."
40 END
```

Which programs in Exercises 10–13, if any, are logically the same as the program the student wrote?

10.
```
10 PE
10 PRINT "THIS IS"
20 PRINT "MY FIRST
30 PRINT "PROGRAM."
40END
20 PRINT "MY FIRST"
```

11.
```
10 PRINT "THIS IS"
20 PRINT
30 PRINT "MY FIRST"
20
20 PRINT "PROGRAM."
50 END
```

12.
```
10 PRINT "THIS IS"
20 PRINT "PROGRAM."
15 PRINT "MY FIRST"
25 END
```

13.
```
1 PRINT "THIS IS"
2 PRINT "PROGRAM."
3 END
2 PRINT "MY FIRST"
3 PRINT "PROGRAM."
4 END
```

Assume that this program is in the computer's memory. For Exercises 14–16, write what must be typed to change the program in the indicated ways.

```
10 PRINT "4"
20 PRINT "3"
30 PRINT "2"
40 "PRINT 1"
50 PRINT "BLAST OFF!"
60 PRINT
70 END
```

14. Correct the syntax error in statement 40.

15. Delete (erase) statement 60.

16. Start the countdown at 5.

Assume that the program below is in the computer's memory.
For Exercises 17–19, write what must be typed to change the program
in the indicated ways.

17. Add a row of six asterisks at the bottom of the output.

18. Delete statement 10.

19. Skip a line in the output between each row of asterisks.

```
10 PRINT
20 PRINT "*"
30 PRINT "**"
40 PRINT "***"
50 PRINT "****"
60 PRINT "*****"
70 END
```

MORE CHALLENGING EXERCISES

20. Suppose that a student types **NEW** and then **LIST** on the computer keyboard. What will the listing show?

COMPUTER LAB ACTIVITIES

Editing Programs

1. Type into a computer the program at the right.
Type **LIST** and check that you entered the lines correctly. Then **RUN** the program.

```
10 PRINT "HERE"
20 PRINT "WE GO"
30 END
```

2. Type **25 PRINT "NOW"** . Then type **LIST** . Where does the new line appear in the listing?

3. Delete line 20 by typing 20 and pressing **RETURN** (or **ENTER**). Type **LIST** to see the program now.

4. Type **10 PRINT "HOW"** and **LIST** the program again to check that the old statement 10 has been replaced by the new 10. Then **RUN** the program.

5. Type **NEW**. Then enter the program lines of Example 1. Type **LIST**. Is the listing the same as that shown in Example 1?

6. Type **NEW**. Enter this program. Then type the lines listed in the solution of Example 2 on page 52. **LIST** the program to see that all changes were made correctly. If they were, **RUN** the program.

```
10 PRINT "THE CAPITAL OF MISSOURI"
20 PRINT
30 PRINT IS JEFFERSON CITY."
40 END
```

Type **NEW.** *Enter the program at the right.*
Refer to this program for Exercises 7–9.

7. Type your answer to Exercise 14 on page 53.
LIST the program. Has the syntax error in
statement 40 been corrected?

8. Type your answer to Exercise 15 on page
53. **LIST** the program. What happens?

9. Type your answer to Exercise 16 on page
53. **LIST** and **RUN** the program. Does the
countdown start at 5?

```
10 PRINT "4"
20 PRINT "3"
30 PRINT "2"
40 "PRINT 1"
50 PRINT "BLAST OFF!"
60 PRINT
70 END
```

Type **NEW.** *Then enter this program. Refer to this program for*
Exercises 10–12.

10. Type your answer for Exercise 17 on page 54.
LIST and **RUN** the program. Is there a row of six
asterisks at the bottom of the output?

11. Type your answer for Exercise 18 on page 54.
LIST the program. Has statement 10 been deleted?

12. Type your answer for Exercise 19 on page 54.
LIST and **RUN** the program. Does the computer
skip a line between each row of asterisks?

```
10 PRINT
20 PRINT "*"
30 PRINT "**"
40 PRINT "***"
50 PRINT "****"
60 PRINT "*****"
70 END
```

EXPLORE: LISTING AND DELETING PARTS OF A PROGRAM

13. On many computers you can list several lines of a program without
listing the entire program. To test this, enter the program of Exercises 14–16 on page 53 into memory. Type **LIST 10–30.** Does the
computer accept the command? If so, what does it do?

14. If your computer accepted **LIST 10–30,** type **LIST 30–.** Does the computer accept the command? If so, what does it do?

15. If your computer accepted the new commands of Exercises 13 and
14, type **LIST–50.** Does the computer accept the command? If so,
what does it do?

If your computer did not accept any of the commands of Exercises
13–15, try these instead. Which does the machine execute?

16. LIST 10,30   **17.** LIST 30,   **18.** LIST,50

19. Type **DELETE 10.** Does the computer accept the command? If so,
type **LIST.** Is statement 10 in the listing?

If your computer accepted **DELETE 10,** *type each of these commands.*
If the computer accepts a command, type **LIST.** *What happens?*

20. DELETE 20–30   **21.** DELETE –40   **22.** DELETE 60–

2-4 OPERATIONS WITH NUMERICAL VARIABLES

OBJECTIVE:

> **To use INPUT, LET, and PRINT statements with numerical variables**

Picture part of a computer's memory as 26 "boxes", each named by a letter. Each box can

A	B	C	$\cdots$	X	Y	Z

hold a number. To store a number in a computer, you must assign the number to a memory location (box). For example, in **BASIC**

$$\texttt{LET X = 10}$$

X
10

puts a 10 in location X (see the box at the right).

A letter such as X that can be given a numerical value is called a **variable**. In this book, single letters (A,B,C,$\cdots$, Z) will be used to name numerical variables.

In a **LET** statement, the = symbol has the meaning of a left arrow ($\leftarrow$). Thus, **LET X = 10** can be thought of as **X $\leftarrow$ 10**. The statement can be interpreted as "let X become 10" or "let X receive 10" or "let X be assigned the value 10." On most computers, the word **LET** is optional. **LET X = 10** can be typed as **X = 10**.

Most versions of **BASIC** use the following operation symbols.

Operation	Symbol	Examples	
		In Mathematics	In Basic
Addition	+	$17 + 12$	$17 + 12$
Subtraction	−	$17 - 12$	$17 - 12$
Multiplication	*	17×12	$17 * 12$
Division	/	$17 \div 12$	$17 / 12$
Raising to a power	↑ or ∧	4^2	$4 ↑ 2$ or $4 ∧ 2$

NOTE: 4^2 means 4×4. Also, 4^3 means $4 \times 4 \times 4$, and so on.

Once numbers are in memory, they can be added, subtracted, multiplied, and so on.

This statement tells the computer to add 7 to the number in X and put the result in Y.

$$LET \ Y \ = \ X \ + \ 7$$

Thus, if X is 10, Y becomes 17. Notice that, after this **LET** command is executed, the variable X on the right of the = <u>has not changed</u> its value. It is still 10. But the variable Y on the left of the = <u>has changed</u> its value.

EXAMPLE 1 What is the value in Y after the computer does these steps?

a. LET X = 9
LET Y = 5 * X

b. LET A = 7
LET B = 4
LET Y = A - B

Solutions: **a.** 45   **b.** 3

To see a number in memory, use the **PRINT** command. For example, **PRINT Y** causes the number in location Y to be shown on the screen or printer.

EXAMPLE 2 Write the output after the computer does these steps.

```
LET  R  =  12
LET  Y  =  R  /  3
PRINT  Y
```

Output 4

NOTE: Although the statement

LET Y = R / 3   can be printed as   **LET Y = R/3,**

it is easier to read when there is additional space between the R and the / and between the / and the 3.

Printing the value of a variable does not change the value. In Example 2, after **PRINT Y** is executed, the value of Y is still 4.

Another way to give a value to a variable is to use the **INPUT** command. For example,

$$10 \ INPUT \ X$$

takes a number typed on the keyboard and stores it in location X. Thus, a program can be written to handle any value a person wishes to enter. Most systems will not accept **INPUT** as a direct command. It must be put into a program with a statement number.

EXAMPLE 3 When the following program is **RUN**, what number will the computer print for **Y** if 20 is entered for **X**?

```
10 INPUT X
20 LET Y = 2 * X
30 PRINT Y
40 END
```

Output   ? 20 ◄─────── *On some machines, there is a*
             40   *space after the ?*

NOTE: In statement 20 above, the * must be typed to show multiplication. **LET Y = 2*X** is acceptable.

When you **RUN** the program in Example 3, the computer will immediately pause and wait for you to type a value for X. Many machines show a ? to "prompt" you to enter a number. On others, the cursor blinks on and off to let you know the computer is waiting for a value. Once you type a number for X (and press **RETURN** or **ENTER**), the computer will print the value it calculates for Y.

NOTE: In Example 3, the **LET** statement of line 20 may <u>not</u> be written **20 LET 2 * X = Y**. The left side of the = must contain a variable only. Any operation signs (+, −, and so on) must be on the right side of the =. (Recall that = in a **LET** statement means ←.)

WRITTEN EXERCISES

Write the value of Y after the computer does the given steps.

1. LET X = 5
    LET Y = X − 2

2. LET A = 7
    LET Y = A + 4

3. LET Z = 10
    LET Y = Z / 2

4. LET R = 9
    LET S = 8
    LET Y = R + S

5. LET M = 20
    LET P = 4
    LET Y = M / P

6. LET N = 12
    LET T = 4
    LET Y = T * N

Write the output after the computer does the given steps.

7. LET X = 14
    LET Y = X / 7
    PRINT Y

8. LET K = 5
    LET Y = K ↑ 2
    PRINT Y

9. LET D = 17
    LET Y = D − 7
    PRINT Y

10. LET J = 6
    LET Y = 3*J
    PRINT Y

11. LET P = 30
    LET Y = 2+P
    PRINT Y

12. LET Q = 15
    LET Y = 60/Q
    PRINT Y

For Exercises 13–18, write the number the computer will print if 10 is entered for X.

13.
```
10 INPUT X
20 LET Y = X * 3
30 PRINT Y
40 END
```

14.
```
10 INPUT X
20 LET Y = 120/X
30 PRINT Y
40 END
```

15.
```
10 INPUT X
20 LET Y = X ↑ 2
30 PRINT Y
40 END
```

16.
```
10 INPUT X
20 LET Y = 4*X
30 PRINT Y
40 END
```

17.
```
10 INPUT X
20 LET Y = 90 - X
30 PRINT Y
40 END
```

18.
```
10 INPUT X
20 LET Y = X/2
30 PRINT Y
40 END
```

19. For Exercises 13–18, what number will the computer print if 30 is entered for X?

MORE CHALLENGING EXERCISES

Write each formula in BASIC.

EXAMPLE: $a = 10s$

Solution: LET A = 10 * S

20. $y = 8x$

21. $w = 12 + z$

22. $t = \dfrac{s}{10}$

23. $m = y^2$

24. $k = 180 - s$

25. $c = 3.1416d$

In Exercises 26–31, which **LET** *statements contain syntax errors? If a statement is incorrect, rewrite it correctly.*

26. LET X − 5 = Y

27. LET Z = 7K

28. LET A = 4

29. LET 180 = L

30. LET J + 1 = 10

31. LET R/7 = S

When executed by the computer, which of the following statements would change the value of X in memory?

32. LET X = 7*Y

33. LET Y = X − 5

34. INPUT X

35. PRINT X

If A = 3, B = 4, and C = 2, what value is assigned to D by each of these **LET** *statements?*

36. LET D = A + B

37. LET D = A * C

38. LET D = B/C

39. LET D = B − A

40. LET D = C↑2

41. LET D = B − C

42. LET D = A / B

43. LET D = A ↑ 3

44. LET D = B * B

What number is in location Y after the computer does these steps?

45.
```
LET Y = 1
LET Y = Y + 1
```

46.
```
LET Y = 11
LET Y = Y - 1
```

47.
```
LET Y = 12
LET Y = 2 * Y
```

LET Statements

1. Type **NEW**. (Be sure to press **RETURN** or **ENTER** after each line you type.) Then type **LET X = 5**. On the next line, type **PRINT X**. Does the computer display 5, the value it stored for X?

2. Type **LET 6 = Y** and press **RETURN** (or **ENTER**). What happens?

3. Type **PRINT Y**. What does the computer display? Explain this result.

4. Type **LET Y = X**. Then enter **PRINT Y**. What does the computer display?

5. Type **PRINT X**. Has the value of X changed since Exercise 1? Explain.

6. Type **LET X = "5"**. How does the computer respond?

7. Type **NEW**. Then enter this program. **RUN** the program, entering 20 for X. Does the computer print 40 for Y?

```
10 INPUT X
20 LET Y = 2 * X
30 PRINT Y
40 END
```

*For Exercises 8–11, **RUN** the program entered in Exercise 7. Type the given values for X. Before running the program, predict the output each time. Then check your prediction against the actual output.*

8. 25   9. 100   10. 45.5   11. −3

EXPLORE: SPECIAL LET STATEMENTS

12. Type **NEW**. Then enter and **RUN** the program shown at the right. What does the computer print for X?

```
10 LET X = 10
20 LET X = X + 1
30 PRINT X
40 END
```

13. What was the effect of statement 20? (Recall that "=" in a **LET** statement should be interpreted as ←.)

14. Retype statement 20 as **20 LET X = X + X** and **RUN** the program again. What is the output?

15. Change line 20 to **20 LET X = X * X**. Before running the program, predict the new output. Is your prediction correct?

16. Change statement 10 to **10 INPUT X**. Then **RUN** the program. Type any value for X. Before pressing **RETURN** (or **ENTER**), predict the output. Is your prediction correct?

17. Type **NEW**. Then enter and **RUN** the program shown at the right. What is the output?

```
10 LET X = 0
20 LET X = X + 1
30 PRINT X
40 IF X < 10 THEN 20
50 END
```

18. Change the program of Exercise 17 so that it counts to 15.

REVIEW: Sections 2–1—2–4

Complete each statement.

1. Each line typed on a computer keyboard is ended by pressing the __?__ key.

2. In **100 PRINT "THIS IS A SENTENCE."**, 100 is the __?__.

3. A special symbol or word that a computer displays to indicate that it is waiting for you to enter something is called a __?__.

4. As you type on a computer keyboard, a symbol called the __?__ marks your place on the screen.

5. In order to display just statement 30 of a program, you would type __?__.

For Exercises 6–8, choose the statements that are direct commands.

6. LIST

7. PRINT "ARE YOU HERE?"

8. 25 PRINT "NOT NOW!"

9. Write the output for this program.

```
100  PRINT "X    X"
110  PRINT " X X "
120  PRINT "  X   "
130  PRINT " X X "
140  PRINT "X    X"
150  END
```

For Exercises 10–11, state which commands are correct and contain no syntax errors.
For any command that is incorrect, give the reason.

10. PRINT "YESTERDAY"?

11. 50 PRINT "TOMORROW"

12. Suppose that a student enters the lines shown at the right. Then the student types **LIST.** What would the listing look like?

```
100  PRINT "R"
130  PRINT "A"
120  PRINT "D"
140  PRINT "R"
150  END
110  PRINT "A"
```

13. Write the value of Z after the computer performs the given steps.

```
LET  T  =  16
LET  Z  =  T  +  4
```

14. Write the output after the computer performs the given steps.

```
LET  A  =  100
LET  C  =  A / 10
PRINT  C
```

15. When the program at the right is **RUN,** write the number that the computer will print if 5 is entered for X.

```
10  INPUT  X
20  LET  Y  =  X * 30
30  PRINT  Y
40  END
```

WORD PROCESSING

Probably the most widespread application of computers is in **word processing**. In numerous offices, computers and word processing software have replaced typewriters. Word processing makes it easier to write a letter, a research paper, or a lab report.

Users of word processors type in correspondence or manuscript on a computer keyboard. If the copy on the computer screen needs rewriting, changes can easily be made. This "editing" can continue until the final copy is printed. Users can also save what they wrote, call it up on the screen, and work on it again at a later time.

There are dozens of word processing programs. However, most have the following features.

Entering What the user types is shown on the screen. Special keys move the cursor back or forward, and up or down. The user can type over words or insert text into what has already been written. The text shown on the screen and stored in memory is automatically adjusted as changes or additions are made.

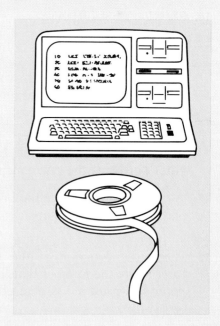

Saving At any point, the user can save what has been written on a disk or tape. Later, the user can load the file and continue working on the text.

Deleting Using certain keys or a combination of keys, the user can delete characters, words, sentences, or entire paragraphs.

Formatting The user can set the left–, right–, top–, and bottom–margins and choose single– or double–spacing between lines and paragraphs. Even if the screen is limited to 40 characters across and 20 lines down, the program will still print wider lines and a full page of text on paper.

Centering The user can tell the computer to center a line or block of lines horizontally or vertically on the printout. The lines do not have to be centered when they are typed.

Moving The user can move sentences or entire paragraphs to new locations in the text.

Searching/ Replacing Most programs will search the text for any strings the user wishes to find. They will even replace one string with another. For example, throughout a letter, the computer will replace the name ''Ronald'' with ''Sam.''

Spelling Some programs contain a file of thousands of words and can search in this dictionary for each word in the manuscript. Any word not found in the dictionary is highlighted on the screen. The user can correct its spelling or, if it is a proper name or technical word (like **RAM** or **ROM**), leave it as it is. The word can even be added to the dictionary.

Help With some programs, the user can request help with forgotten procedures. Some packages have tutorial programs and manuals to teach users how to use the program.

Appendix A Appendix B Appendix A and Appendix B on pages 321–340 of this text contain a self-study introduction to two word-processing programs: and the *Bank Street Writer* for the Apple II + and Apple IIe (Appendix A) and *SCRIPSIT*® for the TRS–80 Model III or 4 (Appendix B).

PROJECTS

1. In what language are most word processing programs written? Why?

2. List the minimum components of a computer system that is used for word processing.

3. Contact a business in your area that uses word processing. Report to the class on how word processing is used by that business.

4. Find the names of at least three word processing programs. List some computers that can run each program.

2-5 STRING VARIABLES

OBJECTIVE: To use INPUT, LET, and PRINT statements with string variables

All variables in the last lesson had numerical values. Non-numerical information cannot be stored in a numerical variable like A or X. Instead, non-numerical information is stored in **string variables.** A **string** is any combination of symbols, such as **"GEORGE WASHINGTON"**, **"1985"**, **"A + B"**, or **"504-283-1561"**, that can be typed into a machine. This type of variable is indicated by a $ following a letter: **A$, B$, C$, . . . Z$.** These variable names are usually read "A string, B string, C string," and so on.

Remember

A, B, C, . . . , X, Y, Z are **numerical variables.**	
A$, B$, C$, . . . , X$, Y$, Z$ are **string variables.**	

EXAMPLE 1 Classify each expression as a numerical variable, a string variable, or not a variable.

Expression	Type	Expression	Type
J	Numerical variable	X$	String variable
$A	Not a variable	7	Not a variable
8$	Not a variable	D	Numerical variable

Just as with numerical variables, string variables can be given "values" by using a **LET** statement or an **INPUT** statement.

Numerical Variables	String Variables
LET X = 7	LET X$ = "END OF PROGRAM"
INPUT Y	INPUT Y$

Notice that the value assigned to a string variable in a **LET** statement must be inside quotation marks. When a string is typed for an **INPUT** command (after the ? prompt), the quotations marks are <u>not</u> used.

EXAMPLE 2 **a.** Write a program to accept a person's name (such as LUCY). Then print **LUCY IS THE GREATEST**.

Program
```
10 INPUT N$
20 PRINT N$;" IS THE GREATEST."
30 END
```

b. Write the output from a **RUN** of the program.

Output
```
?LUCY
LUCY IS THE GREATEST.
```
← *The ? is produced by statement 10.*
The user types LUCY.

Compare statement 20 of the program of Example 2 with the output produced by that statement.

Statement `20 PRINT N$;" IS THE GREATEST."`

↓

Output `LUCY IS THE GREATEST.`

The computer prints the value of N$ in front of the string **IS THE GREATEST**. The value of a string variable can be printed anywhere in a string. Example 3 shows this.

EXAMPLE 3 Write the output of each **PRINT** statement.
Assume that **X$ = "CHRIS"**.

Statement

a. PRINT "THE WINNER IS ";X$

b. PRINT X$;", WHAT IS YOUR LAST NAME?"

c. PRINT "YES, ";X$;", YOU'RE RIGHT!"

Output

a. THE WINNER IS CHRIS

b. CHRIS, WHAT IS YOUR LAST NAME?

c. YES, CHRIS, YOU'RE RIGHT!

The output shown in Example 3 may be slightly different on some machines. Extra spaces might appear. For instance, the output of Example 3a might be as follows with extra space between **IS** and **CHRIS**.

```
THE WINNER IS  CHRIS
```

WRITTEN EXERCISES

Classify each item as a numerical variable, a string variable, or not a variable.

1. A$ **2.** $X   **3.** A   **4.** $

5. X   **6.** 6   **7.** 9$ **8.** Z

State whether a numerical or a string variable should be used for each of these.

9. A distance traveled

10. The name of a month

11. A date in the form 09/14/85

12. Number of points scored

13. A student's grade on a scale of 0 to 100

14. A student's grade on a scale of A, B, C, D, F

For Exercises 15–24, determine which statements are correct and contain no syntax errors. For each incorrect statement, give a reason why it is incorrect.

15. 10 INPUT X$

16. 90 INPUT

17. 45 PRINT Y$

18. 80 PRINT A$ IS TOPS!"

19. 70 PRINT "YOUR AGE, ";$K

20. 100 LET A$ = SARAH

21. 20 LET K$ = "THE WINNER"

22. 55 LET "DECEMBER" = M$

23. 120 INPUT J$ = "09/25/89"

24. 85 PRINT "SORRY, ";L$; YOU'RE WRONG."

*For Exercises 25–32, write the output of each **PRINT** statement. Assume that **A$ = "JUNE"** and **B$ = "PABLO"**.*

25. PRINT A$;" SALES"

26. PRINT "PLEASE START, ";B$

27. PRINT "YOUR GRADE, ";B$;" IS A."

28. PRINT "TOTAL FOR ";A$;" IS 0."

29. PRINT "THAT'S IT, ";B$

30. PRINT A$;" 'S WINNER:"

31. PRINT "TOPS FOR ";A$;" IS ";B$

32. PRINT "SEE YOU, ";B$;", IN ";A$

SEE YOU PABLO IN JUNE

For Exercises 33–38, assume that
L\$ = "JOHN".

Write a **PRINT** *statement involving L\$ that produces each line of output.*

33. JOHN WINS!

34. GOOD LUCK, JOHN

35. IT'S YOUR TURN,   JOHN

36. NO, JOHN , THAT'S NOT IT.

37. NOW, JOHN , IT'S TIME TO START.

38. JOHN'S MOVE.

MORE CHALLENGING EXERCISES

For Exercises 39–43, write a program as indicated. In each exercise, begin by accepting a person's name typed at the keyboard.

39. Write a program that prints the name twice, one below the other.

40. Write a program that prints the name followed by these words.
IS COMPUTER LITERATE

41. Write a program that prints the name indented five spaces from the left margin of the screen or printer.

42. Write a program that prints

 WELCOME TO THE COMPUTER LAB

followed by the person's name.

43. Write a program that prints the name between two rows of stars as shown below.

NOTE: The name may not appear exactly in the center of the rows of stars, depending on how many letters are in the name. If possible, **RUN** the program on a computer.

COMPUTER LAB ACTIVITIES

String Variables

1. Type this direct command.

```
LET A$ = TOM
```

What is the computer's response?

2. Type this direct command.

```
LET "TOM" = A$
```

What does the computer do?

3. The program below accepts a person's name. Enter the program on your computer keyboard. **RUN** it several times. Enter a different name each time.

```
10 INPUT N$
20 PRINT N$;" IS THE GREATEST."
30 END
```

4. Enter this direct command.

```
LET X$ = "CHRIS"
```

Then type each statement of Example 3 on page 65 as a direct command. Does your computer give exactly the same output shown in the Example? Check carefully whether the spaces before and after the word **CHRIS** are the same as in the Example.

5. Enter these direct commands.

```
LET A$ = "JUNE"
LET B$ = "PABLO"
```

Then enter each command of Exercises 25–32 on page 66. Is the output you predicted actually produced each time?

6. Enter this direct command.

```
LET L$ = "JOHN"
```

Then enter the **PRINT** commands you wrote for Exercises 33–38 on page 67. Does each command produce the required output? If not, retype it until it does.

Did You Know?

A **mouse** is a computer input device that moves the cursor. It consists of a small box with one or more buttons on top and is attached to the computer by a cord. When the mouse is rolled on a flat surface such as a table, the rolling movement causes the cursor on the screen to move the same distance and in the same direction. The buttons on the mouse are used for giving commands.

2-6 OPERATIONS WITH STRINGS: LEN AND +

OBJECTIVE: To use the LEN function and the + operation for strings

Computers can perform operations with numbers. They can add, subtract, multiply and divide. They can also perform operations on strings. Two of these operations will be studied in this section.

Just as a calculator has certain keys that you can press to make the calculator perform a built-in operation, so **BASIC** has built-in <u>functions</u> you can use in programs.

In **BASIC**, **LEN(A$)** (read "the length of A-string") gives the number of characters, including blanks, in the value of A$. A **character** is any symbol that can be typed on the computer's keyboard. Some examples are the letters of the alphabet, the digits 0, 1, 2, 3, 4, 5, 6, 7, 8, and 9, punctuation marks, and mathematical symbols such as = or +.

If **A$ = "COMPUTERS"** and **B$ = "COMPUTER PROGRAM"**, then

$$\textbf{LEN(A\$) = 9} \quad \text{and} \quad \textbf{LEN(B\$) = 16.}$$

For **LEN(B$)**, the blank between **COMPUTER** and **PROGRAM** counts as a character. A blank at the beginning or end of a string also counts. For example, if **A$ = "COMPUTERS "**, then **LEN(A$) = 10.**

EXAMPLE 1
a. Write a program to accept a person's name typed at the keyboard. Have the program print the number of characters in that name.

Program
```
10 PRINT "PLEASE TYPE YOUR NAME."
20 INPUT N$
30 LET L = LEN(N$)
40 PRINT L;" CHARACTERS IN YOUR NAME"
50 END
```

b. Write the output from a **RUN** of the program.

Output
```
PLEASE TYPE YOUR NAME.
?MARY BETH
9 CHARACTERS IN YOUR NAME
```

Compare statement 40 with its output.

A statement such as statement 10 in Example 1 is called a **prompt**. If a program starts with an **INPUT** command, then the first thing a user sees on the screen when the program is **RUN** is a **?**. By starting with a **PRINT** statement that tells the user what to type, the program is more "user friendly."

Two strings can be put together to form one longer string. The symbol + is used to join strings. For example, if **A\$ = "COMPUTERS"** and **B\$ = "PROGRAM "**, then

$$A\$ + B\$ = \text{"COMPUTERS"} + \text{"PROGRAM"}$$
$$= \textbf{"COMPUTERS PROGRAM"}.$$

$$B\$ + A\$ = \text{"PROGRAM"} + \text{"COMPUTERS"}$$
$$= \textbf{"PROGRAM COMPUTERS"}.$$

EXAMPLE 2 **a.** Write a program which accepts from the keyboard a person's first name and then the last name. Print the names joined into one string with a space between the first and last names.

Program
```
10 PRINT "TYPE YOUR FIRST NAME."
20 INPUT F$
30 PRINT "NOW TYPE YOUR LAST NAME."
40 INPUT L$
50 LET N$ = F$ + " " + L$
60 PRINT "COMPLETE NAME IS ";N$
70 END
```

b. Write the output from a **RUN** of the program.

Output

	Statement(s) Producing Each Line of Output
TYPE YOUR FIRST NAME.	10
?RICARDO	20
NOW TYPE YOUR LAST NAME.	30
?GARCIA	40
COMPLETE NAME IS RICARDO GARCIA	50 and 60

The key statement of Example 2 is statement 50. Statement 50 joins the first name (F\$), a space, and the last name (L\$). Thus, for the first input of the sample **RUN**, **F\$ = "RICARDO"** and **L\$ = "GARCIA"**.

$$N\$ = \quad F\$ \quad + \text{" "} + \quad L\$$$
$$N\$ = \text{"RICARDO"} + \text{" "} + \text{"GARCIA"}$$
$$N\$ = \text{"RICARDO GARCIA"}$$

EXAMPLE 3 Which statements are correct and contain no syntax errors? When a statement is incorrect, give the reason.

Statement	Correct	Reason
20 INPUT X$,Y$	Yes	
10 INPUT LEN(X$)	No	**LEN** may not appear in an **INPUT** statement.
25 INPUT A$+B$	No	The + sign may not appear in an **INPUT** statement.
50 INPUT A$, C	Yes	
15 LET X = LEN(A$+B$)	Yes	
35 LET Y = LEN(X)	No	X must be X$.
30 LET Z$ = LEN(L$) + LEN(M$)	No	Z$ must be Z.
80 LET LEN(D$) = LEN(C$)	No	**LEN** may not appear on the left of the = sign in a **LET** statement.
95 LET L = LEN(R$) − LEN(T$)	Yes	
70 LET P$ + Q$ = R$	No	A + may not appear on the left of an = in a **LET** statement.

As shown in statement 15 of Example 3, **LEN** and + may be combined in a **LET** statement. For example, if **A$** = "I LOVE" and **B$** = "COMPUTERS", then **LEN(A$+" "+B$)** equals the number of characters in "I LOVE COMPUTERS". Thus, **LEN(A$+" "+ B$) = 16**.

WRITTEN EXERCISES

For Exercises 1–12, suppose that **X$** = "I LIKE" *and* **Y$** = "SCHOOL". *Give the result of each of these operations.*

1. LEN(X$)
2. LEN(Y$)
3. X$ + Y$

4. Y$ + X$
5. LEN(X$+Y$)
6. LEN(Y$+X$)

7. X$ + " " + Y$
8. Y$ + "0 " + X$
9. LEN(X$+" "+Y$)

10. LEN(Y$+"? "+X$)
11. X$ + " " + Y$ + "."
12. LEN(X$+" "+Y$+".")

Which statements are correct and contain no syntax errors?
When a statement is incorrect, give the reason.

13. 90 LET X = LEN(A$)
14. LET L$ = M$ + N$

15. 35 INPUT A,B$
16. 10 INPUT LEN(T$)

17. 74 INPUT T$ + Z$

18. 34 INPUT L$,M

19. 45 LET M$ = LEN(Y$)

20. 98 LET S = LEN(W)

21. 63 LET LEN(B$) = 7

22. 60 LET A$ + B$ = C$

23. 95 LET Y = LEN(C$) + LEN(D$)

24. 70 LET LEN(K$)*LEN(L$) = M

25. Generally in **BASIC**, does **X$ + Y$** equal **Y$ + X$**? Does **LEN(X$ + Y$)** equal **LEN(Y$ + X$)**?

For Exercises 26–29, rewrite statement 40 of the program of Example 1 so that it prints the output as indicated.

26. CHARACTERS IN THE NAME = 9

27. THERE ARE 9 CHARACTERS IN THE NAME

28. THE NAME CONTAINS 9 CHARACTERS

29. MARY BETH CONTAINS 9 CHARACTERS

30. Write two statements that can be added to the program of Example 2 so that it also prints the number of characters in the complete name N$.

31. The program for Example 2 on page 65 is shown on the right. Write a statement that can be added to the program to prompt the user to type a name.

```
10 INPUT N$
20 PRINT N$;" IS THE GREATEST."
30 END
```

MORE CHALLENGING EXERCISES

32. Write a program that accepts a person's first and last names typed separately at the keyboard (for example, **LUCY** and **SMITH**). Print

       I LIKE LUCY SMITH.

33. Write a program that accepts a person's first and last names typed separately at the keyboard. Print the name in the form LAST NAME, FIRST NAME. For example, accept **RICARDO** and **GARCIA**. Print **GARCIA, RICARDO**.

For Exercises 34–37, suppose that **R$** = "GO" *and* **S$** = "TEAM". *Give the result of each of these operations.*

34. R$ + " " + S$ + "!"

35. R$ + " " + S$ ", " + R$ + "!"

36. R$ + ", " + R$ + " " + S$ + "."

37. S$ + ", PLEASE " + R$ + "."

COMPUTER LAB ACTIVITIES

LEN and +

1. Type **NEW**. Then enter this program (see Example 2 on page 70). **RUN** the program and enter the names **RICARDO** and **GARCIA**. Is the output the same as that shown in the output of Example 2?

```
10 PRINT "TYPE YOUR FIRST NAME."
20 INPUT F$
30 PRINT "NOW TYPE YOUR LAST NAME."
40 INPUT L$
50 LET N$ = F$ + " " + L$
60 PRINT "COMPLETE NAME IS ";N$
70 END
```

2. Enter the two statements you wrote for Exercise 30 on page 72. Then **RUN** the program again. Does the program produce the desired output? If not, revise it until it does.

EXPLORE: COMBINING PRINT AND INPUT

3. In many forms of **BASIC**, the two statements on the left below may be combined into the statement on the right.

```
10 PRINT "ENTER YOUR NAME."
20 INPUT N$
```
}
```
10 INPUT "ENTER YOUR NAME.";N$
```

To test whether your computer accepts such a statement, enter and **RUN** the program below. Does the computer accept statement 10?

```
10 INPUT "ENTER YOUR NAME.";N$
20 PRINT "LENGTH = ";LEN(N$)
30 END
```

4. If the computer accepted statement 10, did it print a question mark right after **ENTER YOUR NAME.**? If it did, then you should revise statement 10 to **10 INPUT "WHAT IS YOUR NAME";N$**. In this way the prompt is worded as a question. **RUN** the revised program. Does the output read better now?

5. If the computer printed an error message for

```
10 INPUT "ENTER YOUR NAME.";N$
```

retype it as follows.

```
10 INPUT "ENTER YOUR NAME":N$
```

RUN the program again. Does the computer accept the statement now?

2-7 OPERATIONS WITH STRINGS

OBJECTIVE:

> **To use the LEFT\$ and RIGHT\$ functions**

LEFT\$ ("left string") and **RIGHT\$** ("right string") are **BASIC** functions that work on strings. **LEFT\$** "picks off" characters from the beginning (left end) of a string. **RIGHT\$** "picks off" characters from the right end of a string.

Both **LEFT\$** and **RIGHT\$** require <u>two items</u> in parentheses after the function name. The first item is the *string variable*; the second is the *number of characters* to be picked off.

Suppose that **A\$ = "COMPUTERS"** and **B\$ = "PROGRAM "**.

Expression	Result	Expression	Result
LEFT\$(A\$,1)	"C"	RIGHT\$(B\$,1)	" "
LEFT\$(A\$,4)	"COMP"	LEFT\$(B\$,2)	"PR"
RIGHT\$(A\$,3)	"ERS"	RIGHT(B\$,5)	"GRAM "
LEFT\$(A\$ + B\$,10)	"COMPUTERSP"	RIGHT\$(A\$ + B\$,10)	"RSPROGRAM "

NOTE: **RIGHT\$** does <u>not</u> pick off the letters backward.
RIGHT\$(B\$,5) = "GRAM " and <u>not</u> " MARG".

EXAMPLE 1   **a.** Write a program which accepts a string typed at the keyboard and prints only the last character of the string.

Program
```
10 PRINT "PLEASE TYPE A STRING."
20 INPUT S$
30 LET L$ = RIGHT$(S$,1)
40 PRINT "THE LAST CHARACTER IS ";L$
50 END
```

b. Write the output from a **RUN** of the program.

Output
```
PLEASE ENTER A NAME.
?WASHINGTON
THE LAST CHARACTER IS N
```

After **LEFT\$** or **RIGHT\$** operate on a string, that string is not changed. For instance, suppose that **A\$ = "COMPUTERS"** and the statement LET C\$ = LEFT\$(A\$,2) is executed.

Then C$ = "CO" and A$ is still "COMPUTERS".

EXAMPLE 2　**a.** Write a program which accepts a name typed at the keyboard and prints the first and last characters of the string.

Program
```
10 PRINT "PLEASE TYPE A NAME."
20 INPUT N$
30 LET F$ = LEFT$(N$,1)
40 LET L$ = RIGHT$(N$,1)
50 PRINT "FIRST AND LAST LETTERS:"
60 PRINT F$;"   ";L$
70 END
```

b. Write the output from a **RUN** of the program.

Output
```
PLEASE TYPE A NAME.
?MCPHERSON
FIRST AND LAST LETTERS:
M   N
```

In statement 60, the "　" adds spaces in the output between the first and last letters. Without the "　", many machines would print the letters back-to-back: **MN**.

EXAMPLE 3　Which statements are correct and contain no syntax errors? When a statement is incorrect, give the reason.

Statement	Correct?	Reason
85 LET K$ = RIGHT$(T$,3)	Yes	
62 LET E$ = RIGHT$(J$)	No	**RIGHT$** must have a number in the parentheses after the string variable.
45 LET LEFT$(R$,3)=RIGHT$(U$,3)	No	**LEFT$** and **RIGHT$** may not appear on the left side of = in a **LET** statement.
15 LET X = LEFT$(V$,2)	No	**X** must be a string variable.
25 INPUT RIGHT$(M$,1)	No	**RIGHT$** and **LEFT$** may not appear in an **INPUT** statement.
38 LET K$ = LEFT$(Y,6)	No	**Y** must be **Y$**.
20 LET M$ = RIGHT$(A$+B$,6)	Yes	

WRITTEN EXERCISES

For Exercises 1–13, suppose that **X$** = **"COMPUTER"** *and* **Y$** = **"LITERACY"**. *Give the result of each of these operations.*

1. LEFT$(X$,3)
2. LEFT$(Y$,4)
3. RIGHT$(Y$,2)
4. RIGHT$(X$,6)
5. X$ + Y$
6. Y$ + X$
7. RIGHT$(X$ + Y$,9)
8. LEFT$(Y$ + X$,10)
9. LEFT$(Y$ + X$,7)
10. LEFT$(X$,2) + RIGHT$(X$,4)
11. RIGHT$(X$,3) + LEFT$(Y$,4)
12. LEFT$(Y$,3) + RIGHT$(X$,3)
13. LEFT$(X$,5) + RIGHT$(Y$,6)

Which statements are correct and contain no syntax errors?
When a statement is incorrect, give the reason.

14. 90 INPUT LEFT$(R$,3)
15. 82 LET L$ = LEFT$(M$ + N$,7)
16. 25 LET RIGHT$(C$,2) = J$
17. 10 LET T$ = RIGHT$(M$)
18. 74 LET C$ = RIGHT$(K$,4)
19. 34 LET H = RIGHT$(L$,1)
20. 45 LET M$ = LEFT$(S,3)
21. 98 LET S$ = RIGHT$("P$", 1)
22. 63 LET X$ = LEFT$(4,L$)
23. 60 LET LEFT$(B$,1) = RIGHT$(C$,1)

24. Revise the program of Example 1 so that it prints the first two characters of the input string.

25. In the program for Example 2, which two statements could be in a different order without changing the output of the program?

MORE CHALLENGING EXERCISES

For Exercises 26–28, the input is a person's first and last names (read as separate strings).

26. Write a program that prints only the person's two initials. For example, given **NORMA** and **CANNIZZARO**, print **N. C.**

27. Write a program that prints only the first letter of the first name followed by the last name. For example, given **JOSEPH** and **AUTIN**, print **J. AUTIN**.

28. Write a program that prints the last name followed by a comma and the first initial. For example, given **CLAIRE** and **LEBLANC**, print **LEBLANC, C.**

For Exercises 29–32, suppose that **R$** = **"GO "** *and* **S$** = **"TEAM!"**. *Give the result of each of these operations.*

29. R$ + S$ + RIGHT$(R$,1) + R$ + RIGHT$(S$,1)
30. LEFT$(RIGHT$(S$,4),2)
31. RIGHT$(LEFT$(R$,2),1)
32. LEFT$(LEFT$(S$,4),3)

LEFT$ and RIGHT$

1. Enter this program (see Example 1 on page 74). **RUN** the program and enter **WASHINGTON.** Does the computer give the same output as that shown in Example 1?

```
10 PRINT "PLEASE TYPE A STRING."
20 INPUT S$
30 LET L$ = RIGHT$(S$,1)
40 PRINT "THE LAST CHARACTER IS ";L$
50 END
```

2. Type **NEW.** Then enter the program of Example 2 on page 75. **RUN** the program and enter **MCPHERSON.** Does the output agree with that shown in the output of Example 2?

EXPLORE: MORE ON LEFT$ AND RIGHT$; MID$

3. Enter these direct commands in order.

LET A$ = "BASIC"   LET B$ = LEFT$(A$,6)   PRINT B$

What output, if any, does the computer produce?

4. Type **LET C$ = RIGHT$(A$,6)** and **PRINT C$.** What output, if any, does the computer produce?

5. Enter and **RUN** the program on the right. What is the output?

```
10 LET A$ = "COMPUTER"
20 LET B$ = MID$(A$,4,3)
30 PRINT B$
40 END
```

In the program of Exercise 5, change statement 20 as indicated in Exercises 6 and 7. What is the output each time?

6. 20 LET B$ = MID$(A$,2,4)   **7.** 20 LET B$ = MID$(A$,7,1)

8. Given a string, write a program that prints the second, third, and fourth characters of the string. Then **RUN** the program.

Did You Know?

By 1990, a **digital watch** may have the computing capacity of ENIAC, the electronic computer completed in 1945 by John Mauchly and J. Presper Eckert.

2-8 SOLVING PROBLEMS IN BASIC

OBJECTIVE: **To write BASIC programs to solve problems**

The programs written in this chapter have four logical parts.

Problem-Solving Steps	Program Statements
1. INPUT one or more data values.	10 PRINT "ENTER YOUR NAME." 20 INPUT N$
2. PROCESS the data (**LET**).	30 LET Y$ = LEFT$(N$,2)
3. OUTPUT the answer (**PRINT**).	40 PRINT "FIRST 2 CHARACTERS ARE ";Y$
4. END the program.	50 END

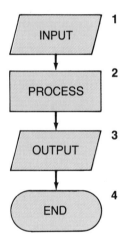

The four steps in the solution of the problem above can be shown as the **flowchart** on the left. In Chapter 5 of this book, you will learn how to draw flowcharts. In the meantime, flow-charting symbols can help to show the problem-solving steps being used.

NOTE: **Processing** can involve calculating a numerical answer. Or it can include manipulating alphabetical information, as in the sample program above.

EXAMPLE 1 Write a program which, given the amount of a purchase (under $1.00), prints the change due from a $1.00 bill.

Solution: The work is in four phases.

Phase 1 Identify the input variable(s) and the output variable. Let

A = the amount of a purchase, and ⟵————— **INPUT variable**
C = the amount of change from $1.00. ⟵————— **OUTPUT variable**

Phase 2 Write a formula for calculating the value of the output variable.

Amount of Change (C) = $1.00 − Amount of Purchase (A)

Phase 3 Write a program.

```
100 PRINT "ENTER AMOUNT OF PURCHASE."
110 INPUT A
120 LET C = 1.00 - A          Do not put a $ in statement 120.
130 PRINT "CHANGE = $";C
140 END
```

Phase 4 Check the program with test values. If the output is not correct, make changes in the program until it produces correct output.

```
ENTER AMOUNT OF PURCHASE.
?.63
CHANGE = $.37
```

Notice how statement 130 of the program labels the output not only with the message **CHANGE =** but also with a **$**.

Programmers usually begin a program by listing the name of the programmer and other information about the program. In **BASIC**, you do this by writing **REM** statements. **REM** is short for **REM**ark. Here are examples.

```
10 REM   GREG ANSLEY    P. 28 #6

34 REM   PROGRAM COMPUTES AREAS OF RECTANGLES.
35 REM   L = LENGTH OF THE RECTANGLE
36 REM   W = WIDTH OF THE RECTANGLE
```

REM statements may appear anywhere in a program. When the computer executes a program, it ignores **REM** statements. They are useful only when a program is listed. They tell people who the programmer is and what the program does.

EXAMPLE 2 Write a program which accepts a person's first, middle, and last names, typed separately at the keyboard. The output is the last name, first name, and middle initial. For example, given **ROBERT LOUIS STEVENSON**, print **STEVENSON, ROBERT L.**

Solution

Phase 1 Identify the input variables and output variable. Let

F$ = first name,
M$ = middle name,
L$ = last name,
A$ = name in the form: last name, first name, middle initial.

Phase 2   Find a way to produce the output from the input.

A$ = L$ + ", " + F$ + " " + LEFT$(M$,1) + "."

Phase 3   Write a program.

```
10 REM  EXAMPLE 2, SECTION 2-8
20 PRINT "ENTER FIRST NAME."
30 INPUT F$
40 PRINT "ENTER MIDDLE NAME."
50 INPUT M$
60 PRINT "ENTER LAST NAME."
70 INPUT L$
80 LET A$ = L$+", "+F$+" "+LEFT$(M$,1)+"."
90 PRINT A$
100 END
```

Phase 4   Check the program with test values. If necessary, make changes in the program until it produces correct output.

```
ENTER FIRST NAME.
?ROBERT
ENTER MIDDLE NAME.
?LOUIS
ENTER LAST NAME.
?STEVENSON
STEVENSON, ROBERT L.
```

It is good programming practice to have a program begin by printing what it does.

EXAMPLE 3   Write a program which accepts a baseball player's times-at-bat and number of hits. Then have the program print the player's batting average.

Solution   Identify the input variables and the output variable.

Phase 1   B = number of times-at-bat   ⟵———— **INPUT variable**
H = number of hits, and   ⟵———— **INPUT variable**
A = batting average.   ⟵———— **OUTPUT variable**

Phase 2   **Batting Average (A) = Number of Hits (H) ÷ Times at Bat (B)**

Phase 3
```
10 REM  EXAMPLE 3, SECTION 2-8
20 PRINT "GIVEN A BASEBALL PLAYER'S"
30 PRINT "NUMBER OF TIMES-AT-BAT AND"
```

```
40 PRINT "NUMBER OF HITS, THIS PROGRAM"
50 PRINT "PRINTS THE BATTING AVERAGE."
60 PRINT "ENTER TIMES-AT-BAT AND HITS."
70 INPUT B, H          ◄────── You may INPUT more than one
80 LET A = H / B               variable in one statement.
90 PRINT "BATTING AVERAGE = ";A
100 END
```

Phase 4 `GIVEN A BASEBALL PLAYER'S`
`NUMBER OF TIMES-AT-BAT AND`
`NUMBER OF HITS, THIS PROGRAM`
`PRINTS THE BATTING AVERAGE.`
`ENTER TIMES-AT-BAT AND HITS.`
`?50,15`
`BATTING AVERAGE = .3` ◄──── **Final zeros after the decimal point are not usually printed.**

WRITTEN EXERCISES

For Exercises 1–4, the commands of a program are listed. They are not necessarily in the correct logical order. Put the commands into the correct order by rewriting them with statement numbers in front of them.

1.
```
INPUT X
PRINT "SQUARE IS ";Y
LET Y = X * X
END
PRINT "TYPE ANY NUMBER."
```

2.
```
LET R = P * Q
INPUT P,Q
PRINT "R = ";R
PRINT "ENTER TWO NUMBERS."
END
```

3.
```
PRINT "LAST 2 LETTERS ARE ";L$
INPUT K$
END
PRINT "PLEASE TYPE A NAME."
LET L$ = RIGHT$(K$,2)
```

4.
```
END
LET Z$ = X$ + X$
PRINT "NEW STRING = ";Z$
INPUT X$
PRINT "ENTER A STRING."
```

Write the missing statement.

5.
```
10 REM   PRINT FULL NAME
20 PRINT "ENTER YOUR LAST NAME."
30  ?
40 LET L$ = "MR. " + N$
50 PRINT "FULL NAME IS ";L$
60 END
```

MR. WILER

Write the missing statement in each program.

6.
```
100 REM   EXERCISE #6
110 PRINT "PLEASE TYPE TWO NUMBERS."
120 INPUT A, B
130   ?
140 PRINT "SUM OF NUMBERS = ";D
150 END
```

7.
```
10 PRINT "THIS PROGRAM MULTIPLIES"
15 PRINT "ANY NUMBER BY PI."
20 PRINT "ENTER A NUMBER."
25 INPUT D
30 LET P = 3.1416*D
35   ?
40 END
```

8.
```
10 PRINT "GIVEN A STRING, THIS"
20 PRINT "PROGRAM PRINTS THE"
30 PRINT "LENGTH OF THE STRING."
40 INPUT S$
50   ?
60 PRINT "LENGTH = ";L
70 END
```

Some farmers use computerized laser-scanning devices to sort the tomato harvest.

Correct any syntax or logic errors in these programs.

9.
```
10 PROGRAMMED BY KENNY WERTHER
20 PRINT "ENTER NO. OF TESTS."
30 INPUT G
40 PRINT "ENTER TOTAL POINTS."
50 INPUT Q.
60 LET Q/G = A
70 PRINT "AVERAGE = A"
80 END
```

10.
```
10 REM   SAMPLE PROGRAM   9/16/87
20       PROGRAMMER:  AMY PUMILIA
30 PRINT "ENTER NAME."
40 INPUT S
50 LET T$ = LEFT$(S,1)
60 PRINT "NAME STARTS WITH ";T$
70 END
```

Computers are used to route mail across the country.

11. Write **REM** and **PRINT** statements for the program of Example 1 to identify the programmer and state what the program does.

12. Revise the program of Example 1 to allow the amount paid to be entered as well as the amount of the purchase. In other words, no longer assume that the purchase is under $1.00.

MORE CHALLENGING EXERCISES

For Exercises 13–17, write a BASIC program. Include at least one REM statement giving your name and the number of the exercise. Each RUN should begin by printing what the program does.

13. Write a program which accepts the number of the month and the day of the month typed separately on the keyboard. The output is the date with the month and the day separated by a slash. For example, given 10 and 30, print 10/30.

OCTOBER						
S	M	T	W	T	F	S
		1	2	3	4	5	6
7	8	9	10	11	12	13
14	15	16	17	18	19	20
21	22	23	24	25	26	27
28	29	30	31			

14. Expand the program of Exercise 13 so that it adds the current year to the date. For example, given 10 and 30, print 10/30/1987.

15. Revise the programs of Exercises 13 and 14 so that the user enters the year as well as the month and day. For example, given 10, 30, and 1987, print 10/30/1987.

16. Write a program which, given the length **S** of one side of a square, prints the perimeter **P**. Use the formula **P = 4S**.

17. Write a program which computes a worker's weekly pay, given the number of hours worked and the rate per hour. Use this formula:

Weekly Pay = Hours Worked × Rate per Hour.

18. Use the **LEFT$** and **RIGHT$** functions in a program that accepts a string typed at the keyboard and prints the <u>second</u> character of the string.

19. Write a program which, given the number of wins and losses of a team computes the winning percentage. Assume that there are no ties. (HINT: Use two LET statements. First calculate the number of games played.)

	W	L	Pct.
Detroit	55	25	?
Toronto	48	32	?
Baltimore	44	37	?
Boston	38	42	?
Milwaukee	38	43	?
New York	35	43	?
Cleveland	33	45	?

COMPUTER LAB ACTIVITIES

Problem Solving

1. Enter and **RUN** this program (see Example 1 on pages 79–80). Use .63 as the value for A. Does the computer produce the output shown in Phase 4 of the solution of Example 1? **RUN** the program several more times, entering different values for A.

```
100 PRINT "ENTER AMOUNT OF PURCHASE."
110 INPUT A
120 LET C = 1.00 - A
130 PRINT "CHANGE = $";C
140 END
```

2. Type **NEW**. Then enter the program of Example 2 on page 80. **RUN** the program, entering **ROBERT, LOUIS,** and **STEVENSON.** Is the output the same as that shown in Phase 4 of the solution for Example 2? **RUN** the program several more times, entering different names each time.

3. Type **NEW**. Then enter this program (see Example 3 on pages 80–81). **RUN** the program, entering 50 times–at–bat and 15 hits. Is the output the same as shown in Phase 4 of the solution for Example 3? **RUN** the program several more times, entering different numbers each time.

```
10 REM  EXAMPLE 3, SECTION 2-8
20 PRINT "GIVEN A BASEBALL PLAYER'S"
30 PRINT "NUMBER OF TIMES-AT-BAT AND"
40 PRINT "NUMBER OF HITS, THIS PROGRAM"
50 PRINT "PRINTS THE BATTING AVERAGE."
60 PRINT "ENTER TIMES-AT-BAT AND HITS."
70 INPUT B, H
80 LET A = H / B
90 PRINT "BATTING AVERAGE = ";A
100 END
```

For Exercises 4–9:
a. *Enter each indicated program, using the statement numbers you chose.*
b. **RUN** *the program. Use any input values you choose.*
c. *Does the program produce correct output? If it does not, revise the program until it does.*

4. Exercise 1 on page 81
5. Exercise 2 on page 81
6. Exercise 3 on page 81
7. Exercise 4 on page 81

For Exercises 8–11:
 a. *Enter each indicated program, including the statement you added.*
 b. **RUN** *the program.*
 c. *Does the program produce correct output? If it does not, revise the program until it does.*

8. Exercise 5 on page 81
9. Exercise 6 on page 82
10. Exercise 7 on page 82
11. Exercise 8 on page 82

EXPLORE: OMITTING SEMICOLONS IN PRINT STATEMENTS

12. In many forms of **BASIC**, the ; may be omitted in a statement like

```
PRINT "ANSWER = ";A
```

To test this on your computer, enter the statement below as a direct command.

```
PRINT "ANSWER = "A
```

Does your computer print an error message or does it execute the statement? (A will be 0.)

13. Enter and **RUN** the program below. Type any value for X.

```
10  INPUT X
20  LET Y = X/2
30  PRINT "X = "X" Y = "Y
40  END
```

Does the computer complete the program or does it print an error message?

14. If the computer printed values for X and Y, then it accepts statement 30 without semicolons. If you received an error message, re-type line 30 as

```
30 PRINT "X = ";X;" Y = ";Y
```

and **RUN** the program again. Does it execute correctly now? In any case, you have learned whether your computer requires semicolons in a **PRINT** statement like statement 30.

15. To test whether the semicolon may be omitted in a **PRINT** statement involving a string variable, enter these direct commands.

```
LET A$ = "TESTING"
```

and then

```
PRINT "OUTPUT IS "A$
```

Does the computer execute the **PRINT** command or does it print an error message?

REVIEW: Sections 2–5—2–8

Classify each item as a numerical variable, a string variable, or not a variable.

1. X$ **2.** 3   **3.** 4$ **4.** N

For Exercises 5–8, determine which statements are correct and contain no syntax errors.
When a statement is incorrect, give the reason.

5. 75 LET K$ = "TAMMY"   **6.** 15 LET LEN(A$) + LEN(B$) = C

7. 40 LET C$ = RIGHT(X$,3)   **8.** 30 PRINT MY NAME IS";N$

For Exercises 9–10, suppose that **X$ = "GEORGE IS A"** *and* **Y$ = "BOOKKEEPER"**. *Give the result of each operation.*

9. X$ + " " + Y$ **10.** LEFT$(X$,7) + RIGHT$(Y$,6)

11. Suppose that **L$ = "MARY"**. Write a **PRINT** statement involving L$ that produces the output at the right.

NO, MARY, I AM NOT GOING.

12. The commands of this program are not in the correct logical order. Put the commands into the correct order by rewriting them with statement numbers in front of them.

```
LET L = LEN(A$)
INPUT A$
END
PRINT "NAME AN ANIMAL."
PRINT A$;" HAS ";L;" CHARACTERS."
```

13. Write the missing statement in the following program.

```
100 REM TRIPLE IT
110 PRINT "PLEASE TYPE A NUMBER."
120 INPUT A
130  ?
140 PRINT "THE NUMBER TRIPLED IS ";T
150 END
```

14. Correct any syntax or logic errors in the following program.

```
100 PROGRAMMED BY JJ
110 PRINT "ENTER A NUMBER."
120 LET N/2 = H
130 PRINT "HALF THE NUMBER ";N;" IS ;H
140 END
```

COMPUTERS AND TYPING

Have you ever wondered why the letters on a typewriter or computer keyboard are arranged the way they are? In the 19th century, the letters were placed where they are in order to slow down typists so the keys wouldn't jam.

QWERTY Keyboard

A new system that improves typing speed and reduces finger fatigue was copyrighted about 50 years ago by August Dvorak. The Dvorak design places the most frequently used letters on the same row of the keyboard.

DVORAK Keyboard

Despite the advantages of the Dvorak system, most people continue to use the QWERTY keyboard. However, computer companies can now change their computer keyboards simply by rewriting software. There are even some companies that are presently marketing a Dvorak keyboard for their computers.

PROJECT

List the advantages and disadvantages of the Dvorak system.

Chapter Summary

Section 2–1

1. **PRINT** statements can be used as direct commands.

2. **PRINT** statements can be included in programs to print messages, numerical results, and designs.

Section 2–2

3. **BASIC** stores the statements of a program in memory in order of statement numbers regardless of the order in which the statements were typed.

4. The statements of a program must be typed exactly.

5. It is good programming practice to include an **END** statement as the last statement of every program.

Section 2–3

6. To change a program statement, retype it using the same statement number.

7. To add a statement, type it with the appropriate statement number.
To delete a statement, type its number and press **RETURN** (or **ENTER**).

8. The common system commands are **NEW**, **LIST**, and **RUN**.

Section 2–4

9. In **BASIC**, a variable represents a location in memory which, at any given moment, can store a single number or string.

10. Values can be put into memory locations by means of **INPUT** and **LET** statements. To see the value of a variable, use the **PRINT** command.

Section 2–5

11. Alphabetical information must be stored in a string variable.

Section 2–6

12. **LEN(X$)** gives the number of characterrs in the value of **X$**.

13. Strings can be joined to form longer strings.

Section 2–7

14. The **LEFT$** function takes characters from the left of a string. The **RIGHT$** function takes them from the right end.

Section 2–8

15. The **BASIC** statements of this chapter can be used to solve problems.

Step 1: Identify the input and output variables.

Step 2: Write a formula for calculating the output variable.

Step 3: Write the program.

Step 4: Check the program with test values.

16. **REM** statements can be used to add comments to a program.

Chapter Review

1. Write a program to produce the output below.

```
        X  X  X  X  X  X
        X              X
Blank line ──────►
        X              X
        X  X  X  X  X  X
```

Correct any errors in these programs.

2.
```
10 PRINT ENTER YOUR NAME
20 INPUT N
30 LET L$ = LEFT(N,1)
40 PRINT "1ST LETTER IS L$
50 END
```

3.
```
100 PRINT "ENTER A NUMBER."?
110 IMPUT X
120 LET Y = X TIMES X
130 PRINT "Y = ";Y
140 END
```

Suppose that a student enters the lines shown and then types **LIST**.
What will the listing look like?

4.
```
10 INPUT X;Y
20 LET Z = X + Y
30 END
25 PRINT "Z = ";Z
10 INPUT X,Y
20 LET Z = X - Y
```

5.
```
10 INPUT A
20 PRINT "FOR A =";A
30 LET B = .75 * A
5  PRINT "GIVE A NUMBER."
40 PRINT "B = ";B
50 END
20
```

6. Write the output of a **RUN** of the program below.
Choose your own values for any input variables.

```
100 PRINT "THIS PROGRAM CONVERTS"
105 PRINT "DECIMALS TO PERCENTS."
110 PRINT "ENTER THE DECIMAL."
120 INPUT D
130 LET P = D * 100
140 PRINT P;"%"
150 END
```

7. Write the output of a RUN of the program below. Choose your own values for any input variables.

```
10 REM CHAPTER 2 REVIEW #7
20 PRINT "PLEASE TYPE YOUR FIRST NAME."
30 INPUT F$
40 LET L$ = RIGHT$(F$,1)
50 PRINT "NAME ENDS IN ";L$
60 END
```

Suppose that **A$ = "BASIC"** *and* **B$ = "PROGRAMMING"**.
Give the result of each of these operations.

8. LEFT$(A$,3)   **9.** RIGHT$(B$,4)   **10.** RIGHT$(A$,1)

11. LEFT$(B$,7)   **12.** A$ + " " + B$ **13.** LEFT$(B$,3)+RIGHT$(A$,2)

14. LEN(A$)   **15.** LEN(B$)   **16.** LEN(A$+B$)

MORE CHALLENGING EXERCISES

For Exercises 17–19, write a **BASIC** *program for each problem.*

a. Prompt all input with a message.

b. Label any output with a message.

c. Include at least one REMark stating your name and the problem number.

d. Have the computer begin a **RUN** *by printing what the program does.*

17. Given the number of runs a baseball player has scored and the number of games played, print the runs-per-game average.

18. Enter a student's number of subjects and the average number of hours per week spent on homework in each subject. Print the total number of hours the student spends on homework each week.

19. Given two strings entered at the keyboard, print the string formed by joining the two strings (in order). Also print the first and last characters of the combined string.

Chapter Test

Correct any errors in these programs.

1.
```
10 CHAPTER TWO TEST, #1
20 INPUT X,
30 LET Y = 5X
40 PRINT ANSWER =;Y
50 END.
```

2.
```
100 PRINT "WHAT IS THE WORD?"
110 INPUT $W
120 LET $L = LEN($W)
130 PRINT "LETTERS IN WORD=";$L
140 END
```

3. Suppose that a student enters the lines shown on the right and then types **LIST**. What will the listing look like?

```
10 IMPUT Y
20 LET Y = X*X
25 PRINT "Y = Y
5  PRINT "TYPE A NUMBER."
30 PRINT "Y = ";Y
25
```

4. Write the output of a **RUN** of the program on the right when 10 is entered for J.

```
10 REM HALVE NUMBERS
20 PRINT "TYPE A NUMBER."
30 INPUT J
40 LET K = J/2
50 PRINT "ANSWER IS ";K
60 PRINT
70 END
```

For Exercises 5–10, suppose that **M$** = **"HAVE"** *and* **N$** = **"FUN"**. *Give the result of each of these operations.*

5. RIGHT$(M$,2)

6. LEFT$(N$,1)

7. M$ + " " + N$

8. LEN(M$)

9. LEN(N$)

10. LEN(M$) – LEN(N$)

EXTRA FOR EXPERTS

For Exercises 11–12, write a **BASIC** *program. Follow these directions.*

a. *Prompt any input with a message.*

b. *Label any output with a message.*

c. *Include at least one REMark stating your name and the problem number.*

d. *Have the computer begin a* **RUN** *by printing what the program does.*

11. Given the number of centimeters in a length, print the corresponding number of meters in the length. Use this formula.

Number of Meters = Number of Centimeters ÷ 100

12. Accept a person's name typed at the keyboard. Print only the first letter.

Computer Lab Projects

STRING PROCESSING APPLICATIONS

1. Given three strings entered at the keyboard, print the string formed by joining the three (in the order in which they were entered).

   DATA   U., S., A.,   I, LIKE , COMPUTERS., EDNA, MARIE, SMITH

2. Given two strings, print the string formed by joining the strings with a blank between them. For example, given **HIGH** and **SCHOOL**, print **HIGH SCHOOL**.

   DATA   HIGH, SCHOOL, UNITED, STATES, JUNIOR, HIGH

3. Given a string, print its first two and last two characters, joined as one string. For example, given **AMERICA**, print **AMCA**.

   DATA   AMERICA, PLAYER, COMPUTERS

4. Expand the program of Exercise 3 so that it also prints the string formed by putting the last two characters first. For **AMERICA**, print **AMCA** and **CAAM**.

   DATA   AMERICA, PLAYER, COMPUTERS

5. Given a person's name and favorite color, print a message like **JOHN'S FAVORITE COLOR IS BLUE.**

   DATA   JOHN, BLUE, AMY, RED, JOLISE, GREEN

6. Given the name of a musical group and the title of one of their songs, print the group's name and the song title with the word **PLAYS** in between.

   DATA   ACES, LOVE DREAM, LED BALLOON, COOL BREEZE, JEFFERSON STARSHIP, COME BACK TO ME

GENERAL APPLICATIONS

7. Given a person's age, print the year of birth.

DATA   11, 13, 25

8. A junior high holds its Student Council election. Given the number of votes a candidate received from the 7th–, 8th–, and 9th–graders, print the total number of votes.

DATA   132, 214, 89,   201, 167, 103,   75, 46, 102

9. Given a person's weight (in pounds) and height (in inches), print the pounds per inch.

DATA   110, 64,   125, 66,   102, 59

10. Given the current year and a person's age this year, print what that person's age will be in the year 2000.

DATA   1985, 13,   1987, 15,   1986, 12

CONSUMER APPLICATIONS

11. Money placed in a savings account earns interest. Given the amount in an account and the rate of interest, print the amount of interest for one year. For example, if the amount is $50 and the interest rate is 6%, the interest for one year equals 50 × .06 = $3.00.

DATA   50, .06,   150, .05,   200, .065

12. Expand the program for Exercise 11 to enter the number of years also.

Amount of Interest = Amount Invested × Interest Rate × Number of Years

DATA   50, .06, 1,   150, .05, 3,   200, .065, 10

13. Suppose that a library charges 15¢ a day for overdue books. Given the number of days a book is overdue, print the amount of the fine for that book.

DATA   3, 5, 10

*An item with a **regular price** of $4.90 is on sale at a 10% **discount**. Thus, the **amount of discount** is $4.90 × 0.10, or **$0.49**. Then the **sale price** (net price) is $4.90 − $0.49 = **$4.41**.*

14. Given the regular price and the sale price, find the amount of discount.

DATA   4.90, 4.41,   50, 46,   9.98, 9.49

15. Given the regular price and the percent of discount, print the amount of discount.

DATA   4.90, .10,   50, .05,   9.98, .20

16. Given the regular price and the amount of discount, find the sale price.

DATA 4.90, .49, 50, 4, 9.98, .49

17. A common practice after a meal in a restaurant is to leave a tip which is 15% of the total bill for the meal. Given the cost of a meal, compute the amount of the tip.

DATA 10, 5.40, 15.20

MORE CHALLENGING COMPUTER LAB PROJECTS

STRING PROCESSING APPLICATIONS

18. The input consists of two numbers or letters followed by an operation symbol. Accept each of these three items as a string. Print the string formed by putting the operation sign between the two numbers. For example, given **3, 6, +**, print **3 + 6**. Given **A, B, X**, print **A × B**. (Notice in the output the blanks before and after the operation sign.)

19. Revise the program of Exercise 18 to accept the operation sign first.

20. Given a string, print only the third character of the string. (HINT: Use **LEFT$** and then **RIGHT$**.)

21. Given a string, print the third and fourth characters of the string. For example, given **COMPUTER**, print **MP**. (HINT: Use **LEFT$** and **RIGHT$**.)

22. Given a three-letter "word," print all six arrangements of the three letters. For example, given **ABC**, print **ABC, ACB, BAC, BCA, CAB**, and **CBA**. (HINT: "Strip off" each of the three letters by using **LEFT$** and **RIGHT$**.)

ALGEBRA APPLICATIONS

Exercises 23–28 require a background in first-year algebra.

23. Given a real number, print its fourth power.

24. Given a real number, print its fifth power.

25. Given a real number, print its additive inverse.

26. Given a non-zero number, print its multiplicative inverse (reciprocal).

27. Given an integer, print the next consecutive integer.

28. Given an integer, print the preceding consecutive integer.

3

MORE INPUT AND OUTPUT METHODS

LESSONS

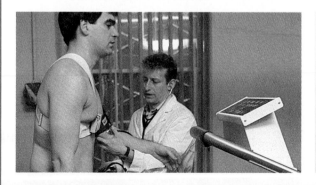

FEATURES

3-1 PROCESSING MORE THAN ONE SET OF DATA

OBJECTIVE:

> **To extend programs to process as many sets of data as the user wishes**

Each program shown up to this point has accepted a set of input data, printed one answer, and stopped. However, a person using a program usually has many sets of data to enter. Example 1 shows how to avoid having to type **RUN** each time you wish to enter new values.

EXAMPLE 1   **a.** Expand the program of Example 1 on page 78 (change from a $1.00 bill) so that it continues accepting input until the user decides to stop.

Program

```
100 PRINT "ENTER AMOUNT OF PURCHASE."
110 INPUT A
120 LET C = 1.00 - A
130 PRINT "CHANGE = $";C
140 PRINT
150 PRINT "WANT TO CONTINUE? (1=YES,0=NO)"
160 INPUT Z
170 IF Z = 1 THEN 100      ◄──── If the value of Z is 1, then
180 END                            go back to statement 100.
```

b. Write the output from a **RUN** of the program.

Output

	Statements Producing the Output
ENTER AMOUNT OF PURCHASE.	100
?.73	110
CHANGE = $.27	120 and 130
	140
WANT TO CONTINUE? (1=YES,0=NO)	150
?1	160
ENTER AMOUNT OF PURCHASE.	100
?.41	110
CHANGE = $.59	120 and 130
	140
WANT TO CONTINUE? (1=YES,0=NO)	150
?0	160

Statement 150 of Example 1 gives the user this code.

Enter 1 to continue running the program; enter 0 to stop.

In statement 160 the answer (1 or 0) is stored as **Z**. Statement 170 is an **IF–THEN** statement. (This type of statement will be considered more fully in Chapter Five.) It is included here to determine whether the user wants to continue.

If **Z = 1**, the computer goes back to statement 100 and executes the steps of the program again.

If at statement 170 **Z** is not 1, the computer ignores **THEN 100** and goes to the next statement in numerical order. This is **180 END**.

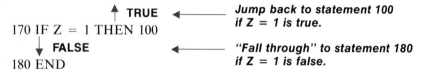

170 IF Z = 1 THEN 100   ↑ **TRUE** ◄────── *Jump back to statement 100 if Z = 1 is true.*

180 END   ↓ **FALSE** ◄────── *"Fall through" to statement 180 if Z = 1 is false.*

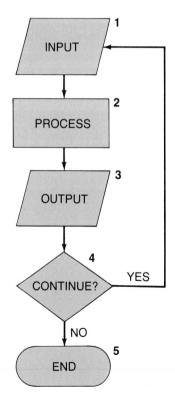

The logic of the program in Example 1 can be shown in the flowchart on the right. The diamond symbol (number 4) shows a **decision point** in the program. A decision has two paths coming from it, called the **YES** branch and the **NO** branch.

NOTE: A decision point in a flowchart corresponds to an **IF–THEN** statement in a **BASIC** program.

In answering the question,

WANT TO CONTINUE?

in the program of Example 1, it is more natural to enter **Y** for yes and **N** for no. For this approach, the variable **Z** in Example 1 must be replaced by a string variable. This is done in Example 2 on the next page.

EXAMPLE 2 **a.** The program of Example 1 on page 69 accepts a person's name and prints the number of characters in that name. Expand that program to continue accepting names as long as the user wishes.

Program

```
10 PRINT "PLEASE TYPE YOUR NAME."
20 INPUT N$
30 LET L = LEN(N$)
40 PRINT L;" CHARACTERS IN YOUR NAME."
50 PRINT "WANT TO CONTINUE (Y/N)?"
60 INPUT Z$
70 IF Z$ = "Y" THEN 10        ← Notice the quotation
80 PRINT "END OF PROGRAM"         marks around Y.
90 END
```

b. Write the output from a **RUN** of the program.

Output

Output	Statements Producing the Output
PLEASE TYPE YOUR NAME.	10
?SAM	20
3 CHARACTERS IN YOUR NAME.	30 and 40
WANT TO CONTINUE (Y/N)?	50
?Y	60
PLEASE TYPE YOUR NAME.	10
?YOLANDA	20
7 CHARACTERS IN YOUR NAME.	30 and 40
WANT TO CONTINUE (Y/N)?	50
?N	60
END OF PROGRAM	80

For now, only the "=" symbol will be used in the **IF** part of an **IF–THEN** statement.

EXAMPLE 3 Which **IF–THEN** statements are correct and contain no syntax errors? For each statement that is incorrect, give a reason.

Statement	Correct?	Reason
85 IF A = B THEN 10	Yes	
40 IF X$ = N THEN 10	No	**N** must be in quotation marks.
70 IF "Y" = Z$ THEN 100	Yes	
90 IF A = "YES" THEN 20	No	The numerical variable **A** cannot equal the string **YES**. A should be A$.
60 IF 1 = K THEN GOTO 30	Probably	

Some computers allow the statement at the left below to be written as the statement at the right.

```
90 IF S = 1 THEN 10    90 IF S = 1 THEN GOTO 10
```

WRITTEN EXERCISES

Write an **IF–THEN** *statement for each of Exercises 1–4.*

1. If **X** is 1, then go to statement **10**.

2. If **A** equals 1, then return to statement **50**.

3. If **T$** equals ''**Y**'', then jump to statement **25**.

4. If **K$** is ''**YES**'', then go to statement **150**.

Determine which **IF–THEN** *statements are correct and contain no syntax errors. For each statement that is incorrect, give a reason.*

5. 100 IF X = 1 THEN 10

6. 80 IF 0 = C THEN 20

7. 120 IF E$ = Y THEN 50

8. 75 IF ''NO'' = S$ THEN 120

9. 155 IF A IS 1 THEN 25

10. 60 IF M = 99, THEN 15

11. 170 IF Q$ = ''NO'' THEN GOTO 5

12. 95 IF J = ''Y'' THEN 40

Complete these programs. Each program should continue processing input until the user wishes to stop.

13. **Problem:** Given a string, print only the last two characters of the string.

```
10 PRINT "TYPE ANY STRING."
20   ?
30 LET C$ = RIGHT$(A$, ? )
40 PRINT "LAST 2 CHARACTERS: "; ?
50 PRINT "ANY MORE STRINGS? (1=YES)"
60 INPUT X
70   ?
80 END
```

14. **Problem:** Given the total charge for a purchase, compute the tax. Assume a tax rate of 6%.

```
10 PRINT "ENTER TOTAL CHARGE."
20 INPUT C
30 LET  ?  = C * .06
40 PRINT "TAX = $";T
50 PRINT "DO ANOTHER? (TYPE Y OR N.)"
60   ?
70 IF K$ =  ?  THEN 10
80 PRINT "THANKS!"
90 END
```

15. Write the output from a **RUN** of the completed program of Exercise 13. Use this input.

AMERICA, 1, COMPUTERS, 0

16. Write the output from a **RUN** of the completed program of Exercise 14. Use this input.

1.00, Y, 5.00, Y, 10.00, N

Correct any errors in these programs.

17.
```
10 REM    EXERCISES 3-1 #17
20         CALCULATE AREA
30 PRINT "ENTER LENGTH OF SIDE."
40 INPUT L
50 LET A = L*L
60 PRINT "AREA = A
70 PRINT "RUN AGAIN?"(Y/N)
80 INPUT R
90 IF R = Y THEN 30
100 END
```

18.
```
10 REM    PROGRAM BY NANAK RAI
15 PRINT "TYPE A WORD".
20 INPUT A$
25 LET D = LEN(A$)
30 PRINT "LETTERS IN WORD =";D
35 PRINT "QUIT? (1/0)"
40 INPUT Q
45 IF 1 = Q THEN 10
50 PRINT "THAT'S ALL!"
55 END
```

19. Add statements to this program to ask whether the user wishes to continue.

```
100 PRINT
110 PRINT "ENTER A NUMBER."
120 INPUT X
130 LET Y = X * X
140 PRINT "SQUARE = ";Y
150 PRINT
```

MORE CHALLENGING EXERCISES

For Exercises 20–22, revise each indicated program. Have each program run until the user indicates there is no more input.

20. Example 1, page 74   **21.** Example 2, page 79   **22.** Example 3, page 80

*Write a **BASIC** program for this problem. The program should continue running until the user indicates there is no more input.*

23. Accept a person's first and last names typed separately at the keyboard. Print the total number of letters in both names.

COMPUTER LAB ACTIVITIES

Processing More Than One Set of Data

1. Enter and **RUN** this program (see Example 1 on page 96). Use input values of $.27 and $.59. Does your computer give the output shown in Example 1?

```
100 PRINT "ENTER AMOUNT OF PURCHASE."
110 INPUT A
120 LET C = 1.00 - A
130 PRINT "CHANGE = $";C
140 PRINT
150 PRINT "WANT TO CONTINUE? (1=YES,0=NO)"
160 INPUT Z
170 IF Z = 1 THEN 100
180 END
```

2. In the program of Exercise 1, replace lines 150, 160, and 170 with this statement.

160 GOTO 100

RUN the program and enter values for **A.** What is the problem now with the program? (In connection with this Exercise, it should be pointed out that every computer has a special key, such as **BREAK**, that stops a program during its **RUN.** Ask your teacher the name of this key for your computer.)

3. Type **NEW.** Then enter and **RUN** the program of Example 2 on page 98. Use these input values: **SAM YOLANDA** is the output the same as that of Example 2?

EXPLORE: IF–THEN, GOTO

4. Type **NEW.** Enter the program of Exercise 1. However, type statement 170 thus.

```
170 IF Z = 1 THEN GOTO 100
```

RUN the program. Does your computer print a syntax error for line 170? If it does not, then your machine accepts this alternate form of the **IF–THEN** statement.

5. Type **NEW.** Then enter the program of Example 2 on page 98. Add this statement.

```
75 IF Z$ <> "N" THEN 50
```

RUN the program. Type any name. Then, after the **WANT TO CONTINUE?** question, type **X.** What happens? What is the only letter you may type to end the program?

3-2 READ AND DATA STATEMENTS

OBJECTIVE: To process DATA by means of READ and DATA statements

Thus far in this text, all data needed by programs has been entered from the keyboard by means of **INPUT** statements. However, **BASIC** offers another way to input values. This method is especially good for long lists of data.

EXAMPLE 1   **a.** Write a program that accepts a name and prints the name and the number of characters in the name. Instead of entering the name by means of an **INPUT** statement, use **READ** and **DATA** statements.

Program
```
100 READ N$
110 LET L = LEN(N$)
120 PRINT N$;" HAS ";L;" CHARACTERS."
130 DATA MARY ANNE
140 END
```

b. Write the output from a **RUN** of the program.

Output   `MARY ANNE HAS 9 CHARACTERS.`

DATA statements allow you to list the input values within the program itself. When a program contains a **DATA** statement, it must have a **READ** statement. Likewise, when a program contains a **READ** statement, it must have a **DATA** statement. **DATA** statements may also contain numerical values. Also, two or more values may be read by a single **READ** statement as shown in the program of Example 2.

EXAMPLE 2   **a.** Write a program which adds any two numbers listed in a **DATA** statement.

Program
```
10 READ A,B
20 DATA 381.6, 278.5
30 LET S = A + B
40 PRINT "SUM = ";S
50 END
```

b. Write the output from a **RUN** of the program.

Output   `SUM = 660.1`

As the programs of Examples 1 and 2 show, a **DATA** statement may appear anywhere in a program before the **END** statement. Also, the order in which the values are listed in the **DATA** statement is important. For the program in Example 2, 381.6 will be read as the value of **A** and 278.5 will be the value of **B**. To obtain the sum of two different numbers, retype statement 20 and **RUN** the program again.

A program may contain more than one **DATA** statement. In Example 2, statement 20 may be replaced by two statements.

```
20  DATA  381.6
25  DATA  278.5
```

The output would be the same as that shown for Example 2.

EXAMPLE 3 Which statements are correct and contain no syntax errors? If a statement is incorrect, give a reason.

Statement	Correct?	Reason
15 READ X$, Y$	Yes	
60 READ A$,B,C	Yes	
10 READ A; B	No	The variables must be separated by a comma, not a semicolon.
23 READ "NUMBER IS";N	No	Only variables are allowed in **READ** statements.
25 READ C+D	No	Operations signs are not allowed in **READ** statements.
90 DATA 2.5, −3, 16	Yes	
82 DATA 3/4,$4.50,6%	No	If the items are numbers, operation signs, %, and $ are not allowed. If the items are strings, the statement is correct.
65 87,91, 80,75, 83,86	No	The word **DATA** must come after the statement number (**65**).
43 DATA 21,18;6,1;7,5	No	Semicolons are not allowed in **DATA** statements except in strings.

A program may read both strings and numbers from **DATA**.

EXAMPLE 4 **a.** Write a program that reads from **DATA** a student's name and year of birth. Print the age of that student in the year 2000.

Program
```
10 REM   PRINT A STUDENT'S AGE IN 2000
20 DATA JIM, 1972
30 READ N$, B
40 LET A = 2000 - B
60 PRINT N$;" WILL BE ";A
70 END
```

b. Write the output from a **RUN** of the program.

Output
```
JIM WILL BE 28
```

WRITTEN EXERCISES

For Exercises 1–14, determine which statements are correct and contain no syntax errors. If a statement is incorrect, give a reason.

1. 10 READ X;Y

2. 85 READ C$, Z

3. 22 READ

4. 15 READ X;

5. 30 READ "ENTER NUMBER."

6. 50 READ X, D$

7. 20 READ K − L

8. 62 DATA 4,7,1, 8,3,2

9. 45 DATA COLTS;BROWNS;JETS

10. 70 DATE 17, 21, 13

11. 25 DATA 2.5,SMITH, 1.7,JONES

12. 52 DATA 4, −3, 0

13. 60 DATA 2*5, 18

14. 77 DATA 6%, 9%, 13%

For Exercises 15–16, complete each program.

15. Problem: Given a person's name and age in 1985, print that person's year of birth.
```
10 READ N$,  ?
20 LET B = 1985 - A
30 PRINT N$;" WAS BORN IN ";  ?
40   ?   DON,14
50   ?
```

16. Problem: Given a string, print the last two characters of the string.
```
100 DATA UNITED STATES
110   ?   X$
120 LET T$ =   ?  (X$,2)
130 PRINT "LAST 2 CHARACTERS ARE";  ?
140 END
```

17. Write the output from a **RUN** of the completed program of Exercise 15.

18. Write the output from a **RUN** of the completed program of Exercise 16.

Correct any errors in the programs of Exercises 19–22.

19.
```
10  READ A;B
20  INPUT A,B
30  LET C = A * B
40  PRINT "PRODUCT =";C
50  END
```

20.
```
100  READ K R
110  DATA 12;  6
120  LET Z = K/R
130  PRINT "QUOTIENT IS  ";Z
140  END
```

21.
```
10  DATA DONNA
15  DATA 95
20  READ N,X
25  LET Y = X * 16
30  PRINT "N WEIGHS ";X;" OUNCES"
35  END
```

22.
```
10  INPUT C$,D
20  LET I = D*.06
30  PRINT C$;"'S INTEREST = ";I
40  DATA 15
50  END
```

MORE CHALLENGING EXERCISES

*For Exercises 23–25, write a **BASIC** program for each problem.*
*Use **READ** and **DATA** statements rather than **INPUT**.*

23. Assume that the school bookstore charges $3.50 for each looseleaf binder. Given the number of binders a student buys, print the cost.

24. Read a person's name and the person's weight in ounces. Print the person's name and the person's weight in pounds, where the number of pounds equals the number of ounces divided by 16.

25. Given two strings, print the string formed by joining the first character of the first string to the last two characters of the second string.

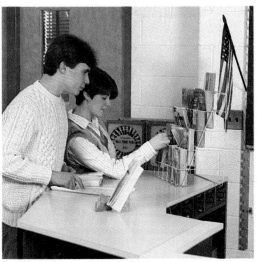

READ and DATA Statements

1. Enter and **RUN** this program (see Example 1 on page 102). Does your computer give the output shown in the Example?

```
100 READ N$
110 LET L = LEN(N$)
120 PRINT N$;" HAS ";L;" CHARACTERS."
130 DATA MARY ANNE
140 END
```

2. In the program of Exercise 1, retype statement 130 as **130 DATA GLENN**. **RUN** the program again. What is the output this time?

3. Type **NEW**. Then enter the program at the right (see Example 2 on page 102). **RUN** the program. Is the output the same as that shown in the Example?

```
10 READ A,B
20 DATA 381.6, 278.5
30 LET S = A + B
40 PRINT "SUM = ";S
50 END
```

4. In the program of Exercise 3, retype statement 20 as **20 DATA 4561, 5987**. **RUN** the program again. What is the output now?

5. In the program of Example 4 on page 104, retype statement 20 as **20 DATA LUPE, 1973**. **RUN** the program again. What is the output?

EXPLORE: DATA AFTER THE END STATEMENT

6. Enter the program of Exercise 1 above. However, instead of typing **140 END**, type **125 END**. **LIST** the program and check that the **DATA** statement now appears after the **END** statement. If it does, **RUN** the program. Is the output the same as the output shown in Example 1 on page 102. If it is, then your computer "finds" the **DATA** even if it is listed after the **END** statement.

Did You Know?

Microprocessor-controlled items such as microwave ovens have **ROM** and **RAM**. The **ROM** has stores instructions that cannot be changed; the **RAM** stores the sequence of buttons a person pushes to "program" the oven.

3-3 GOTO STATEMENTS

OBJECTIVE:

To use GOTO statements in programs

In Section 3–2, each program read from **DATA** only one data value or one set of values. However, as mentioned in Section 3–1, most programs are written to process numerous sets of data. Example 1 uses the **READ/DATA** approach to do this.

EXAMPLE 1 **a.** The program of Example 1 on page 102 read from **DATA** a person's name and printed the number of characters in the name. Expand the program so that it processes more than one name.

Program
```
10 READ N$
20 LET L = LEN(N$)
30 PRINT N$;" HAS ";L;" CHARACTERS."
40 GOTO 10          ◄——————— "10" refers to statement 10.
50 DATA MARY ANNE,YOLANDA,SAM
60 END
```

b. Write the output from a **RUN** of the program.

Output
```
MARY ANNE HAS 9 CHARACTERS.
YOLANDA HAS 7 CHARACTERS.
SAM HAS 3 CHARACTERS.
?OUT OF DATA ERROR IN 10
```

NOTE: The message in the last line of the output above will vary from machine to machine.

In the message

```
?OUT OF DATA ERROR IN 10
```

10 refers to statement 10.

Each time the computer reaches

```
10 READ N$
```

it takes the next value from the **DATA** list and assigns it to N$. The table on the next page traces how the computer executes the program in Example 1.

Statement	What Happens When the Statement Is Executed
10 READ N$	N$ becomes **MARY ANNE**, first name in the **DATA** list.
20 LET L = LEN(N$)	**L** is calculated as 9, the number of characters in **MARY ANNE**.
30 PRINT N$;" HAS ";L;" CHARACTERS."	**MARY ANNE HAS 9 CHARACTERS** is printed.
40 GOTO 10	The computer is sent back to statement 10.
10 READ N$	N$ becomes **YOLANDA** (the next name in the **DATA** list).
20 LET L = LEN(N$)	**L** is calculated as 7.
30 PRINT N$;" HAS ";L;" CHARACTERS."	**YOLANDA HAS 7 CHARACTERS** is printed.
40 GOTO 10	The computer is sent back to statement 10.
10 READ N$	N$ becomes **SAM**.
20 LET L = LEN(N$)	**L** is calculated as 3.
30 PRINT N$;" HAS ";L;" CHARACTERS."	**SAM HAS 3 CHARACTERS** is printed.
40 GOTO 10	The computer is sent back to statement 10.
10 READ N$	Because there are no more names in the **DATA** list, the computer prints **?OUT OF DATA ERROR IN 10** and ends the program.

ADDITIONAL COMMENTS

1. On many systems, **40 GOTO 10** is listed as **40 GO TO 10**.

2. The names in statement 50 could be listed in several **DATA** statements, as in statements 50, 53, and 56.

```
50  DATA  MARY  ANNE
53  DATA  YOLANDA
56  DATA  SAM
```

3. The message **?OUT OF DATA ERROR IN 10** is not the same on all computers. In the program for Example 1, the computer will continue to go back to statement 10 until it has read all the names listed in statement 50.

The program in Example 2 reads both strings and numbers from DATA statements.

EXAMPLE 2 **a.** Write a program which reads from DATA a student's name and year of birth. Print the age of that student in 1985.

Program
```
10 LET C = 1985
20 READ N$, B
30 DATA JIM,1972, DEE,1971, LUCIA,1973
40 LET A = C - B
50 PRINT N$;" IS AGE ";A
60 GOTO 20          ◄─────── Since C is always 1985,
70 END                        there is no need to
                              return to statement 10.
```

b. Write the output from a RUN of the program.

Output
```
JIM IS AGE 13
DEE IS AGE 14
LUCIA IS AGE 12
```

In the DATA list of statement 30, the spaces in front of DEE and LUCIA are not needed. They are included to emphasize that two items in the list are read each time, a name and a birth year. Statement 30 could also be typed as follows.

```
30 DATA JIM,1972,DEE,1971,LUCIA,1973
```

The statement **60 GOTO 20** automatically sends the computer back to statement 20. An IF–THEN statement such as

```
60 IF X = 0 THEN 20
```

tells the computer to go to statement 20 only when $X = 0$. Some computers allow you to type `60 IF X=0 THEN GOTO 20`

WRITTEN EXERCISES

1. Write the output of the program in Example 1 if the DATA statement is changed to the following.

```
50 DATA JOSE,CLAIRE,BRYAN
```

2. Write the output of the program in Example 2 if the DATA statement is changed to the following.

```
30 DATA AKEEM,1974, PAULA,1971, ED,1972, MAMIE,1974
```

3. The program of Example 2 on page 102 added two numbers listed in a **DATA** statement. Modify the program so that it adds as many pairs of numbers as are listed in the **DATA**.

4. Modify the program of Example 4 on page 104 so that it processes as many pairs of names and birth years as are listed in the **DATA**.

For Exercises 5–6, complete each program.

5. **Problem:** Given a person's first and last names, print them in reverse order. Separate the names by a comma.

```
10  READ F$,  _?_
20  LET R$ = L$ + ", " + F$
30  PRINT _?_
40  GOTO _?_
50  _?_  SIDNEY,SMITH,SANDRA,HELM
60  _?_  LAWRENCE,HANDLEY,SARAH,LEE
70  END
```

6. **Problem:** Given the number of tests and total points a student has earned on the tests, print the average.

```
100  _?_  N, T
110  LET A = T/N
120  _?_  "AVERAGE GRADE = ";A
130  DATA 3,270, 5,400, 2,150
140  _?_
150  END
```

7. Write the output from a **RUN** of the completed program of Exercise 5.

8. Write the output from a **RUN** of the completed program of Exercise 6.

Correct any errors in these programs.

9.
```
100  READ X$
110  DATA LINDSEY,DANA,MIKE
120       ELLEN,VICTOR
130  LET L$ = LEFT$(X$)
140  PRINT "FIRST LETTER IS ";L
150  END
```

10.
```
10  134,110,125,122,112,108
20  READ B,A
30  LET B - A = L
40  PRINT "WEIGHT LOSS = L
50  GOTO 10
60  END
```

Athletes use computers to monitor their training.

MORE CHALLENGING EXERCISES

Write a **BASIC** *program for each problem. Use* **READ** *and* **DATA** *statements rather than* **INPUT**. *Include at least three sets of* **DATA** *in each program.*

11. Read a person's name and first initial. Print the first initial, a period, and a space. Then print the last name. For example, for **PERSON,R**, print **R. PERSON**.

12. Given a person's name and present age in years, print the name and how many years it will take for the person to reach the age of 40. For example, it will take a person who is 13 years old 27 more years to reach the age of 40.

13. Given the number of passes attempted by a quarterback and the number completed, print the completion percentage. Use this formula.

$$\textbf{Completion Percentage} = \frac{\textbf{Number Completed}}{\textbf{Number Attempted}}$$

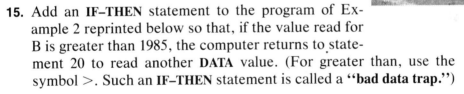

14. Revise the program of Exercise 13 so that the name of the quarterback is included in the **DATA** before the number of attempts and completions. The output should look like this.

```
WOODLEY COMPLETED   .484
BRADSHAW COMPLETED  .5875
FERGUSON COMPLETED  .51875
```

15. Add an **IF–THEN** statement to the program of Example 2 reprinted below so that, if the value read for B is greater than 1985, the computer returns to statement 20 to read another **DATA** value. (For greater than, use the symbol >. Such an **IF–THEN** statement is called a **"bad data trap."**)

```
10 LET C = 1985
20 READ N$, B
30 DATA JIM,1972, DEE,1971, LUCIA,1973
40 LET A = C - B
50 PRINT N$;" IS AGE ";A
60 GOTO 20
70 END
```

16. For the program of Exercise 12 above, write an **IF–THEN** statement to test the value read for the age. If the value is greater than 40, send the computer back to the **READ** statement.

COMPUTER LAB ACTIVITIES

Processing Several Sets of Data

1. Enter and **RUN** this program (see Example 1 on page 107.) Does your computer give the output shown in the Example? Exactly what does your computer print as its **OUT OF DATA** message?

```
10 READ N$
20 LET L = LEN(N$)
30 PRINT N$;" HAS ";L;" CHARACTERS."
40 GOTO 10
50 DATA MARY ANNE,YOLANDA,SAM
60 END
```

2. **RUN** the program of Exercise 1 again, using the data in Exercise 1 on page 109. Is the output you wrote for Exercise 1 produced?

3. Type **NEW**. Then enter and **RUN** the program of Example 2 on page 109. Is the output the same as that shown in Example 2?

4. **RUN** the program of Example 2 again, using the data in Exercise 2 on page 109. Is the output you wrote for Exercise 2 produced?

5. **RUN** the completed program of Exercise 5 on page 110. Was the output you wrote for Exercise 7 on that page actually produced?

EXPLORE: Variations in GOTO and DATA Statements

6. Enter the program of Exercise 1 above. **LIST** the program. How does the computer list statement 40? Does it show either of the following?

```
40 GOTO 10     40 GO TO 10
```

7. Replace statement 50 of the program of Exercise 1 above with these three statements. **RUN** the program again. Is the output the same as that shown in the output of Example 1 on page 107?

```
50 DATA MARY ANNE
53 DATA YOLANDA
56 DATA SAM
```

8. On some machines, a comma at the end of a **DATA** statement will cause no problem. To test this, retype line 50 as follows.

```
50 DATA MARY ANNE,
```

RUN the program. Is the output the same as before? If not, is some kind of error message printed (other than **?OUT OF DATA ERROR**)?

REVIEW: SECTIONS 3–1—3–3

Write an **IF–THEN** *statement for each of Exercises 1–2.*

1. If A is 1, then go to statement 20.

2. If K$ is "YES", then jump to statement 40.

Determine which statements are correct and contain no syntax errors. For each statement that is incorrect, give a reason.

3. 110 7, 36, 18, 45, 62

4. 120 IF T$=YES THEN 50

For Exercises 5–6, complete each program. Each program should continue processing input until the user wishes to stop.

5. **Problem:** Given a string, print the length of the string.

```
10  PRINT "TYPE ANY STRING."
20   ?
30  LET L = LEN(A$)
40  PRINT "THE NUMBER OF CHARACTERS IS ";  ?
50  PRINT "ANY MORE STRINGS? (1=YES)"
60  INPUT X
70   ?
80  END
```

6. **Problem:** Given a person's first and last name, print that person's initials.

```
10  READ   ?  ,L$
20  LET B$ = LEFT$(F$,1)
30  LET C$ =   ?
40  PRINT B$;".";  ?  ;"."
50  GOTO   ?
60  DATA MARY,JONES,  JAMES,SMITH
70  DATA SARA,SANDERS
80   ?
```

7. Write the output of a **RUN** of the completed program of Exercise 5. Use this input: **TOURNAMENT, 1, COUNTRY, 0**.

8. Write the output from a **RUN** of the completed program of Exercise 6.

9. Correct any errors in the program shown at the right.

```
10  PRINT "ENTER THE NAME."
20  INPUT Q
30  LET L = LEN$(Q$)
40  PRINT L
50  PRINT "IS THERE MORE? (1=YES)"
60  INPUT T
70  IF T=1 THEN 80
80  END
```

THE CARE AND HANDLING OF DISKETTES

A **diskette** or **"floppy disk"** is a thin circular piece of plastic about $5\frac{1}{4}$ inches in diameter on which data is recorded as magnetic spots. This data is written in circles called **tracks**. Pie-shaped divisions called **sectors** are also indicated by invisible magnetic marks on the disk.

One track on the disk is reserved for the **directory**. When a disk operating system writes data on a disk, it records in the directory the name of the **file** (a program or set of data) and the **address** (section and track) where the file begins. In this way, when the operating system is asked to load the file into memory, it can find the file on the disk.

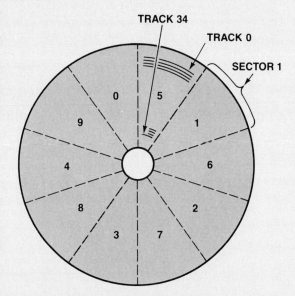

Hundreds of thousands of characters (letters, numbers, special symbols, and so on) can be stored on a disk. Since a tiny dust particle or fingerprint can erase a block of data, diskettes must be handled carefully. Here are some tips for handling floppy disks.

1. Never touch the surface of a disk. Pick up the disk from the side opposite the read/write opening and hold it with your fingers on the jacket.

2. When a disk is not in the drive, keep it in its outer jacket. When you are finished with it, store it in a file box.

3. <u>Never</u> bend or fold a disk. Insert any disk carefully and slowly in the drive to avoid jamming and bending.

4. Do not place any object (such as a bottle, a book, or a pen) on a disk, even when it is in its outer jacket. Avoid spilling food or liquid on a disk.

5. Use a felt-tip pen or marker to write your name or the name of a file on a label of a disk. A pencil or ballpoint pen would make grooves in the surface. Do not use an eraser on a disk.

6. Never expose a disk to heat or to the sun. Never put it near a magnet or unshielded magnetic field.

7. Never put a paper clip or rubber band on a disk.

8. Important programs and files should be "backed up" on two disks.

9. Each disk has a "write-project" notch in its jacket. When this notch is covered with a tab, a drive will not write on that disk. In this way, you protect important files from accidental erasure.

PROJECTS

If the computer you use has a disk drive, consult its manual to answer the next three questions.

1. How many tracks and sectors does it use? What is the maximum amount of information it can store on a disk?

2. How do you obtain a listing of the names of the files on a disk?

3. Before it can be used by a computer, a blank disk must be "initialized" or "formatted." What does this mean? How is this done for your machine?

4. Suppose a disk contains information written by one type of computer. Usually that disk cannot be read by a computer made by a different company. Give several reasons why this is true.

5. What are the differences between a "hard disk" and a "floppy disk"? What are the advantages of a hard disk?

3-4 "PRETTY" PRINTING

OBJECTIVE: To write the output of programs that print in zones

When the output of a program is not neat, it becomes difficult to read. This lesson shows ways to improve printouts.

EXAMPLE 1 Revise the program of Example 1 on page 107 so that the names and the lengths of the names are printed in two columns as shown on the right.

```
MARY ANNE 9
YOLANDA    7
SAM        3
```

Program
```
10 READ N$
20 LET L = LEN(N$)
30 PRINT N$, L
40 GOTO 10
50 DATA MARY ANNE,YOLANDA,SAM
60 END
```

In previous **PRINT** statements, semicolons separated items. A comma between variables or strings in a **PRINT** statement, as in statement 30 above, tells the computer to skip to the next **zone** of the screen or printer. Each computer divides its screen or printer into a fixed number of zones. The effect of statement 30 can be summarized as follows.

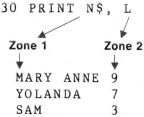

```
30 PRINT N$, L
```

Zone 1   Zone 2

```
MARY ANNE  9
YOLANDA    7
SAM        3
```

The commas spread the output into two columns. If statement 30 were changed as shown at the left below, the numbers would be printed right after the names.

Change	Output
40 PRINT N$; L	MARY ANNE9
	YOLANDA7
	SAM3

EXAMPLE 2 **a.** Write a program to read from **DATA** students' scores on two exams. Print the two scores and the total of the scores in three columns.

Program

```
10 READ X, Y
20 LET T = X + Y
30 PRINT X, Y, T
40 GOTO 10
50 DATA 87,91, 80,75, 83,86, 95,85
60 END
```

b. Write the output from a **RUN** of the program.

Output

87	91	178
80	75	155
83	86	169
95	85	180

EXAMPLE 3 Write the output from this program. List the number of the statement producing each line of output.

```
5  DATA MOO,OINK,BARK
10 PRINT
20 READ X$
30 LET Y$ = X$ + "-" + X$
40 PRINT X$, Y$
50 GOTO 10
60 END
```

Output

		Statements Producing the Output
		10 (blank line)
MOO	MOO-MOO	40
		10 (blank line)
OINK	OINK-OINK	40
		10 (blank line)
BARK	BARK-BARK	40

The output from the program of Example 3 is "double-spaced." This means that every other line is blank.

WRITTEN EXERCISES

1. For the program of Example 1, write the output if the **DATA** statement is replaced by the following.
   50 DATA HORTENSE,WALLY,CRAIG,EMILY

2. For the program of Example 2, write the output if the **DATA** statement is replaced by the following.
   50 DATA 76,68, 80,90, 81,78

3. Suppose that statement **35 PRINT** is added to the program of Example 2. Write the output of the revised program. Use the **DATA** listed in Exercise 2.

4. For the program of Example 3, write the output if the **DATA** statement is replaced by the following.
   5 DATA WALLA,BUZZ,HURRY,GO

5. In the program of Example 3, suppose that statement 50 is changed to **50 GOTO 20**. Write the output of the revised program. Use the **DATA** listed in Exercise 4.

Write the output of each program.

6.
```
10  PRINT
20  READ K$, L$
30  LET S$ = K$ + L$
40  PRINT S$,K$,L$
50  GOTO 10
60  DATA PRO,GRAM,COMP,UTER,AD,AM
70  END
```

7.
```
100  DATA 5, 4, 10 3
110  READ A
120  LET S = A * A
130  PRINT A, S
140  GOTO 110
150  END
```

Complete these programs.

8. **Problem:** Given the number of wins and losses of a baseball team, print the total number of games played.
```
100  DATA 9,1, 5,5, 0,3
110   ?  W, L
120  LET  ?  = W + L
130  PRINT W, L, T
140   ?  110
150   ?
```

9. **Problem:** Given a person's name and age in years, print the name and the age in months.
```
10  READ  ? , Y
20  LET M = 12 *  ?
30  PRINT N$,  ?
40  GOTO  ?
50  DATA RACHEL,12,BOB,13,DOT,11
60  END
```

10. Write the output of the completed program of Exercise 8.

11. Write the output of the completed program of Exercise 9.

Correct any errors in these programs.

12.
```
100 REM   DIVISION OF NUMBERS
200 READ X, Y
300 LET Z = X / Y
400 PRINT X; Y; Z
500 GOTO 10
600 END
```

13.
```
10 REM   PRINT NAME AND 1ST LETTER
20 DATA BOB,CHERI,GARY
40 READ Z$
60 LET L$ = RIGHT(Z$,1)
80 PRINT Z$ L$
100 GOTO 20
120 END
```

```
BOB     B
CHERI   C
GARY    G
```

MORE CHALLENGING EXERCISES

Write a **BASIC** *program for each problem. In each problem, use* **READ** *and* **DATA** *statements.*

14. Given each worker's weekly pay, print the pay and the amount of income tax. Assume that the tax rate is 6%. Print the pay and the tax in two columns.

15. The **DATA** is the number of goals and number of assists of a hockey player. Compute the total points scored. Use this formula.

Total Points = Number of Goals + Number of Assists

Print the output in three columns:

GOALS, AS- SISTS, TOTAL POINTS

16. Expand the program of Exercise 15 so that the name of each player is also included in the **DATA**. If your computer has four zones, print the output in four columns: name, goals, assists, and total points. If your computer has only three zones, print the names on every other line (see below).

```
GRETSKY
28          36          64
HOWE
30          18          48
```
and so on.

COMPUTER LAB ACTIVITIES

Printing In Zones

1. Enter and **RUN** this program (see Example 1 on page 116). Does your computer give the output shown on that page?

```
10  READ N$
20  LET L = LEN(N$)
30  PRINT N$, L
40  GOTO 10
50  DATA MARY ANNE,YOLANDA,SAM
60  END
```

2. Type **NEW**. Enter and **RUN** this program (see Example 2 on page 117). Does your computer give the output shown on that page?

```
10  READ X, Y
20  LET T = X + Y
30  PRINT X, Y, T
40  GOTO 10
50  DATA 87,91, 80,75, 83,86, 95,85
60  END
```

3. Type **NEW**. Then enter and **RUN** this program (see Example 3 on page 117). Is the output shown in the Example actually produced?

```
5   DATA MOO,OINK,BARK
10  PRINT
20  READ X$
30  LET Y$ = X$ + "-" + X$
40  PRINT X$, Y$
50  GOTO 10
60  END
```

4. Enter and **RUN** the programs of Exercises 6–7 on page 118. Is the output you wrote actually produced?

5. Enter and **RUN** the programs you completed for Exercises 8–9 on page 118. Is the output you wrote for Exercises 10–11 on page 119 actually produced?

6. Enter and RUN the corrected programs of Exercises 12–13 on page 119. Were all errors corrected? If not, make further corrections until each program runs correctly.

EXPLORE: ZONES FOR YOUR COMPUTER

To find how many zones your computer has, enter these direct commands. Note the output each time.

7. PRINT 1, 2

8. PRINT 1, 2, 3

9. PRINT 1,2,3,4

10. PRINT 1,2,3,4,5

11. For which commands of Exercises 7–10 did the computer print all the numbers on one line?

12. How many zones does your computer have? Are the zones of equal width? What is done with the extra numbers when there are more numbers than zones?

3-5 PRINTING HEADINGS

OBJECTIVE: **To print output in columns with headings**

It is often helpful to print headings over output organized in columns.

EXAMPLE 1 **a.** Revise the program of Example 1 on page 116 so that the headings **NAME** and **LENGTH** are printed over the two columns.

Program
```
3  PRINT
5  PRINT "NAME","LENGTH"
7  PRINT
10 READ N$
20 LET L = LEN(N$)
30 PRINT N$, L
40 GOTO 10
50 DATA MARY ANNE,YOLANDA,SAM
60 END
```

> NOTE: In statements 5 and 30, commas are used so that the headings will appear above the zones for the name and number of characters.

b. Write the output from a **RUN** of the program.

Output

Output	Statements Producing the Output
	3 (blank line)
NAME LENGTH	5
	7 (blank line)
MARY ANNE 9	30
YOLANDA 7	30
SAM 3	30

> NOTE: Statement 40 causes the headings to be printed only once.

On many machines, positive numbers in a zone print one column to the right of strings.

```
NAME          LENGTH
MARY ANNE      9
YOLANDA        7
SAM            3
```

EXAMPLE 2 Revise the program of Example 2 on page 117 so that the output is printed as shown below.

Output

```
======    ======    =====
EXAM  1   EXAM  2    TOTAL
======    ======    =====
87        91         178
80        75         155
83        86         169
95        85         180
```

Program

```
3   PRINT "======","======","====="
5   PRINT "EXAM 1","EXAM 2","TOTAL"
7   PRINT "======","======","====="
10  READ X, Y
20  LET T = X + Y
30  PRINT X, Y, T
40  GOTO 10
50  DATA 87,91, 80,75, 83,86, 95,85
60  END
```

NOTE: Statements 3, 5, and 7 are executed only once.

Statements 10, 20, 30, and 40 are executed over and over until the **DATA** in statement 50 runs out.

EXAMPLE 3 Write the output from this program.

List the number of the statement producing each line of output.

Program

```
100 REM    READ A PERSON'S NAME AND YEAR OF BIRTH.
110 REM    PRINT THE NAME, YEAR, AND THE PERSON'S
120 REM    AGE IN THE YEAR 2000.
130 DATA KELLY,1972, CARTER,1974, AMY,1971
140 PRINT
150 PRINT "NAME","YEAR","AGE IN 2000"
160 PRINT
170 READ N$, Y
180 LET A = 2000 - Y
190 PRINT N$, Y, A
200 GOTO 160
210 END
```

Output

Output			Statements Producing the Output
			140 (blank line)
NAME	YEAR	AGE IN 2000	150
			160 (blank line)
KELLY	1972	28	190
			160 (blank line)
CARTER	1974	26	190
			160 (blank line)
AMY	1971	29	190
			160 (blank line)

NOTE: If your computer has fewer than three built-in zones, the output from Examples 2 and 3 will not look like the output shown. The **TAB** function (explained in the Section 3–6), must be used to set up the three columns.

WRITTEN EXERCISES

1. For the program of Example 1, write the output if the **DATA** statement is replaced by the following.

   ```
   50 DATA ALVIN,JEANNE,MARY,WILLIAM
   ```

2. For the program of Example 1, suppose that statement **40 GOTO 10** is changed to **40 GOTO 7**. Write the output of the revised program. Use the **DATA** listed in Exercise 1.

3. For the program of Example 2, write the output if the **DATA** statement is replaced by the following.

   ```
   60 DATA 76,68, 80,90, 81,78
   ```

4. In the program of Example 2, suppose that statement **40 GOTO 10** is changed to **40 GOTO 7**. Write the output of the revised program. Use the **DATA** listed in Exercise 3.

5. For the program of Example 3, write the output if the **DATA** statement is replaced by the following statements.

   ```
   130 DATA ARNIE,1970,ROSE,1968
   135 DATA ANNE,1973,SALVADOR,1966
   ```

6. In Example 3, change statement **200** to **200 GOTO 170**. Write the output of the revised program. Use the **DATA** listed in Exercise 5.

Write the output of each program.

7.
```
100 DATA ANDERS,270,SHAW,240
105 DATA SMITH,255,ZAHN,267
110 PRINT "2ND PERIOD CLASS"
120 PRINT "----------------"
130 PRINT "STUDENT","GRADE"
140 READ S$, T
150 LET G = T/3
160 PRINT S$, G
170 GOTO 140
180 END
```

8.
```
10 PRINT
15 PRINT "WORD","FIRST LETTER"
20 PRINT "****","************"
30 READ W$
40 LET F$ = LEFT$(W$,1)
50 PRINT W$, F$
60 GOTO 20
70 DATA OHIO,IOWA,IDAHO
80 END
```

Complete these programs.

9. Problem: Given a player's scores on two tries at a video game, print the scores and the amount of increase or decrease.

```
10 PRINT
20  ?  "GAME 1","GAME 2","CHANGE"
30 READ G, H
40 LET  ?  = H - G
50 PRINT  ? ,  ? , C
60 GOTO  ?
70  ?  185,160, 170,195, 200,215
80 END
```

10. Problem: Given a number of meters, compute the number of centimeters. Print meters and centimeters in labeled columns.

```
100 DATA 38,2.76,99.1
110 PRINT "------","-----------"
120 PRINT " ? "," ? "
130  ?  "------","-----------"
140  ?  M
150 LET C = 100 *  ?
160 PRINT M, C
170  ?  130
180 END
```

11. Write the output of the completed program of Exercise 9.

12. Write the output of the completed program of Exercise 10.

Correct any errors in this program.

13.
```
10 DATA LEON, LESLIE, DANIELLE
20 PRINT
30 READ Z$
40 LET L$ = RIGHT(Z$,1)
50 PRINT "NAME","LAST LETTER"
60 PRINT Z$, L$
70 GOTO 20
80 END
```

MORE CHALLENGING EXERCISES

Write a **BASIC** *program for each problem. In each program, use* **READ** *and* **DATA** *statements.*

14. Given a person's present weight and what the person would like to weigh, compute how much the person must gain or lose to reach the desired weight. Print the output in three labeled columns: **WEIGHT**, **GOAL**, and **DIFFERENCE**.

15. Given a person's name and the number of hours the person slept yesterday, print the number of hours the person was awake. Print the output in three labeled columns: **NAME**, **SLEPT**, **AWAKE**.

16. The **DATA** is the number of games played and the total number of points scored. Compute the number of points per game. Use this formula.

Points per Game = Total Points ÷ Number of Games Played.

Print the output in three labeled columns:

GAMES, POINTS, AVERAGE.

17. Expand the program of Example 1 so that the output is printed as shown at the right. (Each * is in the first column of the second zone. The **LENGTH** is in the third zone.)

```
              *
NAME          *        LENGTH
              *
MARY ANNE     *          9
              *
YOLANDA       *          7
              *            and so on.
```

COMPUTER LAB ACTIVITIES

Printing Headings

1. Enter and **RUN** this program (see Example 1 on page 121). Does your computer give the output shown in the Example?

```
3    PRINT
5    PRINT "NAME","LENGTH"
7    PRINT
10   READ N$
20   LET L = LEN(N$)
30   PRINT N$, L
40   GOTO 10
50   DATA MARY ANNE,YOLANDA,SAM
60   END
```

2. Change the program of Example 1 as indicated in Exercise 2 on page 123. Then **RUN** the revised program. Is the output the same as what you wrote for Exercise 2?

3. In the program of Exercise 1 at the right above, change statement 40 to **40 GOTO 3**. **RUN** the revised program. What is wrong with the output?

4. Type **NEW**. Then enter and **RUN** the program below (see Example 2 on page 122). Is the output the same as that shown in the Example?

```
3    PRINT "======","======","====="
5    PRINT "EXAM 1","EXAM 2","TOTAL"
7    PRINT "======","======","====="
10   READ X, Y
20   LET T = X + Y
30   PRINT X, Y, T
40   GOTO 10
50   DATA 87,91, 80,75, 83,86, 95,85
60   END
```

5. Change the program of Example 2 as indicated in Exercise 4 on page 123. **RUN** the revised program. Is the output you wrote for Exercise 4 produced?

6. Type **NEW**. Then enter and **RUN** the program of Example 3 on page 122. Is the output shown in the Example actually produced?

7. Replace the **DATA** of the program of Example 3 with the **DATA** listed in Exercise 5 on page 123. **RUN** the program. Is the output you wrote for Exercise 5 actually produced?

8. Change the program of Example 3 as indicated in Exercise 6 on page 123. **RUN** the program. Is the output you wrote for Exercise 6 actually produced?

9. Enter and **RUN** the programs of Exercises 7–8 on page 124. Is the output you wrote for each program actually produced?

10. **RUN** the programs you completed for Exercises 9–10 on page 124. Compare the output with your answers to Exercises 11–12 on page 124.

11. Enter the program of Exercise 1 on page 126. Add these statements.

    ```
    15 IF N$="STOP" THEN 60
    55 DATA STOP
    ```

    RUN the program. How does the output differ from that in Exercise 1?

12. A codeword or value like **STOP** at the end of the **DATA** list is called a "sentinel." Why do you think this term is used for such a value?

13. Add these statements to the revised program of Exercise 1.

    ```
    60 PRINT
    70 PRINT "END OF PROGRAM"
    80 END
    ```

    RUN the program again. What is the output now?

Airports use computerized radar for air traffic control.

14. Type **NEW**. Then enter the program of Exercise 4 on page 126. Add these statements.

    ```
    15 IF X = 0 THEN 60
    55 DATA 0,0
    ```

    RUN the revised program. Is an **OUT OF DATA** message printed?

15. Revise the program of Exercise 4 on page 126 so that, after printing 95, 85, and 180, the program skips a line and prints **END OF DATA LIST** before stopping.

16. Revise the program of Example 3 on page 122 so that no **OUT OF DATA** message is printed at the bottom of the output. **RUN** your revised program. If necessary, make corrections until the program produces the desired output.

Did You Know?

A **64K RAM** contains 152,000 components and occupies an amount of space less than that needed for an ant. This photo compares the space occupied by a RAM with the space occupied by a common pin.

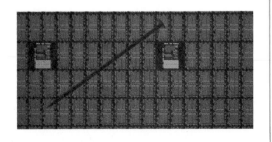

3-6 THE TAB FUNCTION

OBJECTIVE: To write the output of programs containing the TAB function

Example 2 on page 122 shows a program that prints output in three preset zones of the screen or printer. Suppose that the output of a program requires more columns than there are zones. Or suppose that the programmer wants the output in columns but not in the regular zones. The **TAB** function is useful in such cases.

NOTE: Some forms of **BASIC**, such as Atari **BASIC**, do not have the **TAB** function.

EXAMPLE 1 Revise the program of Example 2 on page 122 (total of two tests) so that the three columns are no longer equally spaced. Print the outout as shown below.

Column 1	9	20
↓	↓	↓
EXAM 1	EXAM 2	TOTAL
87	91	178
80	75	155
83	86	169
95	85	180

NOTE: The output will end with the usual **OUT OF DATA** message.

Program
```
 3  PRINT
 5  PRINT "EXAM 1";TAB(9);"EXAM 2";TAB(20);"TOTAL"
 8  PRINT
10  READ X, Y
20  LET T = X + Y
30  PRINT X;TAB(9);Y;TAB(20);T
40  GOTO 10
50  DATA 87,91, 80,75, 83,86
60  END
```

In statements 5 and 30, the expression **TAB(9)** tells the computer to skip to print position 9 (from the left margin) of the current line. Similarly, **TAB(20)** causes the computer to print the next item (A) starting at position 20. In this way, the program creates its own zones.

Many computers number the screen columns starting at 1. That is, the first column at the left margin is position 1. However, other machines start the column numbers at 0. In the programs shown in this book, the first column at the left will be position 1. If your machine starts at 0, subtract one from the number in parentheses after each **TAB** in programs.

Here is exactly what statement 30 of the program in Example 1 tells the computer to do.

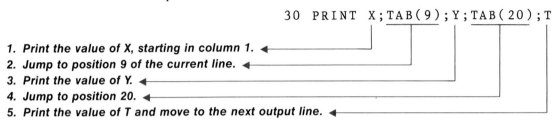

```
30  PRINT  X;TAB(9);Y;TAB(20);T
```

1. *Print the value of X, starting in column 1.*
2. *Jump to position 9 of the current line.*
3. *Print the value of Y.*
4. *Jump to position 20.*
5. *Print the value of T and move to the next output line.*

The **TAB** function is used only in **PRINT** statements. Semicolons should separate a **TAB** expression from any variables or strings before and after it. Do **not** use a comma because the computer would ignore the number in parentheses after **TAB** and would jump to the next built–in zone.

In the table below, assume that X = − 10, Y = 100, N$ = "AN-DERSON", and A = 87.5.

EXAMPLES OF PRINT STATEMENTS INVOLVING THE TAB FUNCTION

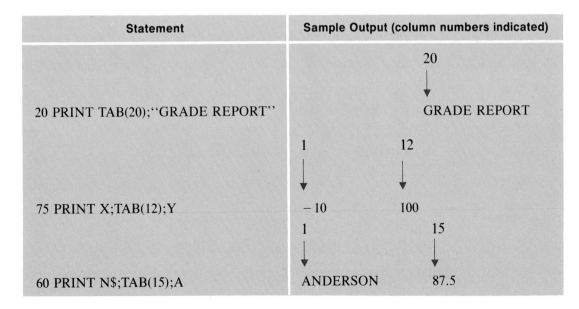

Statement	Sample Output (column numbers indicated)
20 PRINT TAB(20);"GRADE REPORT"	20 ↓ GRADE REPORT
75 PRINT X;TAB(12);Y	1 ↓ −10 12 ↓ 100
60 PRINT N$;TAB(15);A	1 ↓ ANDERSON 15 ↓ 87.5

EXAMPLE 2 Expand the program of Example 1 so that each student's name is included in the **DATA**.

Print the output in this form.

Output   ◄——— *Blank line*

                            GRADE REPORT
                                                              ◄——— *Blank line*
        STUDENT   EXAM 1   EXAM 2   TOTAL
                                                              ◄——— *Blank line*
        ANDERSON   87   91   178
        BROOKS   80   75   155
        CHANEY   83   86   169
        HERNANDEZ   95   85   180

              ↑   ↑   ↑   ↑
Column   1   15   23   31

Program

```
1    PRINT
2    PRINT TAB(13);"GRADE  REPORT"
3    PRINT
5    PRINT "STUDENT";TAB(15);"EXAM 1   EXAM 2   AVERAGE"
8    PRINT
10   READ N$, X, Y
20   LET T = X + Y
30   PRINT N$;TAB(15);X;TAB(23);T;TAB(31);A
40   GOTO 10
50   DATA ANDERSON,87,91,BROOKS,80,75,CHANEY,83,86
60   DATA HERNANDEZ,95,85
70   END
```

In statement 5, it is shorter to type

                "EXAM 1   EXAM 2   AVERAGE"

rather than

        "EXAM 1";TAB(23);"EXAM 2";TAB(31);"AVERAGE"

But to change statement 5 in this way, you must count spaces inside quotation marks carefully. Otherwise, the headings will not be lined up correctly over the output values.

EXAMPLE 3 Which statements are correct and contain no syntax errors? For each statement that is incorrect, give a reason.

Statement	Correct?	Reason
90 PRINT X;TAB;Y	No	**TAB** must have a quantity in parentheses behind it.
75 PRINT TAB(10),A	Yes	However, the comma before **A** will cancel the effect of **TAB(10)** by sending the computer to the next zone after position 10.
50 PRINT M, N; TAB(30); K	Yes	
63 PRINT "ANSWERS ARE";TAB(20);	Yes	
90 PRINT TAB 25;X	No	The number 25 must be in parentheses.
45 PRINT TAB (10);"ANSWER"	Possibly	On some computers the space between **TAB** and **(10)** must be removed.

WRITTEN EXERCISES

Write the output of each **PRINT** *statement. As in Examples 1 and 2, mark the beginning columns of the numbers and strings. Assume that X = 14 and Y = 5.*

1. 30 PRINT X;TAB(12);Y

2. 60 PRINT TAB(10);X;TAB(20);Y

3. 45 PRINT "FIRST";TAB(15);"SECOND"

4. 95 PRINT "XC =";X;TAB(18); "Y =";Y

For Exercises 5–10, determine which statements are correct and contain no syntax errors. For each statement that is incorrect, give a reason.

5. 110 PRINT TAB(10);X,Y

6. 80 PRINT TAB(8);A;TAB(5);R

7. 75 PRINT G,TAB(12),L

8. 140 PRINT K;TAB(9);L;TAB;M

9. 55 PRINT "X =;TAB(10);X

10. 132 PRINT "RESULT =";Z;TAB(20);

11. Revise the program of Example 1 on page 121 so that the column labeled **LENGTH** begins in column 15.

12. Revise the program of Example 3 on page 122 so that the column labeled **YEAR** on page 123 begins in column 15 and the column labeled **AGE IN 2000** begins in column 23.

For Exercises 13–14, write the output. As in Examples 1 and 2, mark the beginning columns of the numbers and strings.

13.
```
10  PRINT
20  PRINT "LENGTH";TAB(12);"WIDTH";TAB(24);"AREA"
30  PRINT "======";TAB(12);"=====";TAB(24);"===="
40  DATA 10,5, 50,15, 25,4
50  READ L, W
60  LET A = L * W
70  PRINT L;TAB(12);W;TAB(24);A
80  GOTO 50
90  END
```

14.
```
100  DATA BERGER,2,CALDWELL,1,PEREZ,0,RODRIGUEZ,4
110  PRINT
120  PRINT TAB(9);"WORKERS' DEPENDENTS"
130  PRINT "NAME";TAB(15);"# OF CHILDREN"
140  READ W$, C
150  PRINT W$;TAB(20);C
160  GOTO 140
170  END
```

For Exercises 15–16, complete the programs.

15. Problem: Given a person's weight last month and weight today, print these weights and the gain or loss.
```
10  PRINT "BEFORE";TAB(12);"AFTER";
20  PRINT TAB(24);"GAIN/LOSS"
30  PRINT
40  READ L, _?_
50  LET _?_ = L - T
60  PRINT L;_?_;T;_?_;G
70  GOTO 30
80  _?_ 110,106,121,125,98,99
90  _?_
```

16. Problem: Acme Storage charges $5 per ounce to store parcels. Given the number of ounces, print the charge.
```
100  DATA 30,10,15
110  PRINT
120  _?_ "OUNCES";TAB(_?_);"CHARGE"
130  READ N
140  LET C = _?_
150  PRINT _?_;TAB(14);_?_
160  PRINT
170  _?_ 130
180  END
```

17. Write the output of the completed program of Exercise 15.

18. Write the output of the completed program of Exercise 16.

Correct any errors in these programs.

19.
```
10  PRINT
20  PRINT "YEARS";TAB15;"DAYS"
30  DATA 13, 11, 9
40  READ Y
60  LET D = 365 * Y
70  PRINT "Y;TAB15;D"
80  GOTO 10
90  END
```

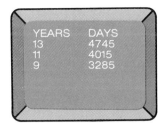

20.
```
100  PRINT TAB (20);"GRADE LIST"
110  PRINT
120  READ S$, G
130  LET X = G * 100
140  PRINT S$,TAB(15),X
150  DATA ADAMS,.67,BELL,.75
151  DATA CRUZ,.88,DANIELS
160  END
```

MORE CHALLENGING EXERCISES

Write a program to print each letter as a large block letter. As in the sample on the right below, use the letter itself to form the large block.

NOTE: *Each program should include the **TAB** function.*

21. N

22. M

23. W

24. Z

```
N               N
N N             N
N   N           N
N     N         N
N       N     N N
N               N
```

*Write a **BASIC** program for each problem. **READ** all input from **DATA** statements. Each program should include the **TAB** function.*

25. In gym class, students do push-ups the first day of the term and again on the last day. Given a student's name and the number of push-ups of that student at the beginning and end of the term, compute the increase or decrease. If your computer's screen is wide enough, the output should look like this.

Column 1	15	22	30
STUDENT	BEGIN	END	CHANGE
-------	-----	---	------
GELE	8	15	7
HOFFMAN	12	20	8
KORNOVICH	14	11	-3
SPERA	10	8	-2	and so on

26. At the end of every work day, each cashier of the Jiffy Super Market turns in bills and coins. Given the I.D. number of each cashier, the amount in bills, and the amount in coins turned in by that cashier, print the total amount turned in. Print the output like this.

Column 1	9	16	23
I.D. #	BILLS	COINS	TOTAL
143	283	44.12	327.12
761	416	38.75	454.75
952	123	27.04	150.04	and so on

*Write the output of each **PRINT** statement for the computer you use. As in Examples 1 and 2, mark the beginning column of each number or string. Assume that A = 1.5, B = −2.3, and C = 10.7.*

27. 23 PRINT A, B;TAB(22); C

28. 90 PRINT A;TAB(10);B,C

29. 87 PRINT TAB(5);A;TAB(12);B,C

30. 55 PRINT "A =","B =";TAB(28);"C ="

31. Revise the program of Exercise 16 on page 119. Use the **TAB** function to fit on one line each player's name, number of goals, assists, and total points.

COMPUTER LAB ACTIVITIES

TAB Function

1. Enter and **RUN** this program (see Example 1 on page 128). Does your computer give the output shown in Example 1?

```
3   PRINT
5   PRINT "EXAM 1";TAB(9);"EXAM 2";TAB(20);"TOTAL"
8   PRINT
10  READ X, Y
20  LET T = X + Y
30  PRINT X;TAB(9);Y;TAB(20);T
40  GOTO 10
50  DATA 87,91, 80,75, 83,86
60  END
```

2. Add these statements to the program of Example 1 (see Example 2 on page 130).

```
1   PRINT
2   PRINT TAB(13);"GRADE REPORT"
10  READ N$, X, Y
30  PRINT N$;TAB(15);X;TAB(23);T;TAB(31);A
50  DATA ANDERSON,87,91,BROOKS,80,75,CHANEY,83,86
60  DATA HERNANDEZ,95,85
70  END
```

RUN the program. Is the output the same as that shown in Example 2?

3. Type **NEW**. Then enter and **RUN** the revised program you wrote for Exercise 11 on page 132. Does the program produce the desired output? If not, revise it until it does.

4. Type **NEW**. Then enter and **RUN** the revised program you wrote for Exercise 12 on page 132. Does the program produce the desired output? If not, revise it until it does.

5. Enter and **RUN** the programs of Exercises 13–14 on page 132. Is the output you wrote for each exercise actually produced?

6. Enter and **RUN** the program you completed for Exercise 15 on page 132. Is the output you predicted in Exercise 17 on that page produced?

EXPLORE: VARIATIONS IN THE TAB FUNCTION

7. What does the computer do if told to **TAB** to a print position beyond the width of the screen? To find out, type the direct command **PRINT 1;TAB(90);2** and press **RETURN** (or **ENTER**). Did the computer execute the command and, if it did, where did it print the 2?

REVIEW: Sections 3–4—3–6

For Exercises 1–2, write the output of each program.

1.
```
10  DATA  6,4,12,3
20  READ  B,C
30  LET  P = B * C
40  PRINT  B,C,P
50  GOTO  20
60  END
```

2.
```
10  PRINT  "EXAM 1","EXAM 2","TOTAL"
20  PRINT  "------","------","-----"
30  READ  E,X
40  LET  T = E + X
50  PRINT  E,  X,  T
60  GOTO  30
70  DATA  56,45,28,55,90,80
80  END
```

3. Complete this program.

Problem: A shoe store charges $25 for a pair of tennis shoes. Given the number of pairs purchased, print the number of pairs and the total price.

```
10   ?   "NUMBER";  ?  (10);"PRICE"
20  READ   ?
30  LET  P = 25*N
40  PRINT   ?  ;TAB(  ?  );P
50  GOTO   ?
60  DATA  2,3,5,12
70  END
```

Correct any errors in these programs.

4.
```
100  REM  MULTIPLICATION  OF  NUMBERS
110  READ  A,B
120  LET  T = A + B
130  PRINT  A,B:T
140  GOTO  120
150  END
```

5.
```
100  REM  COMPUTE  THE  WEEKS
110  PRINT  "DAYS;TAB(8);WEEKS"
120  READ  D
130  LET  W = D/7
140  PRINT  D,TAB(8),W
150  GOTO  120
160  DATA  21,27,18
170  END
```

6. Write the output of the completed program of Exercise 3.

*Write the output for each **PRINT** statement.*

7. PRINT TAB(5);"PROGRAM 1"

8. PRINT "TEST";TAB(15);"WORK"

COMPUTERS AND ROBOTS

You have no doubt seen movies that show how robots might someday be used. Scientists working in the field called **artificial intelligence** have made a number of startling predictions about their use.

- Directed by a microprocessor, the robot of the future will see by television and feel by touch sensors.

- A factory run completely by robots is scheduled for completion in Japan by 1985.

- Robots will be inexpensive to build because other robots will build them.

- You will be able to buy a robot butler who will live in your closet, prepare snacks, clean, and do the dishes.

- Robots could work for long periods of time on the moon. This could help to increase our scientific knowledge at relatively little cost. Other robots might operate undersea food-growing stations or mine minerals in areas too dangerous for humans.

- As humans age, parts of their nervous system could be replaced by robot parts.

PROJECT

Find out if robots are being used in any industry or business in your community. If they are, report to your class how they are being used.

Chapter Summary

Section 3–1
1. Programs containing **INPUT** statements should end by asking whether the user wants to continue. The user can be given a code: 1 = yes, 0 = no. An **IF–THEN** statement can be used to test the input value. An input value of 1 sends the computer back to the beginning of the program.

2. When the computer executes a statement such as

   80 IF X = 1 THEN 10

   it tests the condition X = 1. If the condition is true, the computer jumps to statement 10. If the condition is false, the computer "falls through" to the next statement after 80 in numerical order.

Section 3–2
3. Input values may be put in **DATA** statements in the program itself. Then one or more **READ** statements are used to assign values from the **DATA** list to variables.

4. When all **DATA** values have been used and the computer is asked to **READ** another value, it prints a message like **?OUT OF DATA ERROR IN 10** and ends the program.

Section 3–3
5. Programs use **GOTO** statements to process numerous sets of data.

6. Both strings and numbers can be read from **DATA** statements.

Section 3–4
7. When commas separate items in **PRINT** statements, the numbers or strings are printed in the pre–set zones of the particular computer.

Section 3–5
8. To identify output more clearly, headings should be printed above columns of numbers or strings.

Section 3–6
9. A programmer can set up specific zones with the **TAB** function. A sample statement would be as follows.

```
50 PRINT X;TAB(10);Y;TAB(18);Z
```

Chapter Review

Correct any errors in these programs.

1.
```
5    REM COMPUTE PERCENT OF DISCOUNT
10   PRINT
15   PRINT "COST BEFORE DISCOUNT";C
20   INPUT C
25   PRINT
30   PRINT "DISCOUNT";D
35   INPUT D
40   LET P = D / C
45   PRINT P;" DISCOUNT"
50   PRINT "IS THAT ALL?" (Y/N)
55   INPUT X$
60   IF X$ = Y THEN 5
65   END
```

2.
```
100  MULTIPLY NUMBERS
110  PRINT
120  PRINT "A, B, PRODUCT"
130  PRINT
140  READ A; B
150  LET P = AB
160  PRINT A, B, P
170  GOTO 110
180  END
```

3. Write the output of this program. Use this input.
Fido, 3, 1, Ruff, 10, 0
```
10   PRINT "PROGRAM TO CONVERT DOG"
20   PRINT "YEARS TO HUMAN YEARS."
30   PRINT "ENTER DOG'S NAME."
40   INPUT N$
50   PRINT "ENTER DOG'S AGE."
60   INPUT D
70   LET H = 7 * D
80   PRINT N$;" IS ";H;" HUMAN YEARS."
90   PRINT
100  PRINT "MORE DOGS? (1=YES,0=NO)"
110  INPUT M
120  IF M = 1 THEN 30
130  END
```

Complete each program.

4. Problem: Given a company's gross sales and expenses, compute and print the profit (gross sales minus expenses).

```
10 PRINT "GROSS SALES AND EXPENSES?"
20 INPUT  ?
30 LET  ?  = G - E
40  ?  "PROFIT = $";P
50 PRINT "CONTINUE? (Y/N)"
60 INPUT  ?
70 IF X$ =  ?  THEN  ?
80 END
```

5. Problem: Given an object's weight on Earth, print that object's weight on Mars, where weight on Mars is $\frac{2}{5}$ the weight on Earth.

```
100 PRINT "EARTH";TAB(18);"MARS"
110 READ E
120 LET M =  ?
130 PRINT  ?
140 GOTO  ?
150 DATA 150,65,80
160 END
```

Color Reconstruction of Mars

6. Suppose that a taxpayer is allowed a $500 deduction for each child. Write a program which, given the number of children of a taxpayer, prints the total deduction. Continue processing data from the keyboard until the user wishes to stop.

7. Expand the program of Exercise 6 so that the user enters his or her name before entering the number of children.

8. Write a program which reads from **DATA** a jogger's name and the number of kilometers the jogger has run in one day. Change the kilometers to meters (1 kilometer = 1000 meters). Print the jogger's name and the number of meters.

9. Revise the program of Exercise 8 to print the output like this.

```
-------------------------------------
JOGGER      KILOMETERS RUN    METERS RUN
-------------------------------------

ABELARD         16.5           16500
HELOISE          9.6            9600
```
and so on

Chapter Test

Determine which statements are correct and contain no syntax errors.

For each statement that is incorrect, write the reason.

1. 88 READ X$,A   **2.** 210 IF Y=8 THEN 66   **3.** 130 IF R$=NO THEN 30

4. Complete this program.

Problem: Given a person's name and yearly salary, print the person's yearly salary.

```
10  PRINT "NAME";TAB(15);"WEEKLY SALARY"
20  PRINT
30  READ  _?_,_?_
40  LET W = Y/52
50  PRINT N$;_?_;_?_
60  _?_  30
70  _?_  ELDER,8000,KIM,9800,LEE,10600
80  _?_  MANUEL,11325
90  END
```

Correct any errors in these programs.

5.
```
10  PRINT
20  PRINT "NUMBER, DOUBLE"
30  READ N
40  LET D = 2N
50  PRINT N, D
60  GOTO 10
70  END
```

6.
```
100  PRINT "ENTER YOUR AGE.";X
110  INPUT X
120  LET D = 40 - X
130  PRINT "YEARS TO AGE 40 = ";D
140  PRINT "CONTINUE?" (Y/N)
150  INPUT Z
160  IF Z = Y THEN 100
170  END
```

7. Write the output of the completed program of Exercise 4.

8. Write the output for this **PRINT** statement.

Assume that X = 20 and Y = 5.

60 PRINT TAB(5);X;TAB(10);Y

Cumulative Review: Chapters 1-3

Part 1

Choose the correct answer. Choose a, b, c, or d.

1. Which of these translates each **BASIC** program so that the computer can execute the program?

   a. CRT   **b.** CPU   **c.** interpreter   **d.** printer

2. What does CPU stand for?

   a. cathode primary usage   **b.** central processing unit

   c. computer processing unit   **d.** control point under

3. What is another name for computer memory?

   a. input   **b.** storage   **c.** output   **d.** CPU

4. Which of the following invented the first adding machine?

   a. Blaise Pascal   **b.** Herman Hollerith   **c.** Charles Babbage   **d.** Howard Aiken

5. What is the name of the first high-level language developed for computers?

   a. BASIC   **b.** FORTRAN   **c.** COBOL   **d.** Pascal

6. What is the output of this program?

   a. 10   **b.** 12

   c. 14   **d.** 16

   ```
   10 LET Y = 10
   20 LET X = Y + 4
   30 PRINT X
   40 END
   ```

7. Suppose that **MARY** is entered for **M$** and that **JONES** is entered for **N$**.

   What is the output of this program?

   a. MARES   **b.** MANES
   c. RYSON   **d.** ARYJO

   ```
   10 INPUT M$,N$
   20 LET K$ = LEFT$(M$,2)
   30 LET L$ = RIGHT$(N$,3)
   40 LET T$ = K$ + L$
   50 PRINT T$
   60 END
   ```

8. Which statement is correct and contains no syntax errors?

   a. 10 LET K$=LEFT$(T$,3,2)   **b.** 40 LET T=RIGHT$(M$,3)

   c. 20 LET L$=LEN(N$)   **d.** 55 PRINT TAB(10);"ERROR"

9. Which of the following was the chief component of first generation computers?

   a. vacuum tubes   **b.** transistors

   c. integrated circuits   **d.** microprocessors

10. Which statement is correct and contains no syntax errors?

    a. 45 IF A = B 90
    b. 65 IF A$ = Y THEN 50
    c. 10 IF C = 45? THEN 25
    d. 30 IF A = 10 THEN 90

11. What symbol is placed between variables or strings in a **PRINT** statement to tell the computer to skip to the next zone of the screen or printer?

    a. period
    b. comma
    c. semicolon
    d. colon

12. What is the output of this program at the right?

    ```
    10 DATA 2,5
    20 READ A, B
    30 LET C = A + B
    40 PRINT C
    50 GOTO 20
    60 END
    ```

    a. 10
    ```
    ?OUT OF DATA ERROR IN 20
    ```
    b. 7
    ```
    ?OUT OF DATA ERROR IN 20
    ```
    c. 7
    ```
    ?OUT OF DATA ERROR IN 10
    ```
    d. 10

13. Which word would you type on a computer keyboard to make the computer execute a program in memory?

    a. LIST
    b. NEW
    c. RUN
    d. RETURN

14. To which of the following does **RAM** refer?

    a. random access memory
    b. read altered memory
    c. right access module
    c. random access module

15. Which word would you type if you wished to see all the statements of a program in memory?

    a. SEE
    b. RUN
    c. PRINT
    d. LIST

16. Which of these is a numerical variable?

    a. $B
    b. K$
    c. T
    d. 9

17. Which type of statement is ignored by the computer when a program is run?

    a. INPUT
    b. PRINT
    c. REM
    d. LET

18. Which type of storage allows you to save programs outside the computer?

    a. primary
    b. secondary
    c. ROM
    d. CPU

19. Who was the first computer programmer?

    a. Blaise Pascal
    b. Ada Lovelace
    c. Charles Babbage
    d. Herman Hollerith

20. Which of these functions is useful when the output of a program requires more columns than there are zones or when the programmer wants the output in columns but not in the regular zones?

a. LEFT$　　　　　　　**b.** LEN

c. TAB　　　　　　　　**d.** RIGHT$

Part 2

21. Write the output of this program.

```
10 LET T = 12
20 LET A = T * 2
30 PRINT T, A
40 END
```

22. Write the output of this program when 6 is entered for T.

```
10 INPUT T
20 LET K = T/2
30 PRINT K
40 END
```

23. Write the output of this program when **JACK** is entered for **J$**.

```
10 INPUT J$
20 LET T = LEN(J$)
30 PRINT T
40 END
```

24. Write the output of this program.

```
10 PRINT "YEARS";TAB(10);"DAYS"
20 PRINT "-----"; ? ;"----"
30 READ  ?
40 LET D = 365 * Y
50 PRINT  ? ;TAB(10); ?
60  ?  30
70 DATA 14,21,35
80  ?
```

For Exercises 25–27, correct any errors in each program.

25.
```
10 PRINT "TYPE IN A NAME".
20 INPUT N
30 LET LEN(N$) = K
40 PRINT K
50 END
```

26.
```
10 PRINT "AMOUNT";TAB20;"CHANGE"
20 READ A
30 LET C = 1.00 - A
40 PRINT A;C
50 GOTO 30
60 DATA .05;.55;.78
70 END
```

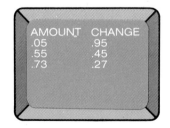

AMOUNT CHANGE
.05　　　.95
.55　　　.45
.73　　　.27

27.
```
10 PRINT ENTER A NAME
20 INPUT A$
30 LET T=LEFT$(A$,2)
40 PRINT FIRST 2 LETTERS ARE ";T
50 END
```

For Exercises 28–30, complete each program.

28. Problem: The user enters a name. The program prints the last two letters of the name. The program then asks whether the user wishes to enter more names.

```
10 PRINT "ENTER A NAME."
20 INPUT  ?
30 LET A$ =  ? (N$,2)
40 PRINT  ?
50 PRINT "ARE THERE MORE NAMES? (1=YES)"
60 INPUT Q
70 IF  ?  = 1 THEN  ?
80 END
```

29. Problem: After reading in the high score and the present score of a video game player, this program computes the difference between the high score and the present score.

```
10 PRINT "HIGH","SCORE","UNDER"
20 READ H,P
30 LET U =  ?
40 PRINT  ?
50 GOTO  ?
60  ?  20100,18765,23987,1099
70 END
```

30. Problem: Given the length of a side of a square, find the area.

```
10  ?  "SIDE";TAB(10);"AREA"
20 READ S
30  ?  A = S * S
40 PRINT S;TAB(10); ?
50 GOTO  ?
60 DATA 2,3,4
70  ?
```

Computer Lab Projects

STRING PROCESSING APPLICATIONS

1. **READ** strings from **DATA**. Print each string, its first character, and its last character, in the three labeled columns as follows.
   STRING, FIRST CHARACTER, SECOND CHARACTER

   DATA   COMPUTERS, ENGLISH, MATHEMATICS

2. Expand the program of Exercise 1 so that the length of each string is printed in a fourth column: **LENGTH OF STRING**

   DATA   COMPUTERS, ENGLISH, MATHEMATICS

3. **READ** from **DATA** the first and last names of several people. Print the first name, the last name, and the complete name in three labeled columns. For example, for **MARY,SMITH**, print
   MARY   SMITH   MARY SMITH.

   DATA   MARY,SMITH, HUBERT,BROWN, SAM,SNODGRASS

4. Revise the program of Exercise 3 so that the complete name is printed in the form **SMITH, MARY**.

5. **READ** from **DATA** the first and last names of several people. Print the first name and its length and the last name and its length in four labeled columns.

DATA   ALAN,STAUB, CHERYL,CAMPBELL, HARRY, BROWN

6. **READ** or **INPUT** a person's name, the type of pet that person has, and the name of the pet. Print the outputs as follows.
SAMMY HAS A PET TURTLE NAMED SPEEDY.

DATA   SAMMY,TURTLE,SPEEDY, LOUELLEN,DOG,SPOT,
        MAY,CAT,SLINKY

7. **READ** from **DATA** the name of the month and the day of the month. Print in three labeled columns the month, the day, and the complete date in the form **OCTOBER 19, 1986**.

DATA   OCTOBER,19, JUNE,21, JANUARY,31

8. Revise the program of Exercise 7 so that the complete date is printed with the day before the month. For example, print **19 OCTOBER 1986**.

9. Given a person's name, join 'S to it. Print the resulting string. For example, given **JOAN**, print **JOAN'S**.

DATA   JOAN, DONNY, DANIEL

10. **READ** from **DATA** the number of the month and the day of the month. Print in three labeled columns:
MONTH NUMBER,   DAY OF THE MONTH,   YEAR
For example, May 16, 1987 would print:
5   16   87
Use these dates.
DATA 5,16,87, 4,9,89, 10,15,93

GENERAL APPLICATIONS

11. **READ** from **DATA** a person's age. Print in two labeled columns the person's age and the year in which the person was born.
(See Exercise 7 on page 93.)

DATA   11, 13, 25

12. The Truman School held Student Council elections. **READ** from **DATA** the number of votes each candidate received from the 6th–, 7th–, and 8th–graders. The output is in four columns: 6th–grade votes, 7th–grade votes, 8th–grade votes, and total votes. (See Exercise 8 on page 93.)

    DATA   132,214,89, 201,167,103, 75,46,102

13. **READ** from **DATA** a person's weight (in pounds) and height (in inches). Print in three labeled columns the weight, height, and pounds per inch. (See Exercise 9 on page 93.)

    DATA   110,64, 125,66, 102,59

14. **READ** from **DATA** a person's age this year. Print in two labeled columns the person's present age and the person's age in the year 2000. (See Exercise 10 on page 93.)

    DATA   13, 15, 12

15. **READ** from **DATA** the total number of times a coin was flipped and the number of flips that were heads. Print in three labeled columns the total number of flips, the number of heads, and the number of tails.

    DATA   100,51, 200,97, 150,80

16. A Computer Literacy test has two parts. **READ** from **DATA** a student's score on each part. Print in three labeled columns the student's score on each part and the student's total score for the test.

    DATA   26,34, 32,40, 29,27

17. **READ** from **DATA** the number of times–at–bat and the number of hits. Print in three labeled columns the times–at–bat, the number of hits, and the batting average.

    DATA   100,25, 50,10, 178,55

18. **READ** from **DATA** the number of points a student lost on a test having the given number of points. Print in two labeled columns the number of points the student lost and the number of points the student earned.

    DATA   100,19, 50,7, 75,10

19. **READ** from **DATA** the number of feet in a measurement. Print in two labeled columns the number of feet and the number of inches in the measurement.

    DATA   15, 24, 75

20. **READ** the number of inches in a measurement. Print in two labeled columns the number of inches and the number of feet in the measurement.

    DATA   120, 75, 102

CONSUMER APPLICATIONS

21. For each worker of a company, **READ** from **DATA** the number of hours worked and the hourly rate of pay. Print in three labeled columns the hours worked, the rate of pay, and the total pay.

    DATA   40,3.50, 45,3.25, 20,4.25

22. **READ** from **DATA** this information about automobiles: license number, miles traveled, and number of gallons of gasoline used. Print the output in four columns: license number, miles, gallons used, and average miles per gallon.

    DATA   234871,100,10, 876102,25,2, 902376,55,5

23. **READ** from **DATA** the amount of an investment and the interest rate. Print in three labeled columns the amount invested, the interest rate, and the interest for one year. (See Exercise 11 on page 93.)

    DATA   50,.06, 150,.05, 200,.055

24. Expand the program of Exercise 23 so that the number of years of the investment is also read. Print an additional column listing the number of years. (See Exercise 12 on page 93.)

25. A library charges 15 cents a day for overdue books. **READ** from **DATA** a person's library card number and the number of days a book is overdue. Print in three labeled columns the library card number, the number of days the book is overdue, and the amount charged. (See Exercise 13 on page 93.)

    DATA   8701,3, 7614,5, 1409,10

26. **READ** from **DATA** the regular price and sale price of an item. Print in three labeled columns the regular price, the sale price, and the amount of discount. (See Exercise 14 on page 93.)

    DATA 4.90,4.41, 50,46, 9.98,9.49

27. **READ** from **DATA** the regular price of an item and the percent of discount. Print in three labeled columns the regular price, the percent of discount, and the net price of the item. (See Exercise 15 on page 93.)

    DATA 4.90,.10, 50,.05, 9.98,.20

28. **READ** from **DATA** the regular price of an item and the amount of discount. Print in three labeled columns the regular price, the amount of discount, and the sales price. (See Exercise 16 on page 94.)

    DATA 4.90,.49, 50,4, 9.98,.49

29. Suppose that a 6% tax is added to the purchase price of any item. **READ** from **DATA** the purchase price of an item. Print in two labeled columns the purchase price and the amount of tax.

    DATA 4.90,12.36,20.50

30. Expand the program of Exercise 29 so that the tax rate is no longer fixed at 6%. The **DATA** now includes the purchase price and the tax rate. Print in three labeled columns the purchase price, the tax rate, and the amount of tax.

    DATA 4.90,.06, 12.36,.05, 20.50,.03

MORE CHALLENGING COMPUTER LAB PROJECTS

STRING PROCESSING APPLICATIONS

31. **READ** from **DATA** two numbers followed by an operation symbol. Print in three labeled columns the two numbers and the string formed by putting the operation sign between the two numbers. (See Exercise 18 on page 94.)

32. Revise the program of Exercise 31 so that the operation sign in the **DATA** is listed before the two numbers. (See Exercise 19 on page 94.)

33. Have the user enter the "password" for today. Then **READ** from **DATA** a list of names. For each name, print something like **JILL, THE PASSWORD IS BASIC**, where **BASIC** was the password. Each person will receive the same password.

34. **READ** strings from **DATA**. Print in four labeled columns each complete string, its first character, its second character, and its third character. (HINT: To "strip off" the second and third characters, use **LEFT$** followed by **RIGHT$**.)

35. Social Security numbers are written in this form: **438–92–0080**. **READ** from **DATA** a person's name and the three parts of the number. Print in two labeled columns the name and the number. (Be sure that the dashes print in the correct places).

GENERAL APPLICATIONS

36. **READ** from **DATA** a student's name and the number of points lost on a 50–point test. Print in three labeled columns the name, the points lost, and the grade. Print the student's grade as a decimal.

37. Expand the program of Exercise 36 so that the total point value of each test is included in the test. Add a fourth column to the output, between the name and points lost, to print the total point value of the test.

38. A coin is flipped a large number of times. **READ** from **DATA** the number of heads and number of tails. Print the output in four columns: number of heads, percent of flips that turn up heads, number of tails, and percent of flips that turn up tails. Print the two percents as decimals.

39. **READ** from **DATA** a baseball player's name, the player's number of singles, number of doubles, number of triples, and number of home runs in one season. Print in three labeled columns the player's name, the total number of hits, and the total number of extra base hits (doubles + triples + home runs).

CONSUMER APPLICATIONS

NOTE: If a formula in a **LET** statement contains both multiplication and addition, the computer does the multiplication first.

40. A plumber charges a base fee of $25 with an additional charge of $11 per hour. **READ** or **INPUT** the number of hours the plumber worked. Compute and print the total charge.

41. **READ** from **DATA** the number of pennies, nickels, dimes, and quarters a person has. Compute the total amount of money the person has. Print the output in five columns labeled **PENNIES, NICKELS, DIMES, QUARTERS, and TOTAL.**

42. A company hires students to work three days a week after school. **READ** or **INPUT** the number of minutes each student worked for each of three days. Compute and print the number of <u>hours</u> the student worked. For example, given 90, 80, and 64, print 3.9 hours. (HINT: First compute the total number of minutes the student worked for the three days.)

43. **READ** from **DATA** a store's cost for an item and the percent of markup. Print in three labeled columns the cost, percent of markup, and amount of markup.

44. **READ** from **DATA** the amount of a purchase and the tax rate. Enter the tax rate as a decimal. Print in three labeled columns the amount of the purchase, the amount of tax, and the total cost of the purchase with the tax added.

ALGEBRA APPLICATIONS

Exercises 45–49 require a background in first–year algebra.

45. **READ** numbers from **DATA**. Print in three labeled columns each number, its square, and its cube (third power).

46. Expand the program of Exercise 45 so that it also prints the fourth power of the number. (See Exercise 23 on page 94.)

47. **READ** from **DATA** non–zero numbers. Print in three labeled columns each number, its additive inverse, and its multiplicative inverse (reciprocal). (See Exercises 25 and 26 on page 94.)

48. **READ** from **DATA** pairs of numbers **X** and **Y**. Print in four labeled columns **X,Y, X – Y,** and **Y – X.**

49. **READ** integers from **DATA**. Print in three labeled columns each integer, the next consecutive integer, and the preceding consecutive integer. (See Exercises 27 and 28 on page 94.)

4

LOOPS AND GRAPHICS

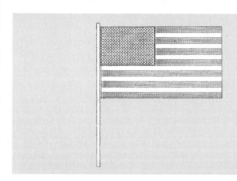

FEATURES

Sprites
Windows
One-Chip Computer
Plotter
Light Pen
Computers and the
   Cashless Society
LOGO

LESSONS

4-1 FOR-NEXT LOOPS

OBJECTIVE:
> **To write programs containing FOR–NEXT loops.**

Computers are great at repeating things using a **FOR–NEXT loop**.

EXAMPLE 1 Write a program to print **COMPUTERS ARE FUN!** ten times.

Program
```
10 FOR I = 1 TO 10
20 PRINT "COMPUTERS ARE FUN!"
30 NEXT I
40 END
```

The variable **I** in the program is a **counter**. In this case, it counts from 1 to 10. Statements 10, 20, and 30 form a **FOR–NEXT** loop. All statements between the **FOR** statement and the **NEXT** statement are done over and over until the counter reaches its final value.

EXAMPLE 2　**a.** Write a program that asks a person's name and then prints the name three times. Skip a line before each printing of the name.

Program
```
10 PRINT "WHAT IS YOUR NAME?"    Beginning statements:
20 INPUT N$                      done once each
30 FOR J = 1 TO 3
40 PRINT                         Loop statements:
50 PRINT N$                      done 3 times each
60 NEXT J
70 PRINT                         Final statements:
80 END                           done once each
```

b. Write the output of a **RUN** of the program.

Output

	Value of J	Statements Producing the Output
WHAT IS YOUR NAME?	0	10
JUAN	0	20
	1	40
JUAN	1	50
	2	40
JUAN	2	50
	3	40
JUAN	3	50
	4	70

In the program of Example 2, the counter is J. Note that the variable after the word **FOR** must be the <u>same</u> as the variable after the word **NEXT**. Two statements, 40 and 50, make up the "body" of the loop. The **body of a loop** consists of all the statements between **FOR** and **NEXT**. These are the statements that are repeated during execution. In long programs, the body of a loop may contain hundreds of statements.

A **NEXT** statement always marks the end of a **FOR–NEXT** loop. During the execution of a program it also has two other effects. First, it tells the computer to change the loop counter to its next value. Then it sends the computer to the top of the loop. When the next value of the counter is beyond the last number in the **FOR** statement, the computer "exits" the loop and jumps to the first statement after **NEXT**.

EXAMPLE 3 Which statements are correct?
When a statement is incorrect, give the reason.

	Statements	Correct?	Reason
a.	50 FOR X = 1, 100	No	The "," should be replaced with "**TO**"
b.	20 FOR M = 0 TO 50	Yes	
c.	100 FOR L = 0 TO 5 110 PRINT L 120 NEXT I	No	The words "**NEXT I**" should be replaced with "**NEXT L**"
d.	75 NEXT J + 1	No	Operations such as + are not allowed in a **NEXT** statement.
e.	60 FOR 2 TO 20	No	The statement needs a variable (counter) to take on values from 2 to 20.

A useful feature of many programs is the **delay loop** (also called a **pause loop** or a **wait loop**). Such a loop is used to slow down the execution of a program. The following is an example of a delay loop.

```
100 FOR I = 1 TO 1000
110 NEXT I
```

The delay loop has no body. You simply want the computer to count to 1000. This causes a delay in the execution of the program.

WRITTEN EXERCISES

For Exercises 1–3, first identify the counter. Then list the number(s) of the statements that make up the body of the loop.

1.
```
10 FOR I = 1 TO 5
20 PRINT "HI!"
30 NEXT I
40 END
```

2.
```
10 PRINT
20 FOR X = 1 TO 3
30 PRINT "HELLO"
40 PRINT
50 NEXT X
60 END
```

3.
```
100 PRINT "NAME?"
110 INPUT N$
120 FOR J = 2 TO 4
130 PRINT "HI, ";N$
140 NEXT J
150 END
```

Write the output of each program.

4. Exercise 1   **5.** Exercise 2   **6.** Exercise 3

State how many times each of these statements is executed when the program of Exercise 2 is RUN.

7. 10   **8.** 30   **9.** 40   **10.** 60

State how many times each of these statements is executed when the program of Exercise 3 is RUN.

11. 100   **12.** 110   **13.** 130   **14.** 140

Correct any errors in these programs.

15.
```
20 PRINT
40 FOR M = 1,15
60 PRINT M
80 M NEXT
100 END
```

16.
```
100 PRINT "NAME?"
110 INPUT X
120 FOR 1 TO 20
130 PRINT X
140 NEXT Q
150 END
```

17.
```
10 FOR K = 1 TO 5
20 PRINT "I LIKE RED."
30 PRINT
40 NEXT L
50 END
```

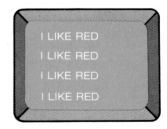

Complete these programs.

18. Problem: Print **I LOVE COMPUTERS** 10 times down the screen or paper.

```
10 FOR I = 1 TO  ?
20 PRINT   ?
30 NEXT    ?
40 END
```

19. Problem: Ask a person's name (such as Joe). Print **HAPPY BIRTHDAY, JOE** five times.

```
100   ?   "TYPE YOUR NAME."
110 INPUT N$
120 FOR  ?  = 1 TO 5
130 PRINT "HAPPY BIRTHDAY, ";  ?
140 NEXT J
150 END
```

For Exercises 20–23, write line numbers before the statements to show the correct order.

20. Problem: Print **CRUSADERS #1** six times down the screen or printer.

```
PRINT "CRUSADERS #1"
FOR C = 1 TO 6
END
NEXT C
```

21. Problem: Skip a line. Then print **BE MY VALENTINE** eight times.

```
NEXT A
PRINT
FOR A = 1 TO 8
PRINT "BE MY VALENTINE"
END
```

22. Problem: Ask for a person's favorite color. Print the name of that color five times.

```
FOR Y = 1 TO 5
INPUT C$
END
PRINT "ENTER YOUR FAVORITE COLOR."
NEXT Y
PRINT C$
```

23. Problem: Ask for a person's favorite team. Print that team's name 15 times down the screen or printer.

```
INPUT T$
NEXT N
FOR N = 1 TO 15
PRINT T$
END
PRINT "WHAT IS YOUR FAVORITE TEAM?"
```

Loops and Graphics **157**

Modify the program of Example 1 in the following ways.

24. Print **COMPUTERS ARE FUN!** 10 times on <u>every other line</u> of the screen or printer.

25. Print **COMPUTERS ARE FUN!** 15 times.

26. Add a delay loop to make the computer pause after each printing of **COMPUTERS ARE FUN!**

Modify the program of Example 2 in the following ways.

27. Do not skip a line before each printing of the name.

28. Change the loop counter from J to K.

29. Print the name five times.

30. Add a delay loop to make the computer pause after printing each name.

Write a program containing a **FOR–NEXT** *loop to produce the output shown.*

31.
```
WHOOPEE!
WHOOPEE!
WHOOPEE!
WHOOPEE!
WHOOPEE!
```

32.
```
YOU'RE  GREAT!
```
← Blank line
```
YOU'RE  GREAT!
```
← Blank line
```
YOU'RE  GREAT!
```
← Blank line

MORE CHALLENGING EXERCISES

For each of Exercises 33–38, write a program containing a **FOR–NEXT** *loop.*

33. Write a program that prints 10 asterisks (*) down the screen or printer. Print one asterisk per line.

34. Add a delay loop to the program of Exercise 33 so that the computer pauses about one second after printing each asterisk.

35. Write a program that asks the user to type a letter of the alphabet. Then print that letter 15 times down the screen or printer.

36. Modify the program of Exercise 35 so that the computer pauses after printing the letter each time.

37. Write a program that prints the counting numbers from 1 to 10 down the screen or printer. Print one number per line.

38. Write a program that prints the display on the right.

1	1
2	1
2	2
3	1
3	2
3	3
4	1
4	2
4	3
4	4

FOR–NEXT Loops

For Exercises 1–3, enter and **RUN** *this program (see Example 1 on page 154).*

a. Modify the program as indicated in each given exercise.

```
10 FOR I = 1 TO 10
20 PRINT "COMPUTERS ARE FUN!"
30 NEXT I
40 END
```

b. **RUN** *the modified program after each change.*

c. Check that the modified program does what it is asked to do.

1. Exercise 24, page 158   **2.** Exercise 25, page 158   **3.** Exercise 26, page 158

4. Type **NEW**. Then enter and **RUN** the program of Example 2 on page 154 (reprinted below). With the exception of your name, is the output similar to that shown in the output of Example 2?

```
10 PRINT "WHAT IS YOUR NAME?"
20 INPUT N$
30 FOR J = 1 TO 3
40 PRINT
50 PRINT N$
60 NEXT J
70 PRINT
80 END
```

For Exercises 5–7:

a. Modify the program of Example 2 as indicated.

b. **RUN** *the modified program.*

c. Check that the modified program does what it is asked to do.

5. Exercise 27, page 158   **6.** Exercise 28, page 158

7. Exercise 29, page 158   **8.** Exercise 30, page 158

For Exercises 9–11, type **NEW**. *Then* **RUN** *the indicated program.*

9. Exercise 1, page 156. Does the output agree with your answer to Exercise 4 on page 156?

10. Exercise 2, page 156. Does the output agree with your answer to Exercise 5 on page 156?

11. Exercise 3, page 156. Does the output agree with your answer to Exercise 6 on page 156?

For Exercises 12–14:

*a. Enter and **RUN** the indicated program.*

b. Check whether all the errors were corrected. If not, make further changes until each program runs correctly.

12. Exercise 15, page 156   **13.** Exercise 16, page 156   **14.** Exercise 17, page 156

For Exercises 15–16:

*a. Enter and **RUN** the indicated program you completed.*

b. Check whether you completed the program correctly.

15. Exercise 18, page 157   **16.** Exercise 19, page 157

For Exercises 17–20:

*a. Using the line numbers you chose, enter and **RUN** the program.*

b. Check whether the program runs correctly. If it does not, change the line numbers until the program does run correctly.

17. Exercise 20, page 157   **18.** Exercise 21, page 157

19. Exercise 22, page 157   **20.** Exercise 23, page 157

EXPLORE: NEXT WITHOUT A VARIABLE

*When writing a program for some computers, you may omit the variable after **NEXT**. The computer uses the same variable as that used for the loop–counter in the last preceding **FOR** statement.*

21. Enter the program of Example 1 on page 154. Type line 30 as **30 NEXT**. **RUN** the program. Does your computer accept **NEXT** without a variable?

Did You Know? _____

A **sprite** is a computer drawing of a shape that can be moved around the screen as a single unit. The shape might be a spaceship or a smiling face. Sprites allow programmers to generate particular shapes and to move them about quickly. Without the ability to store a shape in memory, objects displayed on the screen would have to be redrawn line-by-line every time the user wished to move them.

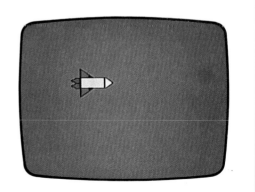

4-2 MORE ON LOOPS

OBJECTIVE: To use a variable with FOR–NEXT loops.

In the previous lesson, each loop was repeated a <u>fixed number</u> of times. However, loops can be executed a <u>variable number of times</u>.

EXAMPLE 1 **a.** Write a program to print **COMPUTERS ARE FUN!** as many times the user wants. Refer to Example 1 on page 154.

Program
```
3   PRINT "HOW MANY TIMES";        ←── The semicolon keeps the
6   INPUT N                            cursor on the same line.
10  FOR I = 1 TO N
20  PRINT "COMPUTERS ARE FUN!"
30  NEXT I
40  END
```

b. Write the output from a **RUN** of the program.

Output
```
HOW MANY TIMES?4        ←──── The question mark produced by
COMPUTERS ARE FUN!            statement 6 is on the same
COMPUTERS ARE FUN!           line as HOW MANY TIMES.
COMPUTERS ARE FUN!
COMPUTERS ARE FUN!
```

In Example 1, statement 10 is the key. The counter does not automatically count from 1 to 10 or to any pre–chosen number. Instead, it goes from 1 to N, where N has the value entered at statement 6.

The beginning value of a loop counter can be selected by the user.

EXAMPLE 2 **a.** Write a program to count from any starting value to any final value. Have the user enter the beginning and ending values.

Program
```
10  PRINT "I WILL COUNT FOR YOU."
20  PRINT "WHERE SHOULD I BEGIN";
30  INPUT B                        ←──── Beginning value
40  PRINT "WHERE SHOULD I END";
50  INPUT E                        ←──── Ending value
60  FOR I = B TO E
70  PRINT I;" ";                   " " is added to create some space
80  NEXT I                  ←────  between the values printed.
90  PRINT
100 END
```

b. Write the output from a **RUN** of the program.

Output
```
I WILL COUNT FOR YOU.
WHERE SHOULD I BEGIN?5
WHERE SHOULD I END?16
   5   6   7   8   9   10   11   12   13   14   15   16
```
NOTE: The numbers 5, 6, 7, 8, and so on, may be spaced further apart on your machine and may spill over to a second line.

Often an **INPUT** (or **READ**) statement is part of the body of a loop.

EXAMPLE 3 **a.** The three children of the Palmer family play a video game. Write a program that accepts each player's scores on four games and prints the total score of each player.

Program
```
10 FOR I = 1 TO 3
20 PRINT "ENTER THE 4 SCORES OF PLAYER ";I
30 INPUT A, B, C, D
40 LET T = A + B + C + D
50 PRINT "TOTAL IS ";T
60 PRINT
70 NEXT I
80 PRINT "END OF PROGRAM"
90 END
```

b. Write the output from a **RUN** of the program.

Output	Value of I	Statements Producing the Output
ENTER THE 4 SCORES OF PLAYER 1	1	20
?350,400,360,410	1	30
TOTAL IS 1520	1	40 and 50
	1	60
ENTER THE 4 SCORES OF PLAYER 2	2	20
?375,325,405,390	2	30
TOTAL IS 1495	2	40 and 50
	2	60
ENTER THE 4 SCORES OF PLAYER 3	3	20
?310,350,340,360	3	30
TOTAL IS 1360	3	40 and 50
	3	60
END OF PROGRAM	4	80

WRITTEN EXERCISES

In Exercises 1–3, identify the loop counter for each Example indicated. Then list the number(s) of all statements that make up the body of the loop.

1. Example 1   **2.** Example 2   **3.** Example 3

When the program of Example 1 is run, suppose that 5 is entered for N. How many times is each of these statements executed during that run?

4. 3   **5.** 6   **6.** 10   **7.** 20   **8.** 30

When the program of Example 1 is run, suppose that 10 is entered for N. How many times is each of these statements executed during that run?

9. 3   **10.** 6   **11.** 20

When the program of Example 2 is run, 1 is entered for B and 10 for E. How many times is each of these statements executed during that run?

12. 30   **13.** 40   **14.** 50   **15.** 70   **16.** 90

When the program of Example 2 is run, suppose that 4 is entered for B and 12 is entered for E. How many times is each of these statements executed during that run?

17. 30   **18.** 40   **19.** 50   **20.** 70   **21.** 90

During any run of the program in Example 3, how many times is each of these statements executed?

22. 20   **23.** 40   **24.** 50   **25.** 60   **26.** 80

Modify the program of Example 1 in the following ways.

27. Skip a line after each printing of **COMPUTERS ARE FUN!**.

28. After printing **COMPUTERS ARE FUN!** N times, print **THAT'S ALL, FOLKS!**

Modify the program of Example 2 as indicated.

29. Print the values of I down the screen or printer instead of across.

30. After printing the values requested, print on the next line the message **END OF LIST**.

31. **READ** from a **DATA** statement the values of B and E.

Modify the program of Example 3 as indicated.

32. Each player plays only three games.

33. There are four players.

34. Allow the user to enter the number of players.

35. **READ** from **DATA** statements the four scores of each of the three players.

36. **READ** from **DATA** the number of players and the four scores of each player.

Correct any errors in these programs.

37.
```
10 PRINT "NUMBER OF TIMES";X
15 INPUT X
20 FOR X = 1 TO X
25 PRINT "HAVE A NICE DAY."
30 NEXT X
35 END
```

38.
```
10 FOR T = A TO B
20 PRINT "START, END";
30 INPUT A, B
40 PRINT T
50 NEXT T+1
60 END
```

39.
```
10 TOTAL SCORES OF 4 PLAYERS
20 FOR 1 TO 4
30 READ X, Y, Z
40 LET A = X+Y+Z
50 PRINT "TOTAL = ;A
60 NEXT P
70 END
```

40.
```
100 REM   COUNT FROM J TO K
110 PRINT "ENTER J AND K."
120 INPUT J;K
130 FOR L = K TO J
140 PRINT L;"   ";
150 PRINT "END OF PROGRAM"
160 NEXT J
170 PRINT
180 END
```

Complete each program.

41. Problem: Print **I LOVE AMERICA** as many times as the user requests.

```
10 PRINT "HOW MANY TIMES";
20 INPUT  ?
30 FOR I =  ?  TO N
40 PRINT "I LOVE AMERICA"
50 NEXT  ?
60  ?
```

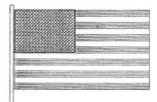

Computer–generated drawing

42. Problem: Count from **1** to **E**. Have the user enter the value of E.

```
100 PRINT "END OF COUNT";
110  ?  E
120 FOR  ?  = 1 TO  ?
130 PRINT  ? ;"   ";
140 NEXT K
150 END
```

In Exercises 43–44, the statements of the given program are not in the correct order. Write line numbers in front of the statements to show their correct order.

43. Problem: Print **YEA, TIGERS!** as many times as requested.

```
PRINT "YEA, TIGERS!"
FOR I = 1 TO Y
PRINT "HOW MANY TIMES";
NEXT I
INPUT Y
END
```

44. Problem: Count from B to 100. Have the user enter B.

```
INPUT B
NEXT G
FOR G = B TO 100
PRINT "STARTING NUMBER";
END
PRINT G;"   ";
```

MORE CHALLENGING EXERCISES

For each of Exercises 45–52, write a program that contains a
FOR– NEXT *loop.*

45. Write a program that prints as many asterisks (*) down the screen as the user requests.

46. Modify the program of Exercise 45 so that it prints the asterisks across the screen.

47. Write a program that prints *N* lines of dashes, where the user enters *N*. Make each line of dashes fill a line of your screen or printer. Skip a line between each row of dashes.

48. Modify the program of Exercise 47 so that the user can select the number of dashes per line as well as the number of lines.

49. Write a program that asks the user to type a character such as #. Have the program ask how many times to print the character. Print the character down the screen the required number of times.

50. Write a program that prints the display below.

X
XX
XXX
XXXX
XXXXX

51. Modify the program of Exercise 49 so that it prints across, instead of down, the screen.

52. Modify the program of Exercise 50 so that the user selects which letter of the alphabet to use for the display.

COMPUTER LAB ACTIVITIES

Loops

1. Enter and **RUN** this program (see Example 1 on page 161).

```
3   PRINT "HOW MANY TIMES";
6   INPUT N
10  FOR I = 1 TO N
20  PRINT "COMPUTERS ARE FUN!"
30  NEXT I
40  END
```

For Exercises 2–3:

a. Modify the program of Example 1 as indicated in each exercise.

*b. **RUN** the modified program.*

c. Check that the program does what it is supposed to do.

2. Exercise 27, page 163

3. Exercise 28, page 163

4. Type **NEW**. Then enter and **RUN** this program (see Example 2 on page 161).

```
10  PRINT "I WILL COUNT FOR YOU."
20  PRINT "WHERE SHOULD I BEGIN";
30  INPUT B
40  PRINT "WHERE SHOULD I END";
50  INPUT E
60  FOR I = B TO E
70  PRINT I;"   ";
80  NEXT I
90  PRINT
100 END
```

For Exercises 5–7:

a. Modify the program of Example 2 as indicated in each exercise.

*b. **RUN** the modified program.*

c. Check that the program does what it is supposed to do.

5. Exercise 29, page 163   **6.** Exercise 30, page 163   **7.** Exercise 31, page 164

8. Type **NEW**. Then enter and **RUN** this program *(see Example 3 on page 162)*.

```
10 FOR I = 1 TO 3
20 PRINT "ENTER THE 4 SCORES OF PLAYER ";I
30 INPUT A, B, C, D
40 LET T = A + B + C + D
50 PRINT "TOTAL IS ";T
60 PRINT
70 NEXT I
80 PRINT "END OF PROGRAM"
90 END
```

For Exercises 9–12:

a. Modify the program of Example 3 as indicated in each exercise.

*b. **RUN** the modified program after each change.*

c. Check that the program does what it is supposed to do.

9. Exercise 32, page 164   **10.** Exercise 33, page 164

11. Exercise 34, page 164   **12.** Exercise 35, page 164

For Exercises 13–16:

*a. Enter and **RUN** the indicated program.*

b. Check whether all the errors were corrected. If not, make further changes until each program runs correctly.

13. Exercise 37, page 164   **14.** Exercise 38, page 164

15. Exercise 39, page 164   **16.** Exercise 40, page 164

Did You Know?

A **window** is a section of a CRT screen that is used to display information. For example, in graphics mode, a computer may reserve a "text window" of several lines at the bottom of a screen. Questions can be asked of the user or information presented in the text window.

4-3 STEPS OTHER THAN ONE

> **To use STEPS other than one in FOR–NEXT loops**

So far, any loop counter has counted by one's. By adding a new word to your **BASIC** vocabulary, you can make a variable count by two's, by three's, and so on. This new word is **STEP**. The word **STEP** may appear <u>only at the end of a **FOR** statement.</u>

EXAMPLE 1

a. Write a program that counts by two's from 2 to 10.

Program
```
10 FOR I = 2 TO 10 STEP 2
20 PRINT I;"   ";
30 NEXT I
40 PRINT
50 END
```

b. Write the output from a **RUN** of the program.

Output   2   4   6   8   10   ← *These numbers may be spaced farther apart on your machine.*

In all **FOR** statements of the previous two lessons, the **STEP** was understood to be 1. The statement

$$10 \text{ FOR } I = 1 \text{ TO } 10$$

has the same effect as

$$10 \text{ FOR } I = 1 \text{ TO } 10 \text{ STEP } 1$$

If no **STEP** is listed, the computer assumes a step of 1.

To make a loop counter count backwards, use a negative **STEP**. For example, the loop below imitates the countdown to a rocket blast-off.

```
10 FOR K = 10 TO 1 STEP -1
20 PRINT K
30 NEXT K
40 PRINT "BLAST-OFF!"
50 END
```

EXAMPLE 2 **a.** Write a program to count from any starting value to any final value, with any **STEP** between counts. Let the user enter the beginning and ending values and the **STEP**.

Program

See Example 2, pages 161–162.

```
10 PRINT "I WILL COUNT FOR YOU."
20 PRINT "WHERE SHOULD I BEGIN";
30 INPUT B
40 PRINT "WHERE SHOULD I END";
50 INPUT E
53 PRINT "WHAT STEP SHOULD I USE";
56 INPUT S
60 FOR I = B TO E STEP S
70 PRINT I;"   ";
80 NEXT I
90 PRINT
100 END
```

b. Write the output of a **RUN** of the program.

Output

```
I WILL COUNT FOR YOU.
WHERE SHOULD I BEGIN?5
WHERE SHOULD I END?16
WHAT STEP SHOULD I USE?3
5   8   11   14
```

These numbers may be spaced further apart on your machine.

NOTE: The number 14, not 16, is the last number printed. Counting by 3's, the next count after 14 is 17. But 17 is greater than 16.

EXAMPLE 3 Which statements are correct? Give the reason for each answer.

	Statement	Correct?	Reason
a.	50 FOR X = 1, 100, 2	No	The statement should read: 50 FOR X = 1 TO 100 STEP 2
b.	20 FOR M = 20 TO 1	No	To count from 20 to 1, a negative **STEP** must be included.
c.	100 FOR L = X TO Y+1 STEP 2	Yes	This assumes that X is less than Y + 1. Expressions containing operations, such as Y + 1, are allowed in **FOR** statements.
d.	65 FOR D = 1 TO 50 STEP −1	No	The **STEP** should be 1 *or* the count should go from 50 to 1.

FOR (but not **NEXT**) statements may contain operations.

90 FOR X = B/2 TO Y*Y STEP K+1

An expression with variables may appear in any of these places.

The following is the general form of a **FOR** statement.

FOR variable = starting value **TO** ending value **STEP** increment

An **increment** (increase) refers to the difference from one count to the next. The increment may be positive or negative.

WRITTEN EXERCISES

Complete each statement.

1. If no **STEP** is listed at the end of a **FOR** statement, the computer will use a **STEP** of __?__.

2. The word **STEP** may be used in a **BASIC** program only inside quotation marks or in a __?__ statement.

3. Expressions such as **2*K+1** may appear in any of __?__ (how many?) places in a **FOR** statement.

4. To make a loop counter count backwards, use a __?__ **STEP**.

5. The difference from one count to the next is called the __?__.

For each statement in Exercises 6–11, identify the loop counter. Then list the values the counter will have for the loop.

6. 20 FOR I = 6 TO 11

7. 15 FOR X = 2 TO 6 STEP 1

8. 55 FOR J = 10 TO 20 STEP 2

9. 70 FOR Y = 10 TO 5 STEP −1

10. 90 FOR A = 100 TO 50 STEP −10

11. 85 FOR M = 15 TO 31 STEP 3

*For Exercises 12–19, write a **FOR** statement that will cause the given loop counter to take on the values listed.*

12. K = 2, 3, 4, 5, 6, 7

13. D = 1, 3, 5, 7, 9, 11, 13

14. L = 5, 10, 15, 20, 25, 30, 35

15. N = 5, 4, 3, 2, 1

16. R = 12, 10, 8, 6, 4, 2

17. W = 4, 1, −2, −5

18. Z = 20, 30, 40, 50, 60, 70, 80

19. Q = −6, −3, 0, 3, 6, 9

Which statements are correct? If a statement is not correct, give the reason.

20. 15 FOR B = 10 TO 1

21. 30 FOR M = 2 TO 16 BY 2

22. 50 LET V = 1 TO 7

23. 65 FOR L = C TO D STEP 2

24. 90 FOR T = 3, 21, 3

25. 45 FOR 20 TO 10 STEP −1

26. 105 FOR E = 100 TO 200 STEP −1

27. 33 FOR F = 50 TO 0 STEP −5

Modify the program of Example 1 in each of the following ways.

28. Count from 2 to 20 by two's.

29. Count from 2 to 20 by four's.

30. Print each count on a separate line down the screen or printer.

31. Count backwards from 10 to 2 by two's. Print the counts on the same line.

32. Count backwards from 10 to 2 by two's. Print each count on a separate line.

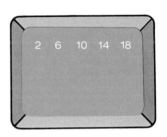

Correct any errors in these programs.

33.
```
100 FOR G = 5 TO 25 STEP 5
110 PRINT G
120 PRINT
130 END
```

34.
```
10 REM 1 TO 100 IN STEPS OF N
20 FOR I = 1 TO 100 STEP N
30 INPUT N
40 PRINT I;"   ";
50 NEXT N
60 END
```

Complete these programs.

35. Problem: Count from X to Y in steps of N.
```
10 PRINT "ENTER X, Y, AND N."
20  ?  X, Y, N
30 FOR J =  ?  TO Y  ?  N
40 PRINT J
50 NEXT  ?
60 END
```

36. Problem: Print the odd numbers from 1 to X.
```
100 PRINT "FINAL ODD NUMBER";
110  ?
120 FOR N = 1 TO X STEP  ?
130 PRINT  ? ,
140  ?
150 PRINT
160 END
```

In Exercises 37–38, the statements of the given program are not in the correct order. Write line numbers in front of the statements to show the correct order.

37. Problem: Print the even numbers from S to 200.

```
INPUT S
NEXT L
PRINT L;"   ";
END
PRINT "STARTING VALUE";
FOR L = S TO 200 STEP 2
```

38. Problem: Count backwards from J to 0 by one's.

```
END
FOR R = J TO 1 STEP -1
NEXT R
INPUT J
PRINT "WHAT IS J";
PRINT R
```

MORE CHALLENGING EXERCISES

For Exercises 39–43, write a program that contains a **FOR–NEXT** *loop.*

39. The multiples of five are 0, 5, 10, 15, and so on. Print the multiples of five from 0 to N, where the user enters N. Print the multiples across the screen in the built-in zones of your machine. HINT: Insert a comma instead of a semicolon at the end of a **PRINT** statement.

40. Modify the program of Exercise 39 to print the multiples of five from J to N. Have the user enter both J and N.

41. Count backwards from 100 to B, where the user enters B. Print the count down the screen. Print one number per line.

42. Modify the program of Exercise 41 to count from 100 to **B** in steps of −C. Have the user enter B and C.

43. Write a program that prints the display below. Have the program continue for as many lines as the user wishes.

```
      *
     ***
    *****
   *******
```

An adult care center computerizes patient records and accounting functions.

COMPUTER LAB ACTIVITIES

Steps Other Than One

1. Enter and **RUN** this program (see Example 1 on page 168).

```
10 FOR I = 2 TO 10 STEP 2
20 PRINT I;"   ";
30 NEXT I
40 PRINT
50 END
```

In Exercises 2–6:

a. Modify the program as you indicated in each given exercise.

*b. **RUN** the modified program.*

c. Check that the modified program does what it is supposed to do.

2. Exercise 28, page 171

3. Exercise 29, page 171

4. Exercise 30, page 171

5. Exercise 31, page 171

6. Type **NEW**. Then enter this program. **RUN** the program several times. Type different values for B, E, and S each time.

```
10 PRINT "I WILL COUNT FOR YOU."
20 PRINT "WHERE SHOULD I BEGIN";
30 INPUT B
40 PRINT "WHERE SHOULD I END";
50 INPUT E
53 PRINT "WHAT STEP SHOULD I USE";
56 INPUT S
60 FOR I = B TO E STEP S
70 PRINT I;"   ";
80 NEXT I
90 PRINT
100 END
```

In Exercises 7–8:

*a. Enter and **RUN** the indicated program you corrected.*

b. If necessary, make corrections until each program runs correctly.

7. Exercise 33, page 171

8. Exercise 34, page 171

In Exercises 9–10:

*a. Enter and **RUN** the indicated program you completed.*

b. Check whether you completed the program correctly.

9. Exercise 35, page 171

10. Exercise 36, page 171

Correct any errors in the programs of Exercises 1–2.

1.
```
10 PRINT "WHERE TO START?"
20 IMPUT S
30 FOR S=S TO 10
40 PRINT "T"
50 NEXT T
60 END
```

2.
```
10 FOR I=1 TWO 10
20 PRINT "GREAT!"
30 NEXT T
40 END
```

For Exercises 3–4, write the output for each program.

3.
```
10 FOR K=1 TO 4
20 PRINT "HOW ARE YOU?"
30 PRINT
40 NEXT K
50 END
```

4.
```
100 FOR T=1 TO 20 STEP 4
110 PRINT T
120 NEXT T
130 END
```

For Exercises 5–6, identify the loop counter.
Then list the values the counter will have for the loop.

5. 20 FOR T = 10 TO 2 STEP −2

6. 40 FOR K = 2 TO 6 STEP 3

For each of Exercises 7–8, write a **FOR** *statement so that the given loop counter will take on the values listed.*

7. K = 1,4,7,10,13

8. Z = 35,30,25,20,15

9. Complete this program.

Problem: Print the whole numbers from 1 to 25.
```
10 FOR  ?  =1 TO 25
20 PRINT K
30 NEXT K
40  ?
```

10. Complete this program.

Problem: Print "I LOVE SCHOOL" as many times as the user wishes.
```
10 PRINT "HOW MANY TIMES?"
20 INPUT  ?
30 FOR I=1 TO T
40  ?  "I LOVE SCHOOL"
50  ?  I
```

Did You Know? _____

This **one–chip computer** is smaller than a paper clip.
But the chip contains everything it needs to store and process data.

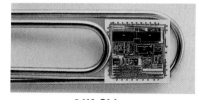

64K Chip

COMPUTERS AND THE CASHLESS SOCIETY

Point-of-sale (POS) terminals found in many retail stores and supermarkets are similar to cash registers. However, there are important differences. Each POS terminal is linked to a central computer system. Consumers will soon be able to make use of some POS terminals to transfer funds from their bank accounts to a retailer. Here's how it works!

1

A store clerk enters each purchase and the total cost into a POS terminal.

2

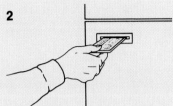

The customer uses a special "bank" card to input a personal identification number (ID) and authorize the purchase.

3

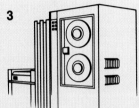

A central computer receives the information from the merchant plus the customer's ID and authorization. The computer sends the data to the customer's bank.

4

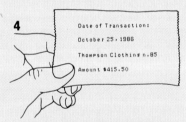

The customer's bank receives the data and confirms the transaction. The bank sends approval to the central computer.

5

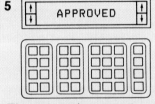

The central computer relays the approval to the merchant's POS terminal.

6

The sales clerk completes the approved transaction. The total purchase amount is subtracted from the customer's bank account and added to the merchant's account.

```
DATE OF TRANSACTION:
OCTOBER 25, 1986
THOMPSON CLOTHING N. 85
AMOUNT $415.50
```

The customer receives a receipt for the purchases and a POS receipt. The customer also receives a monthly bank statement showing all transactions.

PROJECT

Find out the names of businesses in your community that have POS terminals as described on this page. Report to the class on your findings.

4-4 SOME FANCY PRINTING

OBJECTIVE: To write programs with FOR–NEXT loops that produce "fancy" output, given the desired output

FOR–NEXT loops can produce interesting output. In particular, using a loop counter in the TAB function can create some nice effects.

EXAMPLE 1 a. Write a program to print 10 asterisks diagonally from the upper left toward the lower right of the screen or printer.

Program
```
10 FOR I = 1 TO 10
20 PRINT TAB(I);"*"
30 NEXT I
40 PRINT
50 END
```

b. Write the output from a RUN of the program.

Output
```
*
 *
  *
   *
    *
     *
      *
       *
        *
         *
```
←──────── **Blank line**

NOTE: As I counts from 1 to 10, TAB(I) in statement 20 causes the first * to be printed in position 1, the second * to be printed in position 2, and so on. The final * is printed in position 10.

The program in Example 1 could be made more flexible by allowing the user to choose how many asterisks to print. It could also allow the user to choose which symbol to print instead of the *. (See Exercises 6–8 on page 178.)

EXAMPLE 2 Write a program that prints a row of asterisks across the screen or printer. Print an asterisk in every other position. Begin by asking the user to enter the width of the screen or printer.

Program
```
10  PRINT "HOW WIDE IS THE SCREEN/PRINTER";
20  INPUT W
30  PRINT
40  FOR P = 1 TO W STEP 2
50  PRINT TAB(P);"*";
60  NEXT P
70  PRINT
80  END
```

STEP 2 causes the computer to skip every other print position.

b. Write the output from a **RUN** of the program.

Output
```
HOW WIDE IS THE SCREEN/PRINTER? 40

*  *  *  *  *  *  *  *  *  *  *  *  *  *  *  *  *  *  *  *
```

Blank line

Some versions of **BASIC** number the print positions starting from 0 rather than 1. For such a system, statement 40 can be changed to:

```
40  FOR P = 0 TO W-1 STEP 2
```

EXAMPLE 3   Write a program that prints any symbol (letter of the alphabet, counting number from 1 to 9, asterisk, and so on) that the user chooses. Print this symbol in a "backwards" diagonal from the upper right toward the lower left. Have the user also enter the width of the screen or printer.

Program
```
10  PRINT "HOW WIDE IS THE SCREEN/PRINTER";
20  INPUT W
30  PRINT "PRINT WHICH CHARACTER";
40  INPUT C$
50  PRINT
60  FOR I = W-1 TO 1 STEP -1
70  PRINT TAB(I);C$
80  NEXT I
90  END
```

Start printing at the right end of the line (position W−1) and move left (STEP −1).

NOTE: There is no ";" at the end of statement 70. For systems that number print positions from 0, statement 60 should be changed to:

```
60  FOR I = W-1 TO 0 STEP -1
```

WRITTEN EXERCISES

Write the output for each program.

1.
```
10 FOR J = 1 TO 5
20 PRINT TAB(5);"X"
30 NEXT J
40 PRINT
50 END
```

2.
```
10 FOR R = 1 TO 6
20 PRINT "#";TAB(9);"#"
30 NEXT R
40 PRINT
50 END
```

3.
```
10 PRINT
20 FOR S = 1 TO 7
30 PRINT "= ";
40 NEXT S
50 END
```

4.
```
100 PRINT "Z Z Z Z Z"
110 FOR I = 9 TO 1 STEP -2
120 PRINT TAB(I);"Z"
130 NEXT I
140 PRINT "Z Z Z Z Z"
150 END
```

5.
```
10 FOR C = 1 TO 6
20 PRINT TAB(C);"*";TAB(13-C);"*"
30 NEXT C
40 PRINT
50 END
```

For Exercises 6–8, modify the program of Example 1 as indicated.

6. Instead of printing 10 asterisks, ask the user how many to print.

7. Instead of printing asterisks, ask the user which symbol to print.

8. Combine Exercises 6 and 7 by asking the user which symbol to print and how many times to print it.

For Exercises 9–14, write a program that prints each display.
Each program should contain at least two **FOR–NEXT** *loops.*

9.
```
L
L
L
L
L
L
L L L L L L
```

10.
```
T T T T T T T
      T
      T
      T
      T
      T
      T
```

11.
```
          J
          J
          J
          J
          J
          J
J J J J J J
```

12.
```
U           U
U           U
U           U
U           U
U           U
U           U
U U U U U U
```

13.
```
F F F F F F
F
F
F F F F
F
F
F
```

14.
```
1 1 1
    1
    1
    1
    1
    1
1 1 1 1 1
```

MORE CHALLENGING EXERCISES

For Exercises 15–20, write a program for each exercise.
Each program should contain at least one FOR–NEXT loop.

15. Write a program that prints a line of X's down the middle of the screen from top to bottom.

16. Write a program that prints a row of X's across the middle of the screen from the left edge to the right edge.

17. Write a program that prints a large V filling the screen. Use any symbol you wish to form the "arms" of the V.

18. Write a program that prints a large V filling the screen. Ask the user to type the character to be used to form the V.

19. Write a program that prints a large X filling the screen. Use any symbol you wish to form the "arms" of the X.

20. Write a program that prints a large X filling the screen. Ask the user to type the symbol that is to be used to form the X.

For Exercises 21–23, write a program to produce each display.
Each program should contain at least one FOR–NEXT loop.

21.   **22.**   **23.**

Did You Know?

A **plotter** is an output device that a computer can use to draw graphs, charts, and pictures on paper. Unlike a printer, a plotter can produce continuous lines. The plotter has a mechanical arm to which a pen is attached. The computer moves the pen around the paper.

A **flatbed plotter** draws on a flat piece of paper. A **drum plotter** draws on a piece of paper wrapped around a cylinder.

Computer generated art of Mount St. Helens after eruption.

Fancy Printing

1. Enter and **RUN** this program. Does it produce the output shown in Example 1b on page 176?

```
10 FOR I = 1 TO 10
20 PRINT TAB(I);"*"
30 NEXT I
40 PRINT
50 END
```

    For Exercises 2–4:

    a. *Modify the program of Example 1 (see the program at the right) as indicated.*

    b. **RUN** *the program after each change. If necessary, make further changes until correct output is produced.*

2. Exercise 6, page 178   **3.** Exercise 7, page 178   **4.** Exercise 8, page 178

5. Enter and **RUN** the program of Example 2 on page 177. Does it produce the output shown in Example 2b?

6. Enter this program. **RUN** it several times. Enter different symbols for C$ and different numbers for the screen width.

```
10 PRINT "HOW WIDE IS THE SCREEN/PRINTER";
20 INPUT W
30 PRINT "PRINT WHICH CHARACTER";
40 INPUT C$
50 PRINT
60 FOR I = W-1 TO 1 STEP -1
70 PRINT TAB(I);C$
80 NEXT I
90 END
```

    For Exercises 7–11:

    a. *Enter and* **RUN** *the program of each given exercise.*

    b. *Is the output you predicted for each exercise actually produced?*

7. Exercise 1, page 178   **8.** Exercise 2, page 178   **9.** Exercise 3, page 178

10. Exercise 4, page 178   **11.** Exercise 5, page 178

    For Exercises 12–17:

    a. *Enter and* **RUN** *the program of each given exercise.*

    b. *Modify each program until it produces the desired output.*

12. Exercise 9, page 178   **13.** Exercise 10, page 178

14. Exercise 11, page 178   **15.** Exercise 12, page 178

16. Exercise 13, page 178   **17.** Exercise 14, page 178

4-5 SUBROUTINES

> **To write programs containing subroutines**

EXAMPLE 1 **a.** Write a program that prints a rectangle of asterisks.
The box should have 20 asterisks across and 6 down.

Program

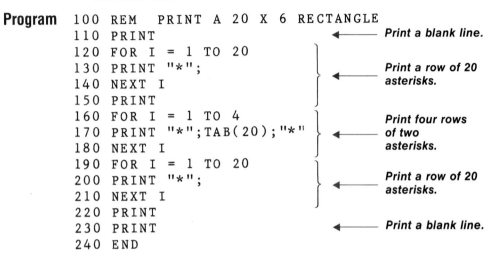

```
100 REM   PRINT A 20 X 6 RECTANGLE
110 PRINT                              ←——— Print a blank line.
120 FOR I = 1 TO 20      ⎫
130 PRINT "*";          ⎬ ←———  Print a row of 20
140 NEXT I              ⎪         asterisks.
150 PRINT               ⎭
160 FOR I = 1 TO 4      ⎫        Print four rows
170 PRINT "*";TAB(20);"*" ⎬ ←——— of two
180 NEXT I              ⎭         asterisks.
190 FOR I = 1 TO 20     ⎫        Print a row of 20
200 PRINT "*";          ⎬ ←———  asterisks.
210 NEXT I              ⎭
220 PRINT
230 PRINT                         ←——— Print a blank line.
240 END
```

b. Draw the output of a **RUN** of the program.

Output

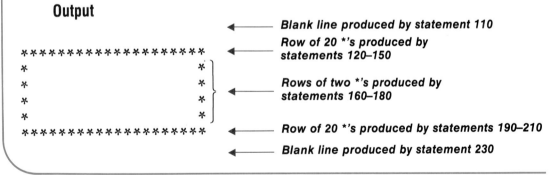

```
                          ←——— Blank line produced by statement 110
                              Row of 20 *'s produced by
********************   ←——— statements 120–150
*                  *  ⎫
*                  *  ⎬    Rows of two *'s produced by
*                  *  ⎪    statements 160–180
*                  *  ⎭
********************   ←——— Row of 20 *'s produced by statements 190–210
                          ←——— Blank line produced by statement 230
```

In the program of Example 1, statements 120–150 and 190–220 do
the same job; that is, they print a row of 20 asterisks. **BASIC** has a
way to write those statements <u>just once</u> but have them executed
<u>more than once</u>. To do this, the statements are put in a subroutine.
A **subroutine** is a group of statements that may be executed at any
point in the program.

The program in Example 2 below contains a subroutine which follows the main program. At two places in the main program, the computer is told to jump to the subroutine. This is done by means of the **GOSUB** (**go** to the **sub**routine) command.

EXAMPLE 2   **a.** Modify the program of Example 1 to include a subroutine.

Program
```
100 REM   LINES 100-240 ARE THE MAIN PROGRAM.
110 PRINT
120 GOSUB 300
160 FOR I = 1 TO 4
170 PRINT "*";TAB(20);"*"
180 NEXT I
190 GOSUB 300
230 PRINT
240 GOTO 400
300 REM   SUBROUTINE TO PRINT 20 ASTERISKS
310 FOR I = 1 TO 20
320 PRINT "*";
330 NEXT I
340 PRINT
350 RETURN
400 END
```

b. Show the order in which the statements are executed.

Statement	What Happens
110	Execution of the main program begins by printing a blank line.
120	The computer is sent to the subroutine beginning at line 300.
300–350	The subroutine to print 20 asterisks is executed. Statement 350 tells the computer to return to the main program.
160–180	Four rows of two asterisks (the vertical sides of the box) are printed.
190	The computer is again sent to the subroutine beginning at line 300.
300–350	The subroutine prints a row of 20 asterisks. Statement 350 again returns the computer to the main program.
230	A blank line is printed.
240	The computer is told to jump over the subroutine to the **END** statement. Line 240 is needed to keep the machine from "falling" into the subroutine again.

A subroutine may contain any **BASIC** statement. Any task that can be done in a main program (for example, reading data from the keyboard or from **DATA** statements) can also be done in a subroutine.

In long programs, subroutines may contain hundreds of lines. However, a subroutine must always end with the **RETURN** command. This sends the computer back to the main program. There the computer executes the first statement after the **GOSUB** that sent it to the subroutine. Whenever the computer hits a **GOSUB** command, it "marks its place" in the program. In this way, it "knows" where to continue execution when it returns from the subroutine.

A program may have more than one subroutine. It is good programming practice to place a subroutine at the end of a program. If there are two or more subroutines, they may be listed in any order. They need not be listed in the order in which they will be executed.

A meter reader uses a portable computer terminal to enter data.

WRITTEN EXERCISES

Complete each statement.

1. Any program that contains a **GOSUB** statement must also contain a __?__ statement.
2. **GOSUB** means "go to the __?__."
3. The last statement of a subroutine is always __?__.
4. A program may contain __?__ (only one/more than one) subroutine.

For Exercises 5–9, modify the program of Example 2 as indicated.

5. Print a 25 × 10 box (rectangle); that is, print 25 asterisks across the top and bottom and 10 asterisks down the sides.
6. Ask the user to enter the dimensions of the box.
7. Instead of printing the box using asterisks, ask the user to type the character to be used.
8. In a subroutine, print ten blank lines before and after the box.

9. Slow down the printing of the box by transferring to a delay loop in a subroutine after printing the top of the box and before printing the bottom.

For Exercises 10–12, draw the output of each program.

10.
```
10  GOSUB 100
20  FOR I = 1 TO 3
30  PRINT "*"
40  NEXT I
50  GOSUB 100
60  PRINT
70  GOTO 150
100 FOR I = 1 TO 4
110 PRINT "* ";
120 NEXT I
130 PRINT
140 RETURN
150 END
```

12.
```
10  GOSUB 100
20  GOSUB 200
30  GOSUB 100
40  GOSUB 200
50  GOSUB 100
60  GOTO 240
100 FOR C = 1 TO 10
110 PRINT "=";
120 NEXT C
130 PRINT
140 RETURN
200 FOR R = 1 TO 5
210 PRINT TAB(10);"="
220 NEXT R
230 RETURN
240 END
```

11.
```
100 FOR J = 1 TO 5
110 PRINT "X";
120 NEXT J
130 PRINT
140 GOSUB 900
150 PRINT
160 GOSUB 900
170 GOTO 999
900 FOR K = 1 TO 5
910 PRINT TAB(K);"X"
920 NEXT K
930 PRINT
940 RETURN
999 END
```

13. When the program below is **RUN**, what is the order in which the statements are executed?
```
10  PRINT "****"
20  GOSUB 200
30  PRINT "XXXX"
40  GOSUB 200
50  GOTO 220
200 PRINT "////"
210 RETURN
220 END
```

14. Write the output of the program of Exercise 13.

Correct any errors in these programs. Then write the output.

15.
```
10  GOSUB 200
20  FOR I = 1 TO 5
30  PRINT "*"
40  NEXT I
50  GOSUB 200
200 FOR I = 1 TO 5
210 PRINT TAB(I);"*"
220 NEXT I
230 PRINT
999 END
```

16.
```
100 FOR K = 5 TO 1
110 PRINT TAB(K);"X"
120 NEXT K
130 GOTO 900
140 GOTO 940
900 FOR K = 1 TO 5
910 PRINT TAB(K);"X"
920 NEXT K
930 RETURN
940 END
```

Complete the program.

17. Problem: Print a large letter C.

```
10  GOSUB  ?
20  FOR I = 1 TO 6
30  PRINT "C"
40  NEXT  ?
50  ?  500
60  GOTO 999
500 REM   SUBROUTINE--PRINT CROSSBAR
510 FOR I = 1 TO 6
520 PRINT "C";
530 NEXT I
540 PRINT
550 ?
999 END
```

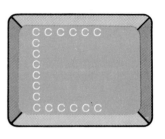

18. Problem: Print a large + sign.

```
100  ?  800
110  FOR X = 1 TO 21
120  PRINT "X";
130  ?  X
140  PRINT
150  GOSUB  ?
160  ?
800  REM SUBROUTINE--VERTICAL BAR
810  FOR X = 1 TO 10
820  PRINT TAB(10);"X"
830  ?  X
840  RETURN
850  ?
```

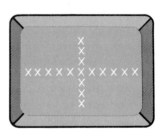

For Exercises 19–27, write a program to print each array.
*Use at least one subroutine and at least two **FOR–NEXT** loops.*

19.
```
I  I  I  I  I  I  I
   I
   I
   I
   I
   I
   I
   I
I  I  I  I  I  I  I
```

20.
```
H                 H
H                 H
H                 H
H                 H
H H H H H H H
H                 H
H                 H
H                 H
H                 H
```

21.
```
Z  Z  Z  Z  Z  Z  Z  Z
                        Z
                     Z
                  Z
               Z
            Z
         Z
      Z
Z  Z  Z  Z  Z  Z  Z
```

22.
```
G G G G G G G
G
G
G
G       G G G
G             G
G             G
G             G
G G G G G G G
```

23.
```
E E E E E E E
E
E
E
E E E E E
E
E
E
E E E E E E E
```

24.
```
O O O O O O
O                 O
O                 O
O                 O
O                 O
O                 O
O                 O
  O O O O O O
```

25.
```
8 8 8 8 8 8
8               8
8               8
8               8
  8 8 8 8 8 8
8               8
8               8
8               8
  8 8 8 8 8 8
```

26.
```
5 5 5 5 5 5 5
5
5
5
5 5 5 5 5 5 5
              5
              5
              5
5 5 5 5 5 5 5
```

27.
```
3 3 3 3 3 3
              3
              3
              3
  3 3 3 3 3
              3
              3
              3
  3 3 3 3 3 3
```

MORE CHALLENGING EXERCISES

For Exercises 28–32, write a program for each problem.
Each program should contain at least one subroutine.

28. Ask the user to type a letter. Then print that letter 10 times down the screen. Ask the user to type a second letter. Print the second letter 10 times down the screen.

29. Print **I LIKE COMPUTERS** slowly. Allow a pause between each word.

30. Print a tic-tac-toe board.

31. Given an integer **N**, print the integers **1** through N^2 as shown at the right.

```
1  1  1
2  2  2
3  3  3
.  .  .
.  .  .
.  .  .
9  9  9
```

32. Write a program that draws a stairway

```
  _ _ _ _ _ _ _
              !
              !
          _ _ _ _ _ _
                    !
                    !
```

and so on across the screen or printer.

COMPUTER LAB ACTIVITIES

Subroutines

1. Enter and **RUN** the program of Example 2 on page 182. Does it produce the output shown in Example 1 on page 181? If it does not, change the program until the correct output is obtained.

For Exercises 2–6:

a. Modify the program as you indicated in each given exercise.

b. **RUN** *the modified program. If necessary, make further changes until the correct output is produced.*

2. Exercise 5, page 183   **3.** Exercise 6, page 183   **4.** Exercise 7, page 183

5. Exercise 8, page 183   **6.** Exercise 9, page 184

For Exercises 7–9:

a. Enter and **RUN** *the program of each indicated exercise.*

b. Check whether the output is the same as the output you predicted.

7. Exercise 10, page 184   **8.** Exercise 11, page 184   **9.** Exercise 12, page 184

10. Enter and **RUN** the program of Exercise 13 on page 184. Is the output the same as the output you predicted in Exercise 14 on page 184?

For Exercises 11–12:

a. Enter and **RUN** *the program you corrected.*

b. Check whether all the errors were corrected. If not, make further changes until the program runs correctly.

11. Exercise 15, page 184   **12.** Exercise 16, page 184

For Exercises 13–14:

a. Enter and **RUN** *the programs you completed.*

b. Check whether you completed the program correctly.

13. Exercise 17, page 185   **14.** Exercise 18, page 185

For Exercises 15–20:

a. Enter and **RUN** *the program for each exercise indicated.*

b. When necessary, modify each program until it produces the desired output.

15. Exercise 19, page 185   **16.** Exercise 20, page 185   **17.** Exercise 21, page 185

18. Exercise 22, page 186   **19.** Exercise 23, page 186   **20.** Exercise 24, page 186

4-6 GENERAL GRAPHICS METHODS

OBJECTIVE: **To learn graphics commands and general graphics methods**

Probably the most exciting form of programming is graphics. **Graphics** refers to producing charts, diagrams, shapes, colors, and animation on computer screens and printers.

Graphics programming differs greatly from one type of computer to the other. Commands that work on one computer will not be understood by another. This lesson will discuss some general principles of graphics. The following lessons will show techniques in graphics for some of the major types of microcomputers.

CURSOR

Each screen displays a **cursor** to mark your place as you type. The cursor may be a dash (—), an underscore (_), or a solid block (■). The cursor may blink on and off. Keyboards usually have arrow keys for moving the cursor in any direction. Some also have a **HOME** key. Pressing this key moves the cursor to its "home" position at the upper left corner of the screen. On many systems, the **BASIC** command **HOME** does the same thing.

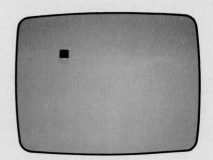

CLEARING THE SCREEN

Most keyboards have a **CLEAR** key for clearing the screen. Each form of **BASIC** also has a way to clear the screen from within a program. **CLS** is a common command used to do this. It is a good habit to begin programs by clearing the screen. The screen can also be cleared after the user has entered some input and before the output is displayed.

SCREEN SIZE

Each form of **BASIC** divides the screen into a fixed number of **columns** (left to right) and **rows** (top to bottom). For example, one popular system has 40 columns and 25 lines. Some systems number the columns from 0; others number from 1. Similarly, the top row may be numbered 0 or 1.

Each letter, digit, or special symbol the user types occupies one block. This is called **text mode**. Text mode is in effect when you turn on a machine and enter a program.

Each character on a screen is composed of tiny dots. Each point is a **pixel** (**picture element**), the smallest block the machine can light.

GRAPHICS MODES

Most machines can switch from text mode to **graphics mode**. In graphics mode, the computer can light smaller blocks. The size of the block determines the **resolution** (sharpness) of the display; that is, *the smaller the pixel, the higher the resolution*.

Some machines have a **high resolution (hi-res)** mode and a **low resolution (low-res)** mode. For example, one computer divides the screen into 280 columns and 192 rows for hi-res. Low-res on this computer has 40 columns and 40 rows.

On a computer having a graphics mode, the **BASIC** has commands to switch to and from that mode. For example, **GR** might change to low-res graphics and **HGR** to high-res graphics. **TEXT** returns to text mode. On another system, **GRAPHICS 5** might change the computer to fifth graphics mode.

COLOR

Some systems have the hardware and software to create color displays. The 8 or 16 colors commonly available on computers are numbered. For example, **color 0** might be **black**, **color 1** might be **magenta**, **color 2** might be **dark blue**, and so on. There is usually a **BASIC** command, such as **COLOR = 5** or **COLOR 5**, to set the color.

On some machines, you can set a **foreground color** and a **background color**. The command, **COLOR 5,2**, might tell the machine to set foreground color 5 and background color 2.

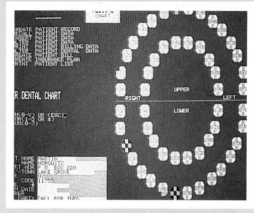

Computer graphics are used in dentistry.

LIGHTING AND UNLIGHTING POINTS

Various **BASIC**'s have commands to light points on a screen. For example, **PLOT 10,15** might light the block in column 10, row 15 with the color specified in the latest **COLOR** command. On another machine, **SET(10,15)** might have the same effect.

To unlight a point on some machines, the user might plot the point using the background color. On another machine, the command **RESET(10,15)** would remove the point.

DRAWING LINES

Some **BASIC**'s have commands to connect points with straight line segments. For example,

LINE(10,15)–(20,30)

might connect the point at (10,15) with the point at (20,30). The command

HPLOT 10,15 TO 20,30

might also have the same effect. Without commands like these, the programmer must write a loop to light each point in the path of the line segment.

DRAWING CIRCLES

A few system have built-in commands for plotting circles. The command **CIRCLE(20,20),10** might draw a circle centered at (20,20) with a radius of 10 dots.

REVERSE VIDEO

Screens usually display light shapes on a dark background. Printing dark characters on a light background is known as **reverse video** or **inverse video**. On some machines, the user can press a key to accomplish this.

FLASHING VIDEO

A common graphics method is to make a figure or word flash on and off. This can be done by displaying something, erasing it, displaying it again in the same position, erasing it again, and so on.

KEYBOARD INPUT

Video game players press keys to move a rocket ship or to fire lasers. They do not have to press the **RETURN** or **ENTER** key. Some versions of **BASIC** have a command for accepting a single key input immediately without waiting for **RETURN** to be pressed. One command commonly used for this is **GET**. Another is **INKEY$**.

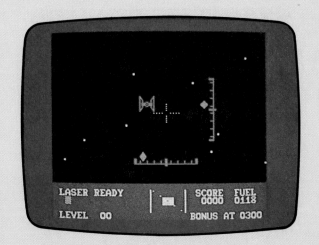

CHARACTER CODES

Every computer codes letters and other symbols as numbers in its memory. The most common code used is **ASCII (American Standard Code for Information Interchange)**. For example, in ASCII, **A** is **65**, **a** is **96**, and **/** is **47**.

PEEK AND POKE

Each location in a computer's memory is numbered. **BASIC** has the **POKE** command which puts a character in **ASCII** code directly into a memory location. For example, **POKE 12345,47** puts a / in location 12345.

The **PEEK** function shows what is in a memory location. For example, **PRINT PEEK(12345)** displays the character coded in location 12345.

Each type of microcomputer uses part of its memory to store what is on the screen. A common way to display something quickly on the screen is to **POKE** the code for the symbol into the appropriate memory location.

WRITTEN EXERCISES

Complete each statement.

1. Producing charts, diagrams, and animation on computer screens and printers is called __?__.

2. Each computer displays a __?__ to mark your place on the screen.

3. To move the cursor to the upper left corner of the screen, some keyboards have a __?__ key.

4. To erase the screen, many keyboards have a __?__ key.

5. Each point which can be lighted on a screen is called a __?__.

6. The size of the lighted blocks determines the __?__ of the display.

7. Many machines have two ''modes'' of operation: the __?__ mode and the __?__ mode.

8. On some computers you can set a __?__ color and a __?__ color.

9. Printing dark characters on a light background is called __?__ video.

10. The **BASIC** command to put a character directly into a memory location is __?__.

11. The **BASIC** function that shows what is in a memory location is __?__.

*In Exercises 12–22, list the **BASIC** commands your computer has, if any, for each of the following operations.*

12. Send the cursor to the upper left corner of the screen.

13. Put the computer into various graphics modes.

14. Put the computer into text mode.

15. Erase the screen.

16. Specify the foreground color.

17. Specify the background color.

18. Light a point on the screen.

19. Unlight a point on the screen.

20. Convert to reverse video.

21. Make a word or figure flash on/off.

22. Accept a typed symbol without **RETURN** (or **ENTER**) being pressed.

Answer these questions about the computer you use.

23. In text mode, how many columns and rows does the screen have?

24. In its various graphics modes (if it has any), how many columns and rows of screen blocks does it have?

REVIEW: Sections 4–4—4–6

1. Write the output for this program.

```
10 GOSUB 200
20 FOR I = 1 TO 3
30 PRINT "5"
40 NEXT I
50 GOSUB 200
60 FOR I = 1 TO 3
70 PRINT TAB(9);"5"
80 NEXT I
90 GOSUB 200
100 GOTO 999
200 PRINT "5 5 5 5 5"
210 RETURN
999 END
```

2. Complete this program.

Problem: Print a large **E.**

```
10 PRINT "E E E E"
20 GOSUB   ?
30 PRINT "E E E E"
40   ?   500
50 PRINT "E E E E"
60 GOTO 540
500 FOR I=1 TO 4
510 PRINT "E"
520 NEXT   ?
530   ?
540 END
```

For Exercises 3–9, complete each statement.

3. On some computers, a program can set a background and a   ?   color.

4. The size of the screen blocks in graphics mode determines the   ?   of the display.

5. The most common code used by computers to code letters and other symbols in its memory is called   ? .

6. What command(s) are used on your computer to clear the screen?

7. What command(s) are used on your computer to draw a vertical line?

8. What command(s) are used on your computer to draw a horizontal line?

LOGO

If you happen to hear students in the computer lab talking about a "turtle," you can almost be sure that they are talking about the computer language LOGO. When LOGO is loaded into a computer from a tape, disk, or cartridge, it displays a special symbol called a **turtle** in the center of the screen. As it moves, the turtle leaves a trail on the screen. The turtle responds to a few simple commands.

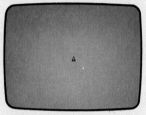

SHOWTURTLE

SHOWTURTLE makes the turtle appear.

FORWARD 100

FORWARD moves the turtle forward a given number of "turtle steps" in the direction it is pointing.

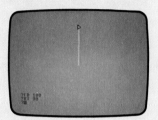

RIGHT 90

RIGHT 90 rotates the turtle 90° clockwise.

FORWARD 150
LEFT 45

LEFT 45 rotates the turtle 45° counter-clockwise.

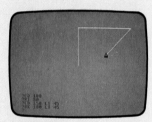

BACK 100
LEFT 45

BACK moves the turtle in the opposite direction to which it is pointing.

PENUP
FORWARD 50
PENDOWN
FORWARD 50
HIDETURTLE

PENUP and PENDOWN raise and lower the pen.
The turtle does not leave a trace when the pen is up. HIDETURTLE makes the turtle disappear.

This table shows some other commonly used LOGO commands. Each command may be entered in direct mode or used in a program.

Command	Short Form	What the Command Does	Example
CLEARSCREEN	CS	Clears the screen.	CS
HOME	HOME	Moves the turtle to the center of the screen, pointing straight up.	HOME
BACKGROUND	BG	Sets the background color.	BG 4
PENCOLOR	PC	Sets the color of lines the turtle draws.	PC 2

PROJECTS

If you have access to a version of LOGO, try each of the following.

1. Enter and **RUN** these direct commands in order from left to right. After each command, press the **RETURN** (or **ENTER**) key.

   FD 50   RT 90   FD 50   RT 90   FD 50   RT 90   FD 50

   Did you end up with a box (rectangle) on the screen?

2. Enter this program (called a **procedure** in LOGO) into your computer. Then execute the procedure in **RUN** mode by first typing **BOX**. Then press **RETURN** (or **ENTER**).

   TO BOX

      CS

      REPEAT 4 [FD 50 RT 90]

   END

   ⟵ **REPEAT 4** means to repeat the commands in brackets four times. This is a loop in LOGO.

3. If your computer has color, experiment by entering the **BG** and **PC** commands as direct commands with numbers after each. To see the new pencolor each time, enter a direct command such as **FD 50** or **BK 40**.

4-7 APPLE® GRAPHICS

OBJECTIVE: To use Apple BASIC graphics commands in programs

Apple computers have three **modes**.

Mode	Dimensions
Text	40 columns × 25 rows
Low-resolution graphics	40 columns × 40 rows
High-resolution graphics	280 columns × 160 rows

In each mode, the column and row numbers begin at zero. For example, in low-resolution graphics, the graphics rows are numbered 0 (top of screen) to 39 (bottom).

Apple BASIC includes special commands for graphics.

Command	What It Does
GR	Clears the screen and changes to low-resolution graphics.
HGR	Clears the screen and changes to high-resolution graphics.
TEXT	Returns to text mode.
COLOR = n	In low resolution, sets the color. The letter n represents a whole number from 0 to 15 inclusive.
HCOLOR = n	In high resolution, sets the color. The letter n represents a whole number from 0 to 7, inclusive.
HTAB n	Like **TAB**, moves the cursor horizontally to column n (from 0 to 39).
VTAB n	Moves the cursor vertically to row n (from 0 to 24).
PLOT x,y	In low resolution, lights a point at position (x, y), where x = the column (0 to 39) and y = the row (0 to 39).
HLIN a,b AT y	In low resolution, draws a horizontal line from a to b in row y.
VLIN a,b AT x	In low resolution, draws a vertical line from a to b in column x.
HPLOT a,b TO c,d	In high resolution, draws a line from point (a,b) to point (c,d).
GET	Accepts a character typed at the keyboard without waiting for the user to press **RETURN**.

APPLE COLOR CODES

Low-Resolution		High-Resolution	
0 = black	8 = brown	0 = black–1	4 = black–2
1 = magenta	9 = orange	1 = green	5 = depends on tv
2 = dark blue	10 = gray	2 = blue	6 = depends on tv
3 = purple	11 = pink	3 = white–1	7 = white–2
4 = dark green	12 = green		
5 = gray	13 = yellow		
6 = medium blue	14 = aqua	White–1 and –2 and black–1 and –2	
7 = light blue	15 = white	are thicker lines.	

EXAMPLE 1 Write a program that draws a rectangle in low–res graphics mode.

Program
```
100 GR
110 COLOR= 8
120 HLIN 1,30 AT 10
130 VLIN 10,20 AT 1
140 VLIN 10,20 AT 30
150 HLIN 1,30 AT 20
160 VTAB 21
170 PRINT "PRESS 'A' TO SEE IT AGAIN."
180 GET K$
190 IF K$ = "A" THEN 100
999 END
```

Statement	What It Does
100	Clears the screen and switches the computer to low–res graphics mode.
110	Sets the color to 8 (brown).
120	Draws the top of the box.
130	Draws the left side of the box.
140	Draws the right side of the box.
150	Draws the bottom of the box.
160	Moves the cursor to row 21 in the "text window," with four lines reserved for text at the bottom of the low-res screen.
170	Prompts the user to type "A" to repeat the program.
180	Accepts a single character typed at keyboard without **RETURN** being pressed and stores this character as K$.
190	Tests K$. If it is "A", the program is run again; if K$ is any other character, the program ends.

EXAMPLE 2 Expand the program of Example 1 so that, if the user wishes, the inside of the rectangle is "painted" light blue.

Solution Add these statements to the program of Example 1.

```
170 PRINT "PRESS 'P' TO PAINT THE INSIDE."
180 GET K$
190 IF K$ <> "P" THEN 999
200 COLOR= 7
210 FOR Y = 11 TO 19
220 HLIN 2,29 AT Y
230 NEXT Y
```

NOTE: The loop in statements **210–230** draws nine horizontal lines across the inside of the rectangle.

WRITTEN EXERCISES

Write the Apple BASIC command to do each of the following.

1. Clear the screen and change to low-resolution graphics mode.
2. Convert to high-resolution graphics mode.
3. Change to text mode.
4. Set the low-resolution color to color 1.
5. Set the high-resolution color to color 2.
6. Move the cursor horizontally to column 20.
7. Move the cursor vertically to row 15.
8. Light a low-resolution point in column 10, row 12.
9. Draw a high-resolution line from positions 5 to 15 in row 20.
10. Draw a low-res horizontal line from positions 8 to 22 in row 5.
11. Draw a low-res vertical line from positions 4 to 16 in column 13.
12. Accept a character from the keyboard without **RETURN** being pressed and store the character as A$.

Complete these statements about Apple BASIC.

13. In text mode, the screen is divided into __?__ columns numbered __?__ through __?__ .

14. In text mode, the screen is divided into __?__ rows numbered __?__ through __?__ .

15. In low-res graphics mode, the screen contains __?__ columns and __?__ rows.

16. In low-res graphics mode, there are __?__ colors numbered __?__ through __?__ .

17. In high-res graphics mode, the screen contains __?__ columns and __?__ rows.

18. In high-res graphics mode, there are __?__ colors numbered __?__ through __?__ .

Modify the program of Example 1 as indicated.

19. Slow down the drawing of the rectangle by jumping to a delay loop in a subroutine after each horizontal or vertical line is drawn.

20. Instead of setting the color to 8, ask the user what color to draw the rectangle.

21. Set up a **FOR–NEXT** loop to draw the rectangle a different color each time the user presses the **A** key.

Modify the program of Example 2 as indicated.

22. Slow down the painting of the inside of the rectangle by jumping to a delay loop in a subroutine after each horizontal line inside the rectangle is drawn.

23. ''Paint'' the inside of the rectangle by drawing vertical lines instead of horizontal lines.

24. Instead of painting the inside light blue, ask the user what color to use.

In Apple BASIC write a **FOR–NEXT** *loop containing a* **PLOT** *command to do the same job as the following statements.*

25. HLIN 5,15 AT 10

26. VLIN 4,18 AT 12

Describe the output of these programs.

27.
```
100 PRINT "WHAT COLOR";
110 INPUT N
120 GR
130 COLOR= N
140 FOR X = 10 TO 30
150 PLOT X,10
160 NEXT X
170 END
```

28.
```
10 GR
20 COLOR= 4
30 FOR Y = 12 TO 20
40 PLOT 12,Y
50 PLOT 20,Y
60 NEXT Y
70 HLIN 12,20 AT 20
80 END
```

Correct any errors in these programs.

29.
```
1  REM   DRAW A SLANTED LINE
10 GR
20 COLOR 7
30 FOR J = 1 TO 20
40 PLOT (J,J)
50 NEXT J
60 END
```

30.
```
10 REM    DRAW AN "L"
20 GR
30 HCOLOR= 3
40 VLIN 8,20
50 HLIN 5 TO 15
60 END
```

Complete each program.

31. Problem: Draw a large capital T in low–resolution graphics.

```
100   ?
110 COLOR= 5
120 REM   DRAW THE TOP OF THE T
130   ?   10,30 AT 8
140 REM   DRAW THE VERTICAL BAR
150   ?   9,25 AT 20
160 VTAB 22
170 PRINT "PRESS 'A' TO SEE AGAIN."
180   ?   X$
190 IF X$ =  ?  THEN  ?
200 END
```

32. Problem: Draw a solid rectangle in low–resolution graphics.

```
10 GR
20   ?  = 11
30 FOR Y = 7 TO 17
40 HLIN 7,27 AT   ?
50 NEXT   ?
60   ?   23
70 PRINT "PRESS A KEY TO END."
80 GET Z$
90 END
```

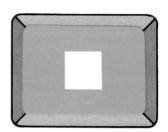

MORE CHALLENGING EXERCISES

*For Exercises 33–36, write a program in Apple **BASIC** to "paint" the screen completely. Have the user select the color.*

33. "Paint" with horizontal lines from the top of the screen to the bottom.

34. "Paint" with horizontal lines from the bottom of the screen to the top.

35. "Paint" with vertical lines that move from left to right.

36. "Paint" with vertical lines that move from right to left.

37. Write an Apple **BASIC** program to make a point in the center of the screen blink on and off. Follow these steps.

a. Change to low–resolution graphics mode.

b. Use any color that does <u>not</u> match the background color of the screen.

c. Light a point at the center of the screen.

d. Pause by executing a delay loop.

e. Execute steps **a** through **d** over and over.

COMPUTER LAB ACTIVITIES

Apple Graphics

NOTE: *A color monitor will help you to obtain the full effects of a* **RUN** *of the programs in these exercises.*

1. Enter and **RUN** this program. If your system has a disk drive, insert a formatted disk and save the program by typing **SAVE RECTANGLE**.

```
100 GR
110 COLOR= 8
120 HLIN 1,30 AT 10
130 VLIN 10,20 AT 1
140 VLIN 10,20 AT 30
150 HLIN 1,30 AT 20
160 VTAB 21
170 PRINT "PRESS 'A' TO SEE IT AGAIN."
180 GET K$
190 IF K$ = "A" THEN 100
999 END
```

2. Add the statements of Example 2 on page 198. **RUN** the new program. If you have a disk drive, save the program by typing **SAVE PAINT**.

For Exercises 3–5:

a. Reload the program of Exercise 1 from the disk by typing **LOAD RECTANGLE**.

b. For each exercise, modify the program as indicated.

c. **RUN** *each program. Make changes to produce correct output.*

3. Exercise 19, page 199   **4.** Exercise 20, page 199   **5.** Exercise 21, page 199

For Exercises 6–8:

a. Reload the program of Example 2 on page 198 from the disk by typing **LOAD PAINT**.

b. For each exercise, modify the program as indicated.

c. **RUN** *each program. Make changes to produce correct output.*

6. Exercise 22, page 199   **7.** Exercise 23, page 199   **8.** Exercise 24, page 199

For Exercises 9–10:

a. Type **NEW**. *Enter and* **RUN** *the program of each exercise.*

b. Is the output you predicted actually produced?

9. Exercise 27, page 199   **10.** Exercise 28, page 199

For Exercises 11–12:

a. *Enter and* **RUN** *the programs you completed in the indicated exercises.*

b. *Did you complete each program correctly?*

11. Exercise 31, page 200

12. Exercise 32, page 200

EXPLORE

13. Enter and **RUN** the program on the right. Stop the **RUN** by pressing the **CONTROL** and **RESET** keys.

For Exercises 14–18, explain briefly what each of the indicated parts of the program does.

14. Lines 50–70

15. Lines 80–100

16. Lines 110–130

17. Lines 140–160

18. Lines 170–180

19. **RND** is **BASIC's** random-number function. Explain the two ways the program uses random numbers.

20. Modify the program to change the effects it produces.

```
10  HOME
20  HGR
30  A = RND(8)*6 + 2
40  HCOLOR = RND(8)*6
50  FOR I = 0 TO 279 STEP A
60  HPLOT 140,159 TO I,0
70  NEXT I
80  FOR I = 0 TO 159 STEP A
90  HPLOT 0,80 TO 279,I
100 NEXT I
110 FOR I = 279 TO 0 STEP -A
120 HPLOT 140,0 TO I,159
130 NEXT I
140 FOR I = 159 TO A STEP -A
150 HPLOT 279,80 TO 0,I
160 NEXT I
170 FOR I = 1 TO 500
180 NEXT I
190 GOTO 30
200 END
```

Did You Know?

Pictures or data on a computer screen can be entered or changed by using a **light pen**. The pen has a light–sensitive cell at its tip. When the light pen touches the screen, it closes a photoelectric current. This enables the computer to identify the point on the screen.

4-8 TRS-80® GRAPHICS

OBJECTIVE:

> **To use TRS-80® BASIC graphics commands in programs**

The **TRS-80®** model I and model III computers operate <u>only</u> in text mode. They display 64 columns of characters in 16 rows. However, smaller blocks can be lit using the **SET** command. For this command, the screen is divided into 128 blocks horizontally and 48 vertically.

Here are some of the graphics commands for TRS-80® Models I and III. Neither of these machines has color capability.

Command	What It Does
CLS	Clears the screen.
SET(x,y)	Lights the block at position (x,y). The letter x represents a column from 0 to 127; the letter y represents a row from 0 to 47.
RESET(x,y)	Unlights the block at position (x,y).
PRINT@n,	Prints the next item starting at position n on the screen, where the top row is numbered 0 to 63, the next row is numbered 64 to 127, and so on down the screen.
INKEY$	Accepts a single character from the keyboard without waiting for the user to press **ENTER**.

EXAMPLE 1 Write a TRS-80® program to draw a rectangle on the screen.

Program
```
100 CLS
110 FOR X = 0 TO 39
120 SET(X,10)
130 NEXT X
140 FOR Y = 11 TO 19
150 SET(0,Y)
160 SET(39,Y)
170 NEXT Y
180 FOR X = 0 TO 39
190 SET(X,20)
200 NEXT X
210 PRINT@12*64,"PRESS 'A' TO SEE IT AGAIN."
220 LET K$ = INKEY$
230 IF K$ = "" THEN 220
240 IF K$ = "A" THEN 100
999 END
```

Statement	What It Does
100	Clears the screen.
110–130	Draws a horizontal line at row 10 of the graphics grid.
140–170	Draws the vertical sides of the box in columns 0 and 39.
180–200	Draws a horizontal line at row 20 of the graphics grid.
210	Prompts the user to type "A" to repeat the program. This prompt begins on the 12th row of the screen (position 12*64).
220	Accepts a single character typed at the keyboard without **ENTER** being pressed. It stores this character as **K$**.
230	As long as **K$** is blank, it returns the computer to statement 220.
240	If **K$** is "A", the program is run again. If **K$** is any other non-blank character, the program ends.

EXAMPLE 2   Add these statements to the program of Example 1 so that, if the user wishes, the inside of the box is "painted" white.

Solution
```
210 PRINT@12*64,"PRESS 'P' TO PAINT THE INSIDE."
240 IF K$ <> "P" THEN 999
250 FOR Y = 11 TO 20
260 FOR X = 1 TO 38
270 SET(X,Y)
280 NEXT X
290 NEXT Y
```

NOTE: Statements 250–290 form a **nested** loop (a loop within a loop). For each value of Y from 11 to 20, X varies from 1 to 38. In this way each point inside the box is lit by statement 270.

The **TRS-80**® **Color Computer** has color capability and additional graphics commands not available on Models I and III.

Color Computer Command	What It Does
CLS n	Clears the screen to color n. (See page 205 for the list of color numbers.)
SET (x,y,c)	Lights the point at location (x,y) using color c.
	The letter x represents a column from 0 to 63; the letter y represents a row from 0 to 31 (both inclusive).

0 = black	**3** = blue	**6** = cyan
1 = green	**4** = red	**7** = magenta
2 = yellow	**5** = buff	**8** = orange

RESET(x,y) works the same way on the Color Computer as on the other models. The **INKEY$** and **PRINT@** commands are also available. For **PRINT@**, the Color Computer screen has only 32 columns across and 16 rows down.

EXAMPLE 3   Modify the programs of Examples 1 and 2 for the TRS–80® Color Computer. Draw a green rectangle on a black background and paint the inside red.

Solution   Add the following statements to the program of Examples 1 and 2.

```
100 CLS 0
120 SET(X,10,1)
150 SET(0,Y,1)
160 SET(39,Y,1)
190 SET(X,20,1)
210 PRINT@12*32,"PRINT 'P' TO PAINT THE INSIDE."
270 SET(X,Y,4)
```

Here is an explanation of these new statements.

Statement	What It Does
100	Clears the screen to color 0 (black).
120	Inside the loop from **100–130**, draws the top of the box in color 1 (green).
150	Draws the left side of the box green.
160	Draws the right side of the box green.
190	Draws the bottom of the box green.
210	Prompts the user to type **"P"** to paint the inside of the box. This prompt begins on the 12th row of the screen (position **12*32**).
170	Accepts a single character typed at the keyboard without **ENTER** being pressed; stores this character as **K$**.
270	Inside the loop from **250–290**, draws red horizontal lines to cover the inside of the box.

WRITTEN EXERCISES

Write the TRS–80® BASIC command to do each of the following.

1. Clear the screen.

2. Light the block in column 40, row 10.

3. Unlight the block in column 12, row 8.

4. Print the value of X at position 260 on the screen.

5. Accept a character from the keyboard without **ENTER** being pressed and store this character as **X$**.

Complete these statements about TRS–80® BASIC.

6. For displaying text, the screen is divided into _?_ columns.

7. For text, the screen is divided into _?_ rows.

8. For the **SET** and **RESET** commands, the screen is divided into _?_ columns numbered _?_ through _?_ .

9. For the **SET** and **RESET** commands, the screen is divided into _?_ rows numbered _?_ through _?_ .

Write the Color Computer BASIC command to do each of the following.

10. Clear the screen to color number 2.

11. Light the point in column 30, row 15 using color number 3.

12. Print **IS THAT WHAT YOU WANTED?** at the beginning of row 12 of the screen.

For Ex. 13–14, modify the program of Example 1 as indicated.

13. Slow down the drawing of the rectangle by jumping to a delay loop in a subroutine after each horizontal or vertical line is drawn.

14. Ask the user to indicate the size of the rectangle by entering the smallest and largest values of X and of Y.

15. Modify the program of Example 3 to ask the user to select the background color, the color of the rectangle, and the color to paint the inside of the rectangle.

For Exercises 16–17, describe the output of each program.

16.
```
100  CLS
110  FOR Y = 6 TO 14
120  SET(12,Y)
130  SET(20,Y)
140  NEXT Y
150  PRINT@64*12,"PRESS KEY TO STOP"
160  LET Z$ = INKEY$
170  IF Z$ = "" THEN 160
180  END
```

17.
```
10  CLS
20  FOR X = 10 TO 30
30  SET(X,10)
40  NEXT X
50  PRINT64*12,"PRESS A KEY TO STOP"
60  LET Z$ = INKEY$
70  IF Z$ = "" THEN 60
80  END
```

A talking computer reads printed books aloud for blind people.

Correct any errors in these programs.

18.
```
1   REM   DRAW A SLANTED LINE
10  CLS
20  FOR J = 10 TO 20
30  SET J,J
40  NEXT J
50  END
```

19.
```
10  DRAW AN "L"
15  CLS
20  FOR Y = 3 TO 13
30  PLOT 5,Y
40  NEXT Y
50  FOR X = 5 TO 15
60  PLOT X,13
70  END
```

Complete this program.

20. Problem: Draw a large capital T.
```
100   ?
110  REM   DRAW THE TOP OF THE T
120  FOR X = 30 TO 90
130   ? (X,5)
140  NEXT  ?
150  REM   DRAW THE VERTICAL BAR
160  FOR  ?  = 5 TO 40
170  SET(60, ? )
180  NEXT Y
190  LET  ?  = INKEY$
200  IF A$ = "" THEN  ?
210  END
```

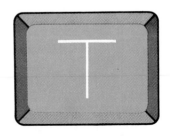

COMPUTER LAB ACTIVITIES

TRS–80® Models I and III

1. Enter and **RUN** the program of Example 1 on page 203. If your system has a disk drive, insert a formatted disk. Then save the program by typing **SAVE "RECTANGLE"**.

   If you have a tape recorder, insert a cassette and save the program by typing **CSAVE "R"**.

2. Add these statements to the program of Example 1. **RUN** the new program.
```
210 PRINT@12*64,"PRESS 'P' TO PAINT THE INSIDE."
240 IF K$ <> "P" THEN 999
250 FOR Y = 11 TO 20
260 FOR X = 1 TO 38
270 SET(X,Y)
280 NEXT X
290 NEXT Y
```

> *For Exercises 3–4:*
> *a. Reload the program of Example 1 on page 203. If you saved it on disk, type **LOAD "RECTANGLE"**.*
> *If you saved it on a cassette, rewind the cassette. Then type **CLOAD "R"**.*
> *b. Modify the program of each exercise as indicated. **RUN** the program.*
> *c. Did the program produce correct output? If not, make further changes until correct output is produced.*

3. Exercise 13, page 206   4. Exercise 14, page 206

> *For Exercises 5–6:*
> *a. Type **NEW**. Then enter and **RUN** the indicated program.*
> *b. Is the output you predicted actually produced?*

5. Exercise 16, page 207   6. Exercise 17, page 207

> *For Exercises 7–8:*
> *a. Enter and **RUN** the corrected program of each indicated exercise.*
> *b. Were all the errors corrected? If not, make further changes until each program runs correctly.*

7. Exercise 18, page 207   8. Exercise 19, page 207

EXPLORE: TRS-80® GRAPHICS

9. Enter and **RUN** the program on the right. Because of line 310, you must stop the program by pressing the **BREAK** key.

10. The subroutine is put in lines 120–150 to make the program run faster. What does the subroutine do?

11. What is the purpose of the decision in line 300? If you cannot answer, delete the line. Then **RUN** the program again. What happens? Retype line 300.

12. Retype line 290, substituting another number for the 5. For example, type $X = X + 10$. **RUN** the program again. What happens? Try other values in place of the 5.

```
1   REM    DIAMONDS ARE FOREVER
100 CLS
110 GOTO 200
120 FOR Y = A TO B STEP C
130 X=X+I:SET(X,Y):SET(X+I,Y)
140 NEXT Y
150 RETURN
200 X=0
210 A=23:B=0:C=-1:I=1
220 GOSUB 120
230 A=0:B=23:C=1
240 GOSUB 120
250 A=24:B=47:I=-1
260 GOSUB 120
270 A=46:B=24:C=-1
280 GOSUB 120
290 X=X+5
300 IF X<81 THEN 210
310 GOTO 310
320 END
```

COMPUTER LAB ACTIVITIES

TRS–80® Color Computer

1. Enter and **RUN** the program of Example 3 on page 205. (You must also enter the appropriate lines from Examples 1 and 2.)

2. Modify the program of Example 3 as indicated in Exercise 15 on page 206. **RUN** the revised program. If necessary, make changes until the correct output is produced.

EXPLORE: COLOR COMPUTER GRAPHICS

3. **a.** Enter the program of Exercises 9–12 above. However, change certain statements as indicated on the right.

```
130 X=X+I:SET(X,Y,3):SET(X+I,Y,3)
210 A=15:B=0:C=-1:I=1
230 A=0:B=15:C=1
250 A=15:B=31:I=-1
270 A=30:B=17:C=-1
300 IF X<32 THEN 210
```

b. **RUN** the program. Because of statement 310, you must stop the program by pressing the **BREAK** key.

4. The subroutine is put in statements 120–150 to make the program run faster. What does the subroutine do?

5. What is the purpose of the decision in statement 300? If you cannot answer, delete statement 300. **RUN** the program again to see what happens. Then retype statemenmt 300.

6. Retype statement 290, substituting another number for the 5. **RUN** the program again to see what happens. Try other values for the 5.

7. Change statement 130 to the statement below. **RUN** the program again. NOTE: **RND** is **BASIC**'s random number generator.

```
130 X=X+I:SET(X,Y,RND(8)):SET(X+I,Y,RND(8))
```

8. To display "thinner" diamonds, change statement 130 to the following and **RUN** the program.

```
130 X=X+I:SET(X,Y,RND(8))
```

9. Make other changes in the program to see what other effects you can produce.

10. Type **NEW**. Then enter and **RUN** the program below.

```
100 CLS
110 PRINT "I WILL START DRAWING CIRCLES"
120 PRINT "MADLY.  PRESS ANY KEY WHEN YOU"
130 PRINT "WANT ME TO STOP."
140 FOR D=1 TO 700:NEXT D
150 PMODE 3,1:B=RND(8):PCLS B
160 SCREEN 1,RND(2)-1
170 X=RND(255):Y=RND(191):R=RND(50)
180 F=RND(3):C=RND(3):COLOR F
190 CIRCLE(X,Y),R
200 K$=INKEY$:IF K$="" THEN 170:END
```

In Exercises 11–13, modify the program above as indicated.

11. Print the opening message (lines 110–130) in the center of the screen. Instead of using the delay loop of line 140, tell the user to **PRESS ANY KEY TO BEGIN**.

12. In line 200, instead of returning to line 170, return to 160 so that the color set can be changed. Add a delay loop after line 190 to slow down the color changes.

13. Make further changes in the program to see what other effects you can produce.

4-9 COMMODORE 64 GRAPHICS

OBJECTIVE:

> **To use the Commodore 64 BASIC graphics commands in programs**

Unlike the Apple and TRS–80® computers, the Commodore 64 has no special **BASIC** commands for plotting points and drawing lines or circles. Instead, graphics is done by **POKE**ing code numbers for shapes in the memory locations for the screen.

The Commodore 64, as its name implies, has 64K positions of **RAM**. Because the screen is divided into 40 columns and 25 rows, 1000 positions starting at address 648 are needed to hold the contents of the screen. Each character on the screen, whether a letter or digit or a graphics shape, is stored as an ASCII code. The Commodore 64 can display characters on the screen in any of 16 colors. The color number of a character is stored at an address that is 54272 <u>more than</u> the address of the character itself.

This table gives some useful commands for the Commodore 64.

Command	What the Command Does
POKE 53280, n	Sets the border color of the screen to color n, where n is a whole number from 0 to 15, inclusive. (See page 212 for the color numbers. The default border color when the machine is turned on is light blue.)
POKE 53281, n	Sets the background color to color n. (The default background color when the machine is turned on is dark blue.)
PRINT CHR$(147)	Clears the screen.
LET S = 256*PEEK(648)	Sets S to the starting location of screen memory.
LET M = S + C + 40*R	Sets M to the memory location holding the contents of the screen location at column C, row R. C is a whole number from 0 to 39, R is a whole number from 0 to 24.
POKE M, n	Puts the character with ASCII code n in screen memory location M.
POKE M + 54272, n	Sets the color for memory location M to color n.
GET K$	Accepts a single character typed at the keyboard without waiting for the user to press **RETURN**.

COMMODORE 64 COLOR CODES

0 = black	4 = purple	8 = orange	12 = medium gray
1 = white	5 = green	9 = brown	13 = light green
2 = red	6 = blue	10 = light red	14 = light blue
3 = cyan	7 = yellow	11 = dark gray	15 = light gray

EXAMPLE 1 Write a Commodore program to draw a white rectangle on a black background.

Program

```
100 POKE 53280, 1
110 POKE 53281, 0
120 PRINT CHR$(147)
130 LET S= 256 * PEEK(648)
140 FOR C = 10 TO 30
150 LET M = S + C + 40*5
160 POKE M+54272, 1
170 POKE M, 120
180 NEXT C
190 FOR R = 5 TO 15
200 LET M = S + 9 + 40*R
210 POKE M+54272, 1
220 POKE M, 225
230 LET M = S + 30 + 40*R
240 POKE M+54272, 1
250 POKE M, 97
260 NEXT R
270 FOR C = 10 TO 29
280 LET M = S + C + 40*15
290 POKE M+54272, 1
300 POKE M, 121
310 NEXT C
320 PRINT CHR$(5)
330 FOR I = 1 TO 16
340 PRINT
350 NEXT I
360 PRINT TAB(8);"PRESS 'A' TO SEE IT AGAIN."
370 GET K$
380 IF K$ = "" THEN 370
390 IF K$ = "A" THEN 120
999 END
```

The table on page 213 explains the program.

Statements	What Happens
100	Sets the border color to white (color 1).
110	Sets the background color to black (color 0).
120	Clears the screen.
130	S is the address where screen memory begins.
140–180	This loop draws the top of the box.
150	M is the address that holds the content of the screen position in column C, row 5.
160	The address in color memory that stores the color of location M is set to 1 (white).
170	The ASCII code for a high horizontal bar, 120, is put in memory location M.
190–260	This loop draws the vertical sides of the box.
200–220	These statements repeat the logic of statements 150–170. They put a white reverse-video vertical bar (code 225) at column 9, row R on the screen.
230–250	A white vertical bar (code 97) is placed at column 30, row R.
270–310	This loop draws the bottom of the box.
280–300	A white low horizontal bar (code 121) is shown at column C, row 15.
320	The color of printed characters is changed to white.
330–360	The cursor is moved to row 16 on the screen so that the sentence **PRESS 'A' TO SEE IT AGAIN** appears below the rectangle.
370–390	When a key is pressed, it is tested. If it is an "A", the program is repeated. Pressing any other key ends the program.

EXAMPLE 2 Expand the program of Example 1 so that, if the user wishes, the inside of the rectangle is "painted" white.

Solution Add these statements to the program in Example 1.

```
360 PRINT TAB(8);"PRESS 'P' TO PAINT THE INSIDE."
390 IF K$<>"P" THEN 999
400 FOR C = 10 TO 29
410 FOR R = 5 TO 15
420 LET M = S + C + 40*R
430 POKE M+54272, 1
440 POKE M, 224
450 NEXT R
460 NEXT C
```

NOTE: The loop in statements **400–460** of Example 2 puts a solid white reverse-video block at each location inside the rectangle.

WRITTEN EXERCISES

Write the Commodore 64 commands to do the following.

1. Clear the screen.
2. Set the screen border color to black.
3. Set the background color to green.
4. Set the background color to color 1.
5. Assign the starting location of screen memory to variable S.
6. Assign to X the memory location for column 10, row 15 on the screen.
7. Assign to L the memory location for column 25, row 12.
8. Put the character with ASCII code 97 in memory location X.
9. Set the color for memory location X to light blue.

Complete these statements about the Commodore 64.

10. The Commodore 64 has __?__ **K** positions of **RAM**.
11. The screen is divided into __?__ columns and __?__ rows.
12. Characters on the screen are usually stored in the 1000 memory positions starting at address __?__ .
13. The color number of a character on the screen is stored at an address __?__ more than the address of the character itself.
14. Characters can be displayed in any of __?__ colors.

For Exercises 15–18, modify the program of Example 1 as indicated.

15. Slow down the drawing of the rectangle by jumping to a delay loop in a subroutine after each **FOR–NEXT** loop is executed.

16. Instead of setting the border and background colors, ask the user what colors to use.

17. Combine the loops that draw the horizontal sides of the rectangle into a subroutine.

18. Set up a **FOR–NEXT** loop to draw the rectangle a different color each time the user presses the **A** key.

For Exercises 19–20, modify the program of Example 2 as indicated.

19. "Paint" the inside of the rectangle by drawing vertical lines.
20. Ask the user to indicate what color to paint the inside of the rectangle.

For Exercises 21–22, describe the output of each program.

21.
```
100  PRINT CHR$(147)
110  POKE 53281, 7
120  POKE 53280, 0
130  LET S = 256 * PEEK(648)
140  FOR X = 15 TO 25
150  LET M = S + X + 40*4
160  POKE M+54272, 4
170  POKE M, 224
180  NEXT X
190  FOR Y = 4 TO 10
200  LET M = S + 20 + 40*Y
210  POKE M+54272, 4
220  POKE M, 224
230  NEXT Y
240  FOR D = 1 TO 1000
250  NEXT D
999  END
```

22.
```
10   POKE 53281, 10
20   PRINT CHR$(147)
30   LET A = 256 * PEEK(648)
40   FOR R = 1 TO 20
50   LET L = A + 1 + 40*R
60   POKE L+54272, 2
70   POKE L, 224
80   NEXT R
90   FOR C = 1 TO 35
100  LET L = A + C + 40*20
110  POKE L+54272, 2
120  POKE L, 224
130  NEXT C
140  FOR D = 1 TO 500
150  NEXT D
160  END
```

Complete each program.

23. Problem: Draw a horizontal line at any row the user selects.
```
100  PRINT "WHAT ROW";
110    ?   R
120    ?   CHR$(147)
130  LET S =   ?   * PEEK(  ?  )
140  FOR C = 0 TO 39
150  LET M = S +  ?  +  ? *R
160  POKE M +  ? , 1
170    ?  M, 224
180  NEXT  ?
190  END
```

24. Problem: Draw a solid box in black on a white background and border.
```
10   PRINT   ? (147)
20   POKE 53280,   ?
30   POKE   ? , 1
40   LET S = 256 *   ? (648)
50   FOR   ?   = 5 TO 30
60   FOR R = 5 TO 15
70   LET M = S+C+40*R
80   POKE M+ ? , 0
90   POKE   ? , 224
100  NEXT   ?
110  NEXT C
120  END
```

25. Correct any errors in this program.

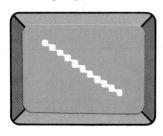

```
1   REM  DRAW A SLANTED LINE
10  PRINT CHR(147)
20  POKE 53280
30  LET S = 256 * PEEK(648)
40  FOR X = 1 TO 20
50  LET M = S + X + X*40
60  POKE M, 127
70  NOTE: 127=CODE OF SLANTED SYMBOL
80  NEXT M
90  END
```

26. Correct any errors in this program.

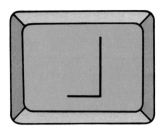

```
10 REM   DRAW A BACKWARDS "L".
20 PRINT CHR$ (147)
30 POKE 1, 53280
40 LET S=PEEK(648)*256
50 FOR Y = 7 TO 23
60 LET M = S+30+40Y
70 POKE 224, M
80 NEXT Y
90 FOR X = 8 TO 30
100 LET M=S+X+40*23
110 POKE 224, M
120 END
```

MORE CHALLENGING EXERCISES

For Exercises 27–30, write programs for the Commodore 64 to "paint" the screen completely. Use whatever color the user selects. Do the painting as follows.

27. Using horizontal lines from top to bottom

28. Using horizontal lines from bottom to top

29. Using vertical lines from left to right

30. Using vertical lines from right to left

31. Write a Commodore 64 program to make a point in the center of the screen blink on and off. Do this as follows.

　a. Clear the screen.

　b. Select any color that does not match the background color of the screen.

　c. Light a point at the center of the screen.

　d. Pause by executing a delay loop.

　e. Light the point again using the background color.

　f. Execute a delay loop.

　g. Execute steps **b** through **f** over and over.

32. Write a Commodore 64 program to draw a rectangle and "move" it down the screen. Do this by continually drawing the rectangle, erasing it, and redrawing it one row lower until it reaches its final position. Use a delay–loop subroutine to slow down the movement.

33. Revise the program of Exercise 32 to move the rectangle across the screen.

34. Combine the programs of Exercises 32 and 33 to allow the user to choose whether the rectangle will be moved down, or across, the screen.

COMPUTER LAB ACTIVITIES

Commodore 64 Graphics

1. Enter and **RUN** the program of Example 1 on page 212. If your system has a disk drive, insert a formatted disk. Save the program by typing

   SAVE "RECTANGLE",8 .

2. Add the statements of Example 2 on page 213 to the program of Example 1. **RUN** the new program. If you have a disk drive, save the program by typing

   SAVE "PAINT",8 .

3. Reload the program of Example 1 from the disk by typing

   LOAD "RECTANGLE",8 .

   Then, if you did any of Exercises 15–18 on page 214, modify the program as indicated in each exercise. RUN the program each time. If necessary, make further changes until correct output is produced.

Disk Storage Unit

4. Reload the program of Example 2 on page 213 from the disk by typing **LOAD "PAINT",8** . Then, if you did any of Exercises 19–20 on page 214, modify the program as indicated there. **RUN** the program each time. If necessary, make further changes until correct output is obtained.

5. Type **NEW**. Then enter and **RUN** the programs of Exercises 21–22 on page 215. Is the output you predicted actually produced?

6. Enter and **RUN** the completed programs of Exercises 23–24 on page 215. Did you complete each program correctly?

7. Enter and **RUN** the corrected programs of Exercises 25–26 on pages 215–216. Were all errors corrected? If not, make further changes until each program runs correctly.

Chapter Summary

Section 4–1   **1.** The computer will repeat statements put between the **FOR** and **NEXT** commands to form a loop. For example, a loop that begins **FOR I = 1 TO 10** will be done 10 times. The loop ends with **NEXT I**.

Section 4–2   **2.** Loops can be made more flexible by varying the starting or ending values or both. For example, a program could do this. **INPUT B, E** and then start a loop **FOR I = B TO E**.

Section 4–3   **3.** The counter variable of a loop does not have to count by 1's. For example, if a loop begins

FOR J = 0 TO 10 STEP 2,

J will take on the values 0, 2, 4, 6, 8, 10. The statement

FOR M = 10 TO 1 STEP −1,

will make **M** count backwards from 10 to 1.

Section 4–4   **4.** **FOR–NEXT** loops can produce interesting output, especially when the loop counter appears in the **TAB** function.

Section 4–5   **5.** A **subroutine** is a set of statements that can be executed at any point in the program. A subroutine is usually placed at the end of the main program. The **GOSUB** command sends the computer to the subroutine, which ends with a **RETURN** statement. The **RETURN** statement sends the computer back to the main program.

Section 4–6
Section 4–7
Section 4–8
Section 4–9

   6. Graphics refers to producing charts, diagrams, and animation on computer screens or printers. The **BASIC** of each microcomputer includes special commands for entering graphics modes, for lighting and unlighting points, and even for drawing lines and circles (on some computers).

Chapter Review

Correct any errors in these programs.

1.
```
10 FOR I = 1, 10
20 PRINT *;TAB I;
30 NEXT I+1
40 END
```

2.
```
100 PRINT "STARTING VALUE";
110 INPUT N
120 FOR J = N TO 1
130 PRINT J
140 NEXT N
150 END
```

3.
```
10 REM   PRINT LINES ACROSS
20 GOSUB 900
30 FOR I = 1 TO 4
40 PRINT
50 NEXT I
60 GOSUB 900
900 FOR I = 1 TO 10
910 PRINT "X ";
920 NEXT I
930 RETURN
999 END
```

4.
```
20 PRINT A LARGE "O"
25 GOSUB 400
30 FOR K = 1 TO 8
35 PRINT "X";TAB(20);"X"
40 PRINT
45 GOSUB 400
400 SUBROUTINE STARTS HERE
410 FOR K = 1 TO 10
420 PRINT "X ";
430 NEXT K
440 PRINT
450 END
```

5. Write the output.
```
10 GOSUB 500
20 FOR L = 1 TO 4
30 PRINT TAB(10);"*"
40 NEXT L
50 PRINT
60 GOSUB 500
70 GOTO 550
500 FOR Q = 2 TO 10 STEP 2
510 PRINT TAB(Q);"*"
520 NEXT Q
530 PRINT
540 RETURN
550 END
```

6. Write the output. Assume that 5 is entered for N.
```
1  REM   COUNTING PROGRAM
10 PRINT "PLEASE ENTER A"
20 PRINT "POSITIVE NUMBER."
30 INPUT N
40 FOR I = 1 TO N
50 PRINT I;"   ";
60 NEXT I
70 PRINT
80 PRINT "END OF PROGRAM"
90 PRINT
99 END
```

7. Complete the program at the right.

Problem: Print a person's name as many times as the person wishes.

```
100 PRINT "WHAT IS YOUR NAME";
110 INPUT   ?
120   ?   "HOW MANY TIMES";
130   ?   T
140 FOR I =   ?   TO   ?
150 PRINT N$
160 NEXT   ?
170 END
```

8. Complete the program shown at the right.

Problem: Print the pattern shown below.

```
********
 * * *
********
```

```
10 GOSUB   ?
20 PRINT "  * * *"
30   ?
40 GOTO 150
100 FOR J = 1   ?   9
110 PRINT "*";
120   ?
130 PRINT
140   ?
150 END
```

9. Write a program that prints the array at the right.

Have the program contain at least one subroutine and at least one **FOR–NEXT** loop.

```
9 9 9 9 9 9
9         9
9         9
9 9 9 9 9 9
          9
          9
9 9 9 9 9 9
```

10. Use graphics commands available on your computer in a program that draws five line segments across the screen. The line segments should be the same distance apart on the screen.

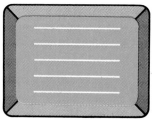

Chapter Test

For Exercises 1–2, write a **FOR** *statement so that the given loop counter will take on the values listed.*

1. K = 1, 3, 5, 7, 9

2. T = 50, 49, 48, 47

For Exercises 3–4, write the output of each program.

3.
```
100 FOR I = 5 TO 1 STEP -1
110 PRINT I
120 NEXT I
130 PRINT
140 FOR I = 2 TO 10 STEP 2
150 PRINT I
160 NEXT I
170 PRINT
180 END
```

4.
```
10 GOSUB 600
20 FOR J = 1 TO 4
30 PRINT "   X"
40 NEXT J
50 GOSUB 600
60 GOTO 640
600 FOR J = 1 TO 2
610 PRINT "XXXXXXX"
620 NEXT J
630 RETURN
640 END
```

Correct any errors in the programs of Exercises 5–6.

5.
```
10  GOSUB 100
20  FOR L = 1 TO 3
30  PRINT
40  GOTO 20
50  GOSUB 100
100 FOR M = 1 TO 10
110 PRINT TAB(M);"-"
120 NEXT M
130 END
```

6.
```
10  PRINT "EVEN NUMBER";
20  INPUT X
30  LET K = 2 TO X BY 2
40  PRINT K;"   ";
50  NEXT X
60  PRINT
70  END
```

For Exercises 7–8, complete each program.

7. Problem: Print the pattern below.

```
I I I I I I I I
              I
              I
              I
              I
I I I I I I I I
```

```
10  GOSUB   ?
20  FOR J = 1 TO 4
30    ?   TAB(14);"I"
40    ?
50    ?
60  GOTO 250
200 FOR   ?   = 1 TO 8
210 PRINT "I ";
220 NEXT Y
230 PRINT
240   ?
250 END
```

8. Problem: Print the pattern below.

```
   K
    K
     K
      K
       K
12345
   K
    K
     K
      K
       K
```

```
10  GOSUB   ?
20  FOR I=1 TO 5
30  PRINT I ?
40  NEXT I
50  GOSUB   ?
60  GOTO 110
70  FOR K=5 TO 9
80  PRINT TAB(K);"  ?  "
90    ?
100   ?
110 END
```

9. Write a program that asks the user to type a letter of the alphabet. Then print the letter ten times in a diagonal from the upper left toward the lower right of the screen or printer. The program should contain at least one **FOR–NEXT** loop.

10. Write a program that prints this array. The program should contain at least one **FOR–NEXT** loop and at least one subroutine.

```
x  x  x  x  x  x  x
   x           x
      x     x
         x
```

Cumulative Review: **Chapters 1–4**

Part 1

*Choose the correct answer. Choose **a, b, c,** or **d.***

1. For which of these functions is the computer keyboard used?
   a. output   **b.** input   **c.** memory   **d.** storage

2. What is another name for programs?
   a. hardware   **b.** software   **c.** graphics   **d.** RAM

3. What is the most common computer language for microcomputers?
   a. FORTRAN   **b.** COBOL   **c.** BASIC   **d.** Pascal

4. What is the name of the English inventor who tried to build a machine he called the analytical engine?
   a. Herman Hollerith   **b.** Charles Babbage
   c. Blaise Pascal   **d.** Howard Aiken

5. What kind of statements can be used to add comments to a program?
   a. IF–THEN   **b.** REM   **c.** LET   **d.** INPUT

6. Which of these was the principal component of second generation computers?
   a. transistor   **b.** integrated circuits
   c. vacuum tube   **d.** relays

7. What is the name of the computer language that consists only of numbers?

   a. FORTRAN   **b.** assembly
   c. machine   **d.** COBOL

8. What is the name given to a group of statements that may be executed more than once at any point in a program?
   a. command   **b.** subroutine   **c.** counter   **d.** string

9. Which of these design computers and related equipment?
   a. programmers   **b.** computer operators
   c. electrical engineers   **d.** salespeople

10. What kind of error results when **BASIC** commands are not typed correctly?

   a. tactical **b.** syntax **c.** logical **d.** decisional

11. What is displayed on a computer screen to mark your place as you type?

   a. dot **b.** place holder **c.** mark **d.** cursor

12. Which **BASIC** command puts a character directly into a memory location?

   a. PRINT **b.** PEEK **c.** POKE **d.** DATA

13. Which of these statements allows you to list input values within a program?

   a. PEEK **b.** POKE **c.** INPUT **d.** DATA

14. What name is given to any symbol that can be typed on the computer's keyboard?

   a. character **b.** letter **c.** number **d.** keystroke

15. Suppose that a loop begins FOR K = 1 TO B. What should be the last statement of the loop?

   a. GOTO 10 **b.** NEXT B **c.** NEXT K **d.** PRINT K

16. What is the loop counter for this statement?   20 FOR J = 1 TO 10 STEP 2

   a. TO **b.** J **c.** STEP **d.** FOR

17. Which of these invented the abacus?

   a. Japanese **b.** British **c.** Chinese **d.** French

18. If no STEP is listed at the end of a FOR statement, what STEP will a computer use?

   a. 0 **b.** 1 **c.** 2 **d.** 3

19. With which **BASIC** command should a subroutine always end?

   a. STOP **b.** END **c.** GOTO **d.** RETURN

20. What is the name given to printing dark characters on a light background?

   a. flashing video **b.** opposite video
   c. reverse video **d.** lighted video

Part 2

For Exercises 21–22, write the output of each program.

21. ```
10 FOR I=1 TO 10 STEP 2
20 PRINT I
30 NEXT I
40 FOR J=20 TO 1 STEP -3
50 PRINT J
60 NEXT J
70 END
```

22. ```
10 GOSUB 500
20 PRINT "****"
30 GOSUB 500
40 GOTO 540
500 FOR I=1 TO 4
510 PRINT "*"
520 NEXT I
530 RETURN
540 END
```

For Exercises 23–24, correct any errors in the programs.

23. ```
10 PRINT "TEST 1","TEST 2","TOTAL"
20 FOR I=1 TO 3
30 READ T;E
40 LET L = T - E
50 PRINT T;E;L
60 GOTO 20
70 DATA 25,30,22,15,54,55
80 END
```

24. ```
10 PRINT "ENTER A NAME."
20 INPUT T$
30 LET L = LEFT$(T$)
40 PRINT L
50 END
```

For Exercises 25–26, identify the loop counter in each statement.

25. 40 FOR J = 20 TO 12 STEP −2

26. 30 FOR T = 1 TO 8 STEP 2

27. For the following statement, list the values the loop counter will have for the loop.

$$50 \text{ FOR } L = 20 \text{ TO } 12 \text{ STEP } -3$$

*For Exercises 28–29, write the **FOR** statement needed so that the given loop counter will take on the values listed.*

28. K = 2,4,6,8,10

29. J = 10,9,8,7,6

30. Write a program that will draw a horizontal line across the middle of your computer's screen or printer page.

Computer Lab Projects

General Instructions

*The exercises in the **Computer Lab Projects** are intended to be used for individual student assignment.*

1. Write a program for each exercise. Follow these directions.
   a. Include at least one **REM** statement. The **REM** statement should list your name and the number of the problem.
   b. Include at least one **FOR–NEXT** loop and at least one subroutine.
   c. Although many figures shown as models are formed by asterisks (*), use any character you wish to "draw" the required pattern. Also, the model figures are intended to give you an idea of the shape of the required pattern. The actual size will vary depending on the dimensions of your screen.
   d. Follow your teacher's directions regarding the use of any special graphics commands that your computer has. Use color if you wish.

2. **RUN** each program. Check whether it produces the required output. If it does not, revise the program until it does.

GRAPHICS APPLICATIONS

For Exercises 1–4, draw a large arrow formed by three line segments (see the figure at the right). The figure should fill the screen and point in the direction indicated.

```
                                    *
                                      *
                                        *
        * * * * * * * * * * *
                                        *
                                      *
                                    *
```

1. To the right
2. To the left
3. Up
4. Down

For Exercises 5–8, draw a large block arrow formed by seven line segments (see the figure at the right). The figure should fill the screen and point in the direction indicated.

```
                    *
                    * *
    * * * * * * *        *
    *                        *
    * * * * * * *        *
                    * *
                    *
```

5. To the right
6. To the left
7. Up
8. Down

9. Print your initials in block letters large enough to fill the screen.

10. Print your initials three times down the screen. Use block letters. If your computer has color, make each set of initials a different color.

For Exercises 11–14, draw a figure that looks like each of the following shapes.

11. A layered birthday cake

12. A five-pointed star

13. A sailboat

14. A fir tree

For Exercises 15–20, print the pattern shown.

15.
```
*   *   *   *
*   *   *   *
*   *   *   *
*   *   *   *   *   *   *
*   *   *   *   *   *   *
*   *   *   *   *   *   *
*   *   *   *   *   *   *
```

16.
```
*   *   *   *   *   *   *
*   *   *   *   *   *   *
*   *   *   *   *   *   *
*   *   *   *   *   *   *
*   *   *
*   *   *
*   *   *
```

17.
```
            *   *   *
            *   *   *
*   *   *   *   *   *   *
*   *   *   *   *   *   *
*   *   *   *   *   *   *
            *   *   *
            *   *   *
```

18.
```
******************
*****        *****
***            ***
*                *
***            ***
*****        *****
******************
```

19.
```
******************
 **************
   **********
    ******
   **********
 **************
******************
```

20.
```
******************
 ******************
        ******
        ******
        ******
 ******************
******************
```

21. Draw three vertical line segments across the screen. The segments should be at equal distances from each other. If your computer has color, make each segment a different color.

22. Draw four diagonal segments slanting from upper left to lower right across the screen. The segments should be at equal distances from each other. If your computer has color, make each segment a different color.

23. Repeat Exercise 22. Have the segments slant from upper right to lower left.

24. Draw a square and both its diagonals (see the figure below). The size of the square will depend on the smaller dimension of your screen.

25. Draw a rectangle and both its diagonals (see the figure below). The dimensions will depend on the size of your screen. Make the rectangle as large as possible.

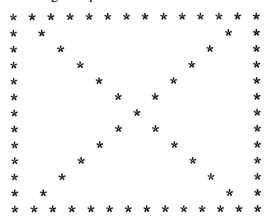

For Exercises 26–29, draw each figure. As far as possible, make all sides of each figure equal in length. Center the figure on the screen.

26.
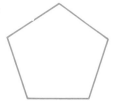

27.
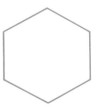

28.
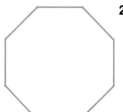

29.
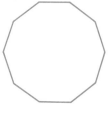

*For Exercises 30–32, use your computer's **BASIC** command for drawing a circle. If your computer does not have this command, omit these exercises.*

30.
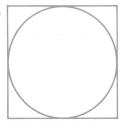

31.

32.
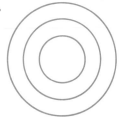

STRING PROCESSING APPLICATIONS

For Exercises 33–47, have each program begin by accepting a name typed at the keyboard.

33. Print the name down the middle of the screen (from the top to the bottom). Print one name per line (row).

34. Print the name once on each line but "staggered" in a diagonal from the upper left of the screen to the lower right (see the display at the right).

```
NANCY
     NANCY
          NANCY
```

35. Print the name "staggered" as in Exercise 34. However, print from upper right to lower left.

36. Combine Exercises 34 and 35. The result will be to form a large X on the screen.

37. Form the display shown at the right. Have the "arms" intersect in the middle of the screen.

```
                    NANCY
                    NANCY
                    NANCY
NANCY    NANCY    NANCY    NANCY    NANCY
                    NANCY
                    NANCY
                    NANCY
```

38. Print **HAPPY BIRTHDAY** to the person whose name was entered. Print the message once per line.

39. Repeat Exercise 38. As in Exercise 34, "stagger" the message in a diagonal from upper left to lower right.

40. Repeat Exercise 38. However, print the message as many times as the user requests.

41. Clear the screen. Print the name in the center of the screen. Make the name "flash" on and off.

42. If your computer has reverse (inverse) video, repeat Exercise 41, making the name alternate between regular and reverse video.

43. In addition to printing the name, accept an adjective describing the person. For example, print **NANCY IS SMART** once per line.

44. Repeat Exercise 43. However, "stagger" the message in a diagonal from upper left to lower right.

45. Repeat Exercise 43. However, print the sentence as many times as the user requests.

46. Use the first letter of a name to form a triangular pattern (see the pattern at the right). Continue the pattern to the bottom of the screen.

```
N
N N
N N N
N N N N
```

47. Repeat Exercise 46. However, form a triangular pattern that resembles the display at the right. Continue the pattern to the bottom of the screen.

```
   N
  N N
 N N N
N N N N
```

MORE CHALLENGING COMPUTER LAB PROJECTS

GRAPHICS APPLICATIONS

For Exercises 48–52, draw a diagram of the playing surface used in each sport.

48. Football   **49.** Tennis   **50.** Baseball   **51.** Basketball   **52.** Hockey

For Exercises 53–54, draw a diagonal from the upper left corner to the lower right corner of the screen. A diagonal from one corner of the screen to the opposite corner divides the screen into two triangles of the same size.

53. "Paint" the lower left half of the screen.

54. "Paint" the upper right half of the screen.

For Exercises 55–56, draw a diagonal from the lower left corner to the upper right corner of the screen.

55. "Paint" the upper left half of the screen.

56. "Paint" the lower right half of the screen.

If two diagonals are drawn on the screen, four quadrants are formed (see the figure at the right). For Exercises 57–60, "paint" the quadrant indicated.

57. I   **58.** II   **59.** III   **60.** IV

61. If your computer has color, combine Exercises 57–60 by "painting" each quadrant a different color.

*If your computer's **BASIC** has a command for drawing a circle, use this command in the programs for Exercises 62–65. If your computer does not have this command, omit these exercises.*

62. Draw a diagram of the sun. That is, draw a circle in the center of the screen with line segments radiating from the circle.

63. Draw the Olympics symbol of five interlocking circles.

64. Draw a large circle in the center of the screen. Then draw smaller circles around that circle. The small circles should touch the large circle and each other in exactly one point.

65. Revise the program of Exercise 64 so that the small circles are touching the large circle on the inside of the large circle.

66. Draw an 8 × 8 checkerboard with alternating dark and light squares.

67. "Weave" a plaid quilt on the screen. No two squares that share a common side should have the same pattern. Part of the quilt might look like the pattern on the right. Continue the pattern down the screen.

68. Draw your initials in block letters that fill the screen. Give each letter a "shadow" as shown in the **N** at the right.

If your computer has color, use it to draw each of the following.

69. The American flag

70. A rainbow

71. The spectrum with color bands extending vertically from the top of the screen to the bottom (the number of colors will depend on your computer's **BASIC** and on its tv monitor).

Draw each three–dimensional figure. If your computer has color, "paint" each face that can be seen a different color.

72.

73.

74.

75.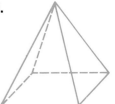

76. If your computer's **BASIC** does not have a command for drawing a circle, draw as close an approximation of a circle as you can.

77. Draw a line segment across the bottom of the screen. Light a point **P** near the top of the screen directly above the midpoint of the segment. Then connect **P** to four equally spaced points on the segment, including the endpoints.

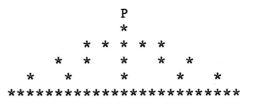

78. Draw a large square (as large as possible for your screen). Then connect the midpoints of the sides of the square to form another square (diamond). Then connect the midpoints of that square to form a third square. Continue this process until you cannot form any smaller squares on your screen.

79. "Tile" the screen with *hexagons*. That is, fill as much of the screen as possible with the "honeycomb" pattern, part of which is shown on the right.

80. "Tile" the screen as in Exercise 79. This time, however, use *equilateral triangles* (triangle with three equal sides).

81. "Tile" the screen with diamonds (see Exercise 79).

82. Draw a snowflake. Follow these instructions.

  a. Draw an equilateral triangle (triangle with three equal sides).

  b. Trisect (divide into three equal segments) each side to form three equilateral triangles. There will be one triangle on each side of the original triangle.

  c. Keep repeating this process until the screen has been filled.

STRING PROCESSING APPLICATIONS

For Exercises 83–85, use the **LEN** *function. Recall that this function gives the number of characters (including blanks) in a string.*

83. Print the letters of the name as shown below.

```
N
NA
NAN
NANC
NANCY
```

84. Repeat Exercise 83. However, display the letters from the end of the name to the front as shown below.

```
Y
CY
NCY
ANCY
NANCY
```

85. "Spell" the name slowly, one letter at a time.

ALGEBRA APPLICATIONS

Exercises 86–94 require a background in first–year algebra.

86. Draw a number line across the middle of the screen. Mark the 0 point near the center of the line. Print the coordinates (1, 2, 3, and so on, and −1, −2, −3, and so on) below the corresponding points on the line. Mark as many positive and negative units as will fit.

For Exercises 87–88, expand the program of Exercise 86 as indicated.

87. Plot (light) any point on the scale whose coordinate is entered by the user.

88. Accept from the user the coordinates of two points on the scale. "Shade" the segment on the number line connecting those two points.

89. Draw the *x*– and *y*–axes of a two–dimensional rectangular (Cartesian) coordinate system. As in Exercise 86, draw a number line across the middle of the screen. Then draw a second number line down the middle of the screen perpendicular to the first. Mark and label the units on each axis. The axes should divide the screen into four quadrants of approximately equal size.

If your computer has color, "paint" each quadrant a different color. Do not cover up the axes and scale markings.

90. Expand the program of Exercise 89 by numbering the quadrants with four large Roman numerals. That is, label the upper right as quadrant I; label the upper left as quadrant II; label the lower left as quadrant III; label the lower right as quadrant IV.

91. Draw a line of your choice on the two–dimensional coordinate system. Print the equation of the line somewhere on the screen.

92. Accept from the user the coordinates of two points. Connect the two points with a line segment. The coordinates the user enters are the coordinates for the axes drawn on the screen, not the row and column numbers used by your computer's **BASIC**.

93. Accept from the user the coordinates of three points. Connect the points to form a triangle. The coordinates the user enters are the coordinates for the axes drawn on the screen, not the row and column numbers used by your computer's **BASIC**.

94. Graph the line for any equation the user enters. Accept the equation in the form y = Mx + B, where the user types M and B each time. (NOTE: **M** represents the **slope** of the line; **B** represents the **y–intercept.**)

5

FLOWCHARTS AND PROGRAMS

LESSONS

FEATURES

Daisy Wheel
Modem
Electronic Spreadsheets
Computers and Crime

5-1 FLOWCHARTS IN DAILY LIFE

OBJECTIVE: **To draw a flowchart that shows the steps in an everyday activity**

Any step-by-step process can be shown in a flowchart. A **flowchart** is an outline of the procedure to be followed to perform a task or solve a problem. Flowcharts do not have to involve computers at all. In this section, you will draw flowcharts for some daily activities. Here are the flowchart symbols you will use.

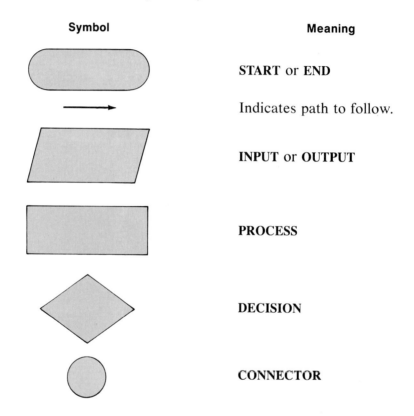

Symbol	Meaning
	START or END
	Indicates path to follow.
	INPUT or OUTPUT
	PROCESS
	DECISION
	CONNECTOR

Note carefully each of the following points about flowcharts in general and particularly about the flowchart of Example 1.

1. Arrows connect the symbols to show the flow of steps.

2. Each symbol in a flowchart, regardless of its shape, is called a flowchart "**box**."

3. Inside each box is a statement of what happens in that step of the procedure.

EXAMPLE 1 Draw a flowchart for making toast.

Solution

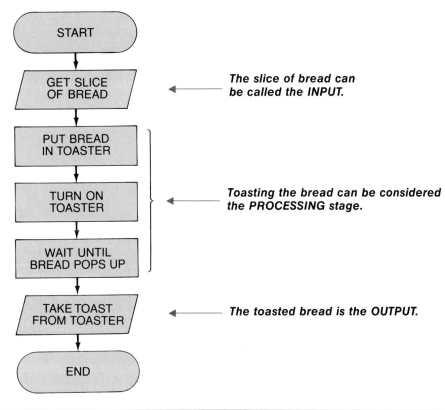

The slice of bread can be called the INPUT.

Toasting the bread can be considered the PROCESSING stage.

The toasted bread is the OUTPUT.

A flowchart can include **decision points**. For example, the flowchart of Example 1 could begin by asking whether any bread is available. The question would be printed inside a decision box.

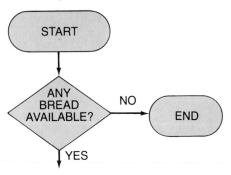

The **decision box** has the shape of a diamond because there must be one path into the decision box and two paths out of it. One path out of the decision box is for a **YES** answer; the second path is for a **NO** answer.

EXAMPLE 2 Draw a flowchart for playing a phonograph record.

Solution

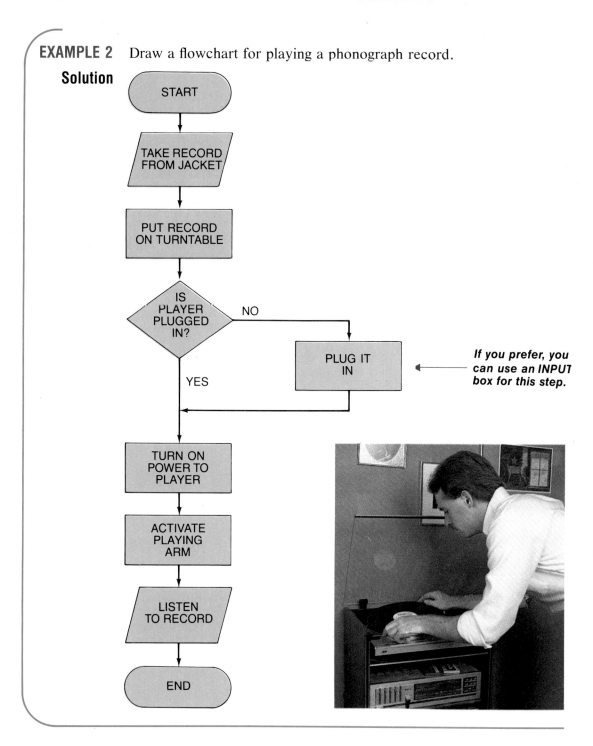

START

TAKE RECORD
FROM JACKET

PUT RECORD
ON TURNTABLE

IS
PLAYER
PLUGGED
IN?

NO

PLUG IT
IN

If you prefer, you can use an INPUT box for this step.

YES

TURN ON
POWER TO
PLAYER

ACTIVATE
PLAYING
ARM

LISTEN
TO RECORD

END

In Example 3, you will draw a flowchart that shows the procedure for making a telephone call.

EXAMPLE 3 Write these steps for making a telephone call in logical order. Then draw a flowchart that shows the procedure.

Wait for dial tone.   Begin conversation.
Answer within 10 rings?   Hang up.
Lift receiver.   Dial the number.
Conversation over?

Solution

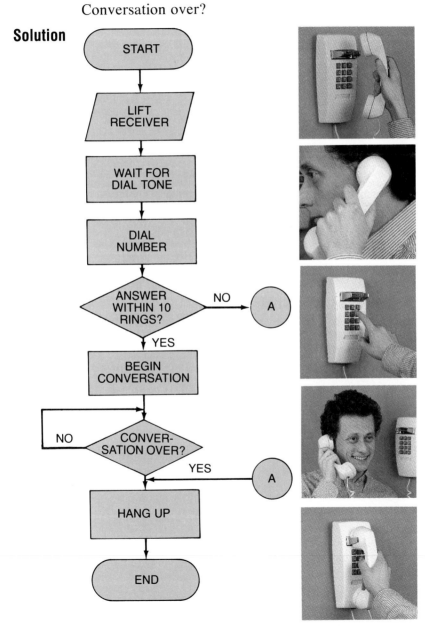

NOTE: The small circles in the flowchart of Example 3 are connectors which are always used in pairs. They save you the trouble of drawing long connecting arrows.

WRITTEN EXERCISES

1. What is a flowchart?

In Exercises 2–7, draw the flowchart symbol for each procedure.

2. Connector　　　　　　**3.** Start　　　　　　**4.** Input/Output

5. Process　　　　　　**6.** End　　　　　　**7.** Decision

For Exercises 8–11, draw a flowchart for each task.
Follow the given steps.

8. Making a peanut butter sandwich

　a. Get two slices of bread.

　b. Get jar of peanut butter.

　c. Get knife.

　d. Spread peanut butter on bread.

　e. Put slices of bread together.

9. Traveling to school

　a. Leave house.

　b. Walk to bus stop.

　c. Wait for bus.

　d. Board bus.

　e. Ride to school.

　f. Get off at school.

　g. Enter school building.

10. Playing a cassette tape

　a. Get cassette tape.

　b. Open recorder.

　c. Insert cassette.

　d. Close recorder.

　e. Recorder plugged in?

　f. If not, plug in recorder.

　g. Push PLAY button.

　h. Listen to tape.

11. Checking a book out of the library

　a. Find card for book in catalog.

　b. Find shelf for that book number.

　c. Is book on shelf?

　d. Take book to checkout counter.

　e. Sign card and have it stamped.

　f. Leave library.

12. Add steps to the flowchart of Exercise 8 to decide whether there are two slices of bread, peanut butter, and a knife available.

13. Expand the flowchart of Exercise 12 to make a peanut butter and jelly sandwich. Include a decision as to whether there is jelly available.

14. Add steps to the flowchart of Exercise 10 to decide whether the correct side of the tape to be played is loaded into the machine.

For Exercises 15–18:
  a. Write the steps of each task in logical order.
  b. Draw a flowchart for the procedure.

15. Repairing a flat tire

Remove flat tire.
Jack up the car.
Get jack from trunk.
Put on spare tire.
Let car down.
Get spare tire from trunk.

16. Entering and running a program

Type RUN.
Are all statements correct?
Is the output correct?
Type the statements of the program.
Retype incorrect statements.
Make changes in the program.

17. Pouring a glass of milk

Is the glass full?
Pour the milk into the glass.
Get glass.
Is a clean glass available?
Get milk.
Is there milk in the refrigerator?
Put carton of milk in refrigerator.

18. Brushing your teeth

Put toothpaste on toothbrush.
All teeth brushed?
Get toothpaste.
Rinse toothbrush.
Get toothbrush.
Rinse mouth.
Dry mouth with towel.
Brush teeth.

MORE CHALLENGING EXERCISES

19. Expand the flowchart of Exercise 9 to start when the student wakes up in the morning.

20. Expand the flowchart of Exercise 15 to decide whether there is a jack and a spare tire in the trunk.

For Exercises 21–25, draw a flowchart for each procedure. Each flowchart should include at least one decision.

21. Taking the Computer Literacy book from a briefcase containing all your textbooks

22. Taking a true-false test

23. Setting the table for supper

24. Buying a quart of milk and a loaf of bread at the grocery store

25. Loading and running a program from a diskette

5-2 FLOWCHARTS AND PROGRAMS

OBJECTIVE: To draw a flowchart to solve a given problem

Before writing a program, a programmer often draws a flowchart that lists the steps to be followed in solving the problem. Flowcharts for actual programs can be made more precise than those for everyday activities. In this lesson, program flowchart boxes (except **START** and **END**) will be numbered to make referencing easier.

EXAMPLE 1 Draw a flowchart for this problem.

Problem Given the number of tee shirts bought at $5.98 each, print the total cost (without tax).

Solution Let T = the number of tee shirts.
Let C = the total cost.

Remember these four basic steps.

1. **INPUT** one or more values.

2. **PROCESS** the data.

3. **OUTPUT** the answer.

4. **END** the program.

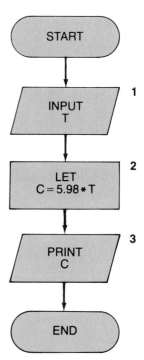

NOTE: Inside each box (except in decision boxes) is a direct command to the computer.

a. In the input box, write the **INPUT** or **READ** command.

b. In the calculate box, write the **LET** command.

c. In the output box, write **PRINT**.

The flowchart of Example 1 outlines a program that prints only one answer and then stops. As you know from earlier chapters, programs are usually written to handle as many sets of data as the user wishes to enter.

EXAMPLE 2 Expand the flowchart of Example 1 so that it handles as many data values as the user wants to enter.

Solution

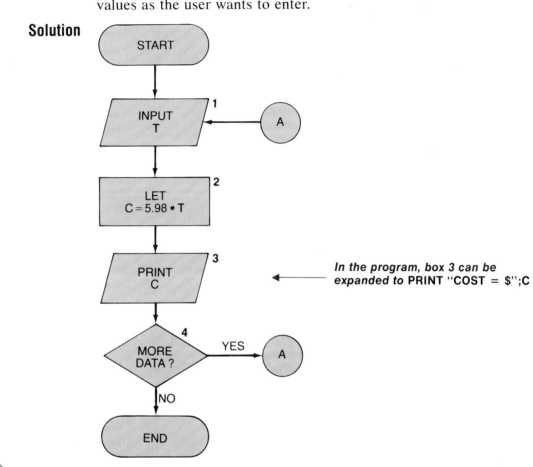

In the program, box 3 can be expanded to PRINT "COST = $";C

NOTE: In a flowchart, it is not necessary to specify exactly how the **MORE DATA?** question will be handled in the program.

A decision box must contain a question which can be answered **YES** or **NO**. Depending on the answer, one of two paths or "branches" is taken. For box 4 in the solution of Example 2, the **YES** branch points to a connector with A inside it. Elsewhere in the flowchart is another connector with an A in it. The two connectors save the programmer the trouble of drawing a long path from box 4 back to box 1.

A flowchart should include only the essential steps of the solution of a problem. For example, the flowchart need not contain the preliminary **PRINT** steps that tell what the program will do. The programmer can "dress up" the program when it is written. The flowchart of Example 2 might give rise to the following program.

```
10  REM   SECTION 5-2, EXAMPLE 2
20  PRINT "GIVEN THE NUMBER OF $5.98 TEE SHIRTS"
30  PRINT "BOUGHT, THIS PROGRAM PRINTS THE"
40  PRINT "TOTAL COST OF THE TEE SHIRTS."
50  PRINT
60  PRINT "HOW MANY TEE SHIRTS WERE BOUGHT";
70  INPUT T                                        ◄——— Flowchart box 1
80  LET C = 5.98 * T                               ◄——— Flowchart box 2
90  PRINT "TOTAL COST = $";C                       ◄——— Flowchart box 3
100 PRINT "MORE PURCHASES (1=YES,0=NO)";
110 INPUT X                                        ◄——— Flowchart box 4
120 IF X = 1 THEN 50
130 END                                            ◄——— Flowchart box 5
```

NOTE: In the program above, statements **10–60** contain the preliminary steps that "dress up" the program for the user. Statements 70–130 are the essential steps for the solution of the problem.

WRITTEN EXERCISES

For Exercises 1–5, choose from the box at the right the word that describes each flowchart symbol.

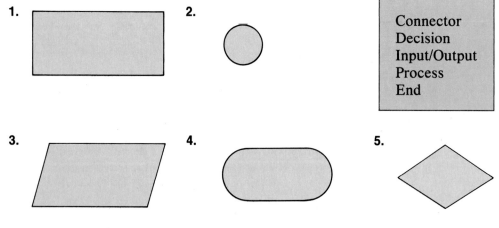

Connector
Decision
Input/Output
Process
End

1.

2.

3.

4.

5.

For each flowchart box, state whether it is correct. If not, explain why.

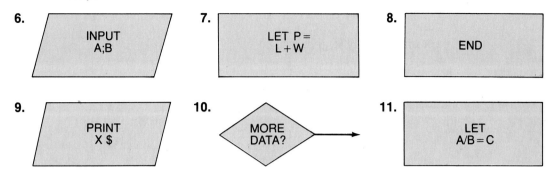

6.
```
INPUT
A;B
```

7.
```
LET P =
L + W
```

8.
```
END
```

9.
```
PRINT
X $
```

10.
```
MORE
DATA?
```

11.
```
LET
A/B = C
```

In Exercises 12–14, a flowcharting problem is stated. Complete the flowchart.

12. Problem: Given a number, square it and print the answer.

```
START

INPUT        1
N            ← A

2
?

PRINT        3
S

MORE      4  YES
DATA?       →  A

?

?
```

13. Problem: Given a number of feet, print the corresponding number of inches.

```
START

?            1
             ← A

LET          2
I = 12 * F

PRINT        3
?

?         4  ?
             →  A

NO

END
```

14. Problem: Input two numbers. Multiply them and print the product.

```
START

INPUT        1
A,B          ← ?

2
?

PRINT        3
P

?         4  ?
             →  A

NO

END
```

Correct any errors in these flowcharts.

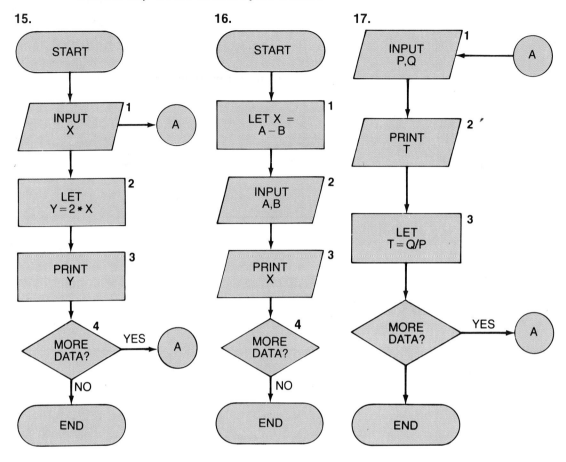

15.

START

INPUT X | 1 → A

LET Y = 2 * X | 2

PRINT Y | 3

MORE DATA? | 4 — YES → A
NO

END

16.

START

LET X = A − B | 1

INPUT A,B | 2

PRINT X | 3

MORE DATA? | 4
NO

END

17.

INPUT P,Q | 1 ← A

PRINT T | 2

LET T = Q/P | 3

MORE DATA? — YES → A

END

For Exercises 18–21, draw a flowchart for each problem.

18. Given the number of words a person can type in one minute, calculate how many words that person can type in one hour.

19. Compute the yearly simple interest on a given investment (principal) at a yearly interest rate of 6%. Use this formula.

Interest = Principal × .06

20. Given a word, print only the first letter of the word.

21. Given two strings, print the string formed by joining the two words. For example, given **FLOW** and **CHART**, print **FLOWCHART**.

MORE CHALLENGING EXERCISES

22. Write a program for each completed flowchart of Exercises 12–14.

23. Write a program for each flowchart you drew for Exercises 18–21.

For Exercises 24–26, draw a flowchart for each program. Each flowchart should include only the essential steps of the program.

24.
```
10 REM   EXERCISE 24
20 PRINT "ENTER YOUR NAME."
30 INPUT X$
40 LET Y$ = RIGHT$(X$,1)
50 PRINT "LAST LETTER IS ";Y$
60 PRINT "CONTINUE (1=YES)";
70 INPUT Z
80 IF Z = 1 THEN 20
90 END
```

25.
```
100 PRINT "GIVEN THE RADIUS OF A
110 PRINT "CIRCLE, THIS PROGRAM"
120 PRINT "COMPUTES THE AREA."
130 INPUT R
140 LET A = 3.1416 * R * R
150 PRINT "AREA = ";A
160 PRINT "MORE CIRCLES (Y/N)";
170 INPUT M$
180 IF M$ = "Y" THEN 130
190 END
```

26.
```
10 PRINT "THIS PROGRAM COMPUTES"
20 PRINT "THE CIRCUMFERENCE OF A"
30 PRINT "CIRCLE."
40 LET P = 3.14159
50 PRINT "WHAT IS THE RADIUS";
60 INPUT R
70 LET C = P * 2 * R
80 PRINT "CIRCUMFERENCE = ";C
90 PRINT "ANY MORE (1=YES)";
100 INPUT Z
110 IF Z = 1 THEN 50
120 END
```

Making a Robot at Summer Camp

5-3 MORE ON FLOWCHARTS

OBJECTIVE: To draw a flowchart containing one or more decisions other than MORE DATA?

EXAMPLE 1 Draw a flowchart for this problem.

Problem Given a student's score on a test, print whether the student passed the test. Assume that 70 is the minimum passing grade.

Solution

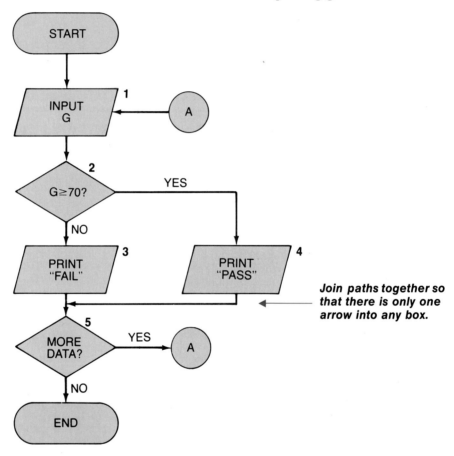

Join paths together so that there is only one arrow into any box.

NOTE: The **YES** branch may come out of any corner of the decision symbol. The **NO** branch may come from any other corner. However, where possible, have the **NO** branch come out of the bottom corner. In this way, flowchart branches will correspond to the way **BASIC**'s **IF–THEN** statement works.

A decision such as that in Box 2 of the flowchart in Example 1 on page 246 may contain any one of these six symbols.

Symbol	Meaning
$=$	equals
$<$	less than
$\leq$	less than or equal to
$>$	greater than
$\geq$	greater than or equal to
$\neq$	not equal to

Here are some decision boxes that may appear in flowcharts.

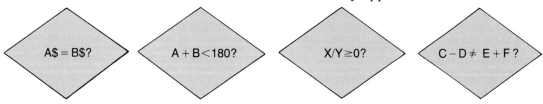

EXAMPLE 2   Draw a flowchart for this problem.

Problem   Given a name, print whether it begins with "**A**".

Solution

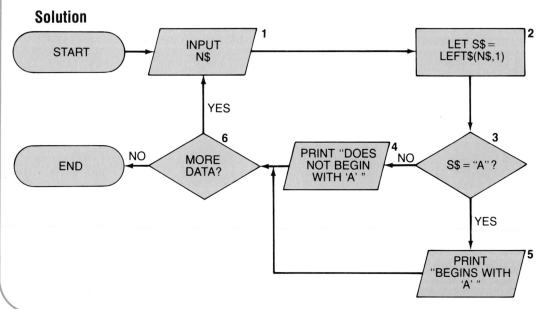

NOTE: A decision question may have operations on either, or both, sides of the equality or inequality symbol. However, a computer can compare only <u>two quantities</u> at a time. Therefore, in a flowchart, decisions such as these are not allowed.

$$A > B > C? \text{ or } A\$ = B\$ = C\$?$$

Such decisions must be broken into two steps. For example, ask $A > B$? Then ask $B > C$? Or ask $A\$ = B\$$? followed by $B\$ = C\$$?

WRITTEN EXERCISES

1. List the six mathematical symbols that may appear in a decision box.

2. In a decision box, on which side or sides of the equation or incequality symbol may operation signs appear?

3. How many quantities can a computer compare at one time?

What is wrong with each of these decision boxes?

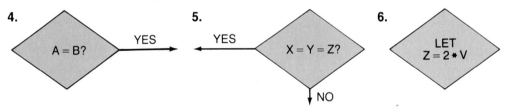

4. A = B? YES →

5. ← YES X = Y = Z? ↓ NO

6. LET Z = 2 * V

7. Complete this flowchart.

Problem: Given two numbers, decide whether either number is 0.

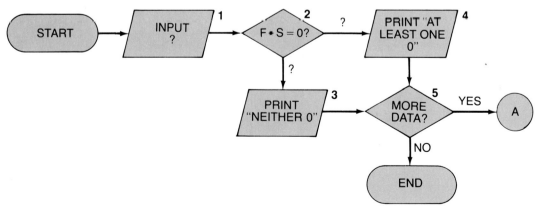

START → INPUT ? → [1] F * S = 0? → ? → [4] PRINT "AT LEAST ONE 0"

F * S = 0? → ? → PRINT "NEITHER 0" [3] → MORE DATA? [5] → YES → A

MORE DATA? → NO → END

8. Complete this flowchart.

Problem: Given two numbers A and B, decide whether their sum equals a given number, C.

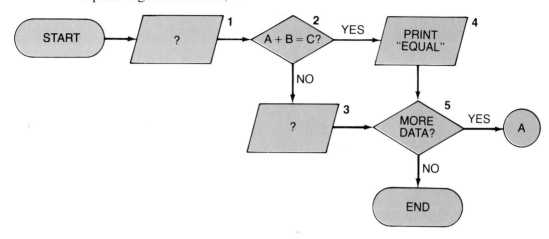

Correct any errors in these flowcharts.

9.

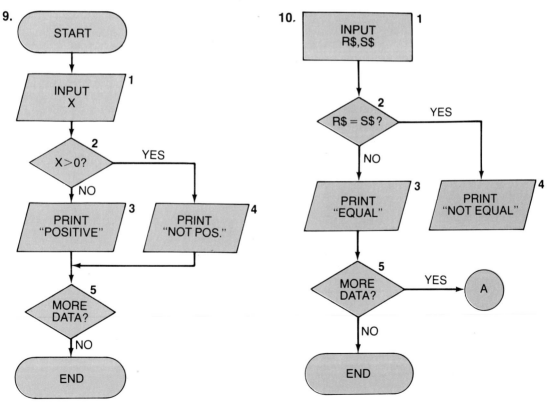

10.

MORE CHALLENGING EXERCISES

For Exercises 11–18, draw a flowchart for each problem. Each flowchart should contain at least one decision in addition to the **MORE DATA?** *decision.*

11. Given a number, decide whether it equals 0. Print either **ZERO** or **NOT ZERO**.

12. Given a word, decide whether it ends with "T".

13. Given a word, decide whether it has the same first and last letters. For example, **ALPHA** begins and ends with an "A"; **BETA** does not begin and end with the same letter.

14. Given two numbers, decide whether their sum is greater than 0.

15. Given two numbers, decide whether the first is more than twice the second.

16. Given the number of hours an employee worked this week, decide whether the number of hours is more than 40. If it is, print **OVERTIME**. If not, print **NO OVERTIME**.

17. Given two numbers, decide whether the second is zero. If it is not, divide the first number by the second and print the quotient. However, if the second number is zero, print **NO QUOTIENT**.

18. Given two words, decide whether the words have the same first letter.

REVIEW: Sections 5–1—5–3

For Exercises 1–4, state what is wrong with each flowchart box.

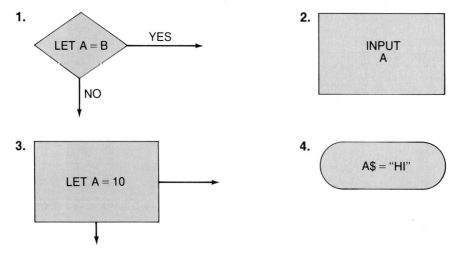

1.

LET A = B   YES

NO

2.

INPUT A

3.

LET A = 10

4.

A$ = "HI"

5. Draw a flowchart for turning on a television set and selecting the channel you want to watch.

6. Complete the flowchart below.

7. Correct any errors in the flowchart below.

Problem: Given a string, print its last two letters.

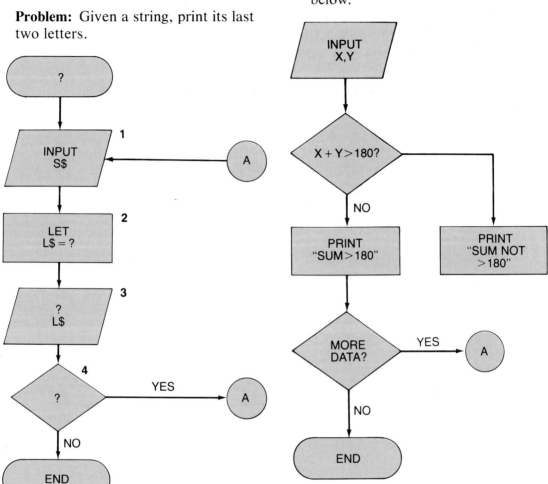

8. Draw a flowchart for this problem.

Problem: Given the length of one side of a square, print the perimeter of the square. Use this formula.

Perimeter = 4 × (length of one side)

ELECTRONIC SPREADSHEETS

For businesses and for the home, an **electronic spreadsheet** is a valuable tool for manipulating numbers. It performs tedious calculations without error and far more quickly than can be done using paper and pencil or a calculator.

Electronic spreadsheets organize data in rows and columns. A row and a column meet at a location called a **cell.** Each cell holds *one piece* of information.

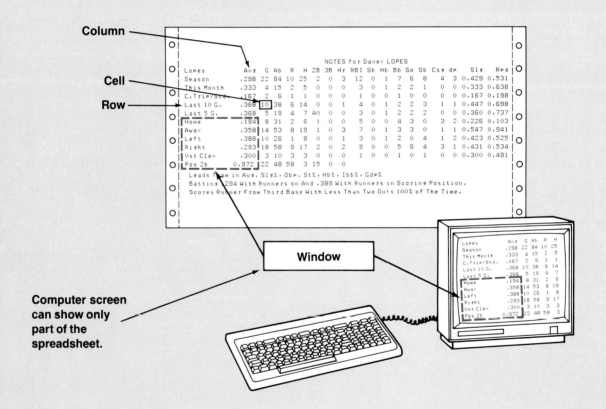

Column

Cell

Row

Window

Computer screen can show only part of the spreadsheet.

To explain how a spreadsheet program works, suppose that a teacher plans a spreadsheet that will calculate the average grades in three tests for each student in a class. A section of the spreadsheet will look like this on the computer screen.

	A	B	C	D	E	F
1		TEST 1	TEST 2	TEST 3	SUM	AVG.
2	ALLEN	88	86	90	264	88
3	BARKER	83	87	88	258	86
4	CARTER	88	93	95	276	92
5	DELANEY	90	84	87	261	87
6	JACOBS	76	78	86	240	80
7	LAUSTRA	88	68	82	237	79
8	PARSON	95	92	92	279	93
9	ROTH	87	94	86	267	89
10	VILLAR	90	92	88	270	90
11	WORSTER	94	89	90	273	91

On the spreadsheet, columns are marked by letters; rows are numbered. Each cell where a column and a row meet is named by a letter and a number. For example, the cell containing ALLEN is A2. The cell containing AVG. is F1. ALLEN and AVG. are called **labels.** To enter ALLEN in cell A2, press the > key. The words **GOTO** will appear at the top of the screen. Then type A2 (the cell where you want the arrow to go) and ALLEN. The computer will put the label ALLEN in cell A2.

A second type of entry is a **value.** For example, to enter a grade of 87 for ALLEN for TEST 1, GOTO cell A3. Then type +87. (The + tells the computer that 87 is a value, not a label.)

A **formula** is a third type of entry. For example, to calculate in cell E2 the sum of Allen's grades on three tests, send the cursor to cell E2. Then type +B2+C2+D2. The formula will appear in the information line at the top of the screen. The computer will calculate the sum immediately and display it in cell E2. When the formula +E2/3 is entered in cell F2, the computer will calculate ALLEN's average on the three tests and display the average in cell F2.

Once all the labels and formulas have been entered, the teacher can enter each student's grade on each test. As each value is entered in each cell, the program will immediately update all other entries. This automatic updating is one of the chief advantages of spreadsheet programs.

PROJECTS

Write the formula that should be entered for each of these cells in the teacher's grade spreadsheet.

1. E4   **2.** F4   **3.** C27   **4.** D28

5. List two ways of using a spreadsheet program.

6. Obtained from a software store the names of two spreadsheet programs and the names of the computers each program runs on.

5-4 TRACING FLOWCHARTS

OBJECTIVE:

> **To trace a flowchart for a given problem**

A flowchart can be checked by a **trace**. The programmer picks **data values** that test all possible outcomes of the flowchart. Example 1 on page 246 displayed a flowchart for this problem.

> **Problem:** Given a student's score on a test, print whether the student passed the test

To check this flowchart, at least one value greater than 70 and at least one value less than 70 should be tested.

EXAMPLE 1 Trace the flowchart of Example 1 on page 246 for the values 95 and 68.

Trace

Flowchart Box Number	Values of Variable G	Decision		Output
		Condition	Yes/ No?	
1	95			
2		95 ≥ 70?	Yes	
4				**PASS**
5		**MORE DATA?**	Yes	
1	68			
2		68 ≥ 70?	No	
3				**FAIL**
5		**MORE DATA?**	No	
END				

To write a trace, pretend that you are the computer carrying out what the flowchart (or program) tells you do do. You do <u>exactly</u> what the flowchart says. In this way, if the flowchart contains an error in logic, some of the test data will produce the wrong output. You can then correct the error and trace the flowchart again.

EXAMPLE 2   **a.** Draw a flowchart for this problem.

Problem   Given three numbers, select and print the largest.

Solutions   **a.** Let A, B, and C be the three given numbers.

1. Select two of the three numbers, say A and B.
2. Compare A to B (box 2).
3. Compare C to whichever number is larger, A or B (boxes 3 and 6).
4. The larger of the two numbers compared in step 3 is the largest of the three numbers.

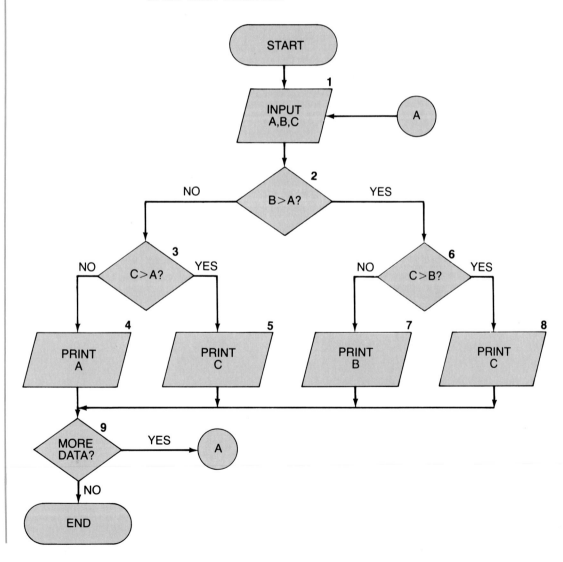

b. Trace the flowchart for these input values.

10, 5, 6   8, 11, 3   1, 2, 3

These sets of values are chosen so that in one of them, **A** is the largest number; in another set, **B** is the largest; in the third set, **C** is the largest.

Trace

Flowchart Box Number	Values of Variables			Decision		Output
	A	**B**	**C**	**Condition**	**Yes/No?**	
1	10	5	6			
2				5 > 10?	No	
3				6 > 10?	No	
4						10
9				MORE DATA?	Yes	
1	8	11	3			
2				11 > 8?	Yes	
6				3 > 11?	No	
7						11
9				MORE DATA?	Yes	
1	1	2	3			
2				2 > 1?	Yes	
6				3 > 2?	Yes	
8						3
9				MORE DATA?	No	
END						

WRITTEN EXERCISES

Trace the flowchart of Example 1 for each set of data.

1. 60, 78, 70

2. 100, 58, 66

Trace the flowchart of Example 2 for each set of data.

3. 2,5,3,   20,22,24,   8,1,2

4. 6,6,1,   2,7,7,   5,5,5

5. Trace the completed flowchart of Exercise 7 on page 248 for this data.

DATA: 0,7, 8,4, 0,0

6. Trace the completed flowchart of Exercise 8 on page 249 for this data.

DATA: 4,5,6, 1,1,2

MORE CHALLENGING EXERCISES

For Exercises 7–9, draw a flowchart for each problem.
Then trace the flowchart for the data listed.

7. The input is values for A and B which are the scores of two players of a video game. If A is larger, print **A WINS**. If B is larger, print **B WINS**. If they are equal, print **TIE**.

DATA: 130,120, 105,105, 140,155

8. Given three numbers, decide whether any of them are equal. Print either **EQUAL** or **NONE EQUAL**. You need not print which two are equal.

DATA: 4,4,4 4,5,6 4,5,4 5,4,4

9. Given three numbers, decide whether any of them is negative. Print either **NEGATIVE** or **NONE NEGATIVE**. You need not print which one is negative.

DATA: −1,4,5 0,−2,3 8,10,6 5,4,−2

For Exercises 10–11, draw a flowchart for each problem. Then select a set of test data and trace the flowchart.

10. Given three numbers A, B, and C, decide whether C is between A and B. That is, determine whether C is greater than A and less than B. In mathematical symbols,

$$A < C < B.$$

11. The input is the length and width of a rectangle, plus an additional number X. If **X = 0**, compute and print the area of the rectangle.

Area = length × width

If **X = 1**, compute and print the perimeter.

Perimeter = 2 × (length + width)

5-5 FROM FLOWCHART TO PROGRAM

OBJECTIVE: **To write a BASIC program for a given flowchart**

A flowchart can help you to write a program.

EXAMPLE 1 Write a program for the flowchart of Example 1 on page 246.

Solution The program is developed in steps.

Step 1 For flowchart box 1 (**INPUT G**), write these statements.

```
10 PRINT "ENTER THE STUDENT'S TEST SCORE."
20 INPUT G
```

Step 2 For box 2 (G ≥ 70?), first write these statements. Statements 30 and 50 will be completed later.

```
30 IF G >= 70 THEN  ?
40 PRINT "FAIL"
50 GOTO  ?
```

In **BASIC**, the statements of the **NO** branch of a decision come right after the **IF–THEN** statement. Therefore, when statement 30 is first written, it is not yet known which line number to write after **THEN**. So leave a blank after **THEN** until the **NO** branch is written. Also leave a blank in line 50 until the **YES** branch of statement 30 is written.

Step 3 Complete statement 30. Then write its **YES** branch.

```
30 IF G >= 70 THEN 60
40 PRINT "FAIL"
50 GOTO  ?
60 PRINT "PASS"
```

Step 4 Complete statement 50 (**GOTO 70**). Then write the statements corresponding to flowchart box 5 (**MORE DATA?**).

```
70 PRINT "ANY MORE STUDENTS (1=YES,0=NO)";
80 INPUT X
90 IF X = 1 THEN 10
100 END
```

The complete program is given on the next page.

Program

```
10  PRINT "ENTER THE STUDENT'S TEST SCORE."
20  INPUT G
30  IF G >= 70 THEN 60
40  PRINT "FAIL"                    ◄──────── NO branch of statement 30
50  GOTO 70
60  PRINT "PASS"                    ◄──────── YES branch of statement 30
70  PRINT "ANY MORE STUDENTS (1=YES,0=NO)";
80  INPUT X
90  IF X = 1 THEN 10
100 END
```

So far in this course, **IF–THEN** statements have been used only as in statement 90 of the program of Example 1. That is, they have been used to indicate whether the user wants to continue the program. In many programs, however, **IF–THEN** statements are needed to decide between two or more possibilities.

SYMBOLS THAT MAY BE USED IN IF–THEN STATEMENTS

Mathematical Symbol	BASIC Symbol	Meaning	Example
$=$	$=$	equals	80 IF A\$ + B\$ = C\$ THEN 15
$<$	$<$	less than	190 IF A + B < C*2 THEN 300
$>$	$>$	greater than	120 IF A $\uparrow$ 2 > 25 THEN 30
$\leq$	$<=$	less than or equal to	70 IF 6 <= K THEN 150
$\geq$	$>=$	greater than or equal to	50 IF X >= 0 THEN 100
$\neq$	$<>$	not equal to	150 IF N\$ <> "N" THEN 10

NOTE: In an **IF–THEN** statement, operation signs may appear on either or both sides of an equation or inequality. This is different from **LET** statements, where all operations must be on the right side of the equality ($=$) symbol.

EXAMPLE 2 Write a program for the flowchart in Example 2 on page 255.

Program
```
10  PRINT "ENTER THREE NUMBERS."
20  INPUT A, B, C
30  IF B > A THEN 70
40  IF C > A THEN 100
50  PRINT "LARGEST IS ";A
60  GOTO 110
```

```
70 IF C > B THEN 100
80 PRINT "LARGEST IS ";B
90 GOTO 110
100 PRINT "LARGEST IS ";C
110 PRINT "ANY MORE DATA (1=YES,0=NO)";
120 INPUT X
130 IF X = 1 THEN 10
140 END
```

There are two common mistakes to be avoided when writing **IF–THEN** statements.

1. An **IF–THEN** statement should almost never be followed by a **GOTO** statement. For example, statements 80 and 90 at the left below should be replaced by statement 80 at the right.

```
80 IF A = B THEN 100 ⎫
90 GOTO 150           ⎬ ────→ 80 IF A <> B THEN 150
```

2. The number after **THEN** should never be the number of the statement immediately after the **IF–THEN** statement. For example, the following "decision" is really no decision at all.

```
70 IF X > 0 THEN 80
80 . . .
```
If X > 0 is true, the computer goes to 80.
If X > 0 is false, the computer goes to the next statement, which is 80.
Either way the computer goes to 80.

WRITTEN EXERCISES

1. Does the program below print the same output as the program of Example 1?

```
10 PRINT "ENTER TEST SCORE."
20 INPUT G
30 IF G < 70 THEN 60
40 PRINT "PASS"
50 GOTO 70
60 PRINT "FAIL"
70 PRINT "MORE STUDENTS (1=YES)";
80 INPUT X
90 IF X = 1 THEN 10
100 END
```

2. Does the program below print the same output as the program of Example 2?

```
10 PRINT "ENTER THREE NUMBERS."
20 INPUT A, B, C
30 IF A < B THEN 70
40 IF A < C THEN 100
50 PRINT "LARGEST IS ";C
60 GOTO 110
70 IF B < C THEN 100
80 PRINT "LARGEST IS ";A
90 GOTO 110
100 PRINT "LARGEST IS ";B
110 PRINT "ANY MORE DATA (1=YES,0=NO)";
120 INPUT X
130 IF X = 1 THEN 10
140 END
```

For Exercises 3–7, write an **IF–THEN** statement for each decision.

3. If **X$** equals **Y$**, then go to statement 50.

4. If A is greater than 0, go to 100.

5. If Y is less than or equal to 100, jump to statement 75.

6. Jump to statement 120 if **C$** does not equal **D$**.

7. Go to 150 if Z is greater than or equal to L.

8. Modify the program of Example 1 so that it reads the input values from **DATA**.

9. Modify the program of Example 2 so that it prints the <u>smallest</u> of the three numbers.

10. Revise the program below to eliminate statement 40.

```
10 PRINT "WHAT IS THE NUMBER";
20 INPUT X
30 IF X < 0 THEN 50
40 GOTO 70
50 PRINT "NEGATIVE"
60 GOTO 80
70 PRINT "NOT NEGATIVE"
80 PRINT "ANOTHER NUMBER (Y/N)";
90 INPUT Z$
100 IF Z$ = "Y" THEN 10
110 END
```

11. Revise the program below to eliminate statement 160.

```
100 PRINT "ENTER YOUR AGE";
110 INPUT A
120 IF A > 18 THEN 150
130 PRINT "UNDER 18"
140 GOTO 200
150 IF A > 21 THEN 170
160 GOTO 190
170 PRINT "OVER 21"
180 GOTO 200
190 PRINT "OVER 18 BUT UNDER 21"
200 END
```

12. Complete the program on the right so that it corresponds to the flowchart on the left.

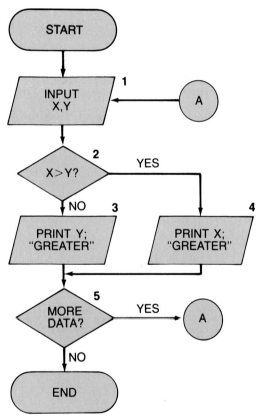

```
10  PRINT "ENTER TWO NUMBERS."
20  ?
30  IF X > Y THEN  ?
40  ?
50  GOTO  ?
60  PRINT X;" GREATER"
70  PRINT "CONTINUE (1=YES)";
80  ?
90  IF K = 1 THEN  ?
100 END
```

For Exercises 13–14, write a program for the flowchart you completed for the indicated exercise.

13. Exercise 7 on page 248

14. Exercise 8 on page 249

15. Modify the program of Example 2 so that it reads the input values from **DATA**. Print the output in four labeled columns: **A**, **B**, **C**, and **LARGEST**.

For Exercises 16–19, write a program for the flowchart you drew for each indicated exercise.

16. Exercise 7 on page 257

17. Exercise 8 on page 257

18. Exercise 9 on page 257

19. Exercise 10 on page 257

For Exercises 20–21:
a. Draw a flowchart.
b. Write a program.

20. Given a number X, print its recipocal $\frac{1}{X}$ if X is not 0. If **X** is 0, print **NO RECIPROCAL**.

21. Given the scores of a student on two tests, decide whether the sum is 140 or more. If it is not, print **FAIL**. If the sum is 180 or more, print **PASS WITH HONORS**. If the sum is between 140 and 180, print **PASS**.

Did You Know?

Character printers, such as a **daisy wheel printer**, are like typewriters in that they print lines across a page character by character. The daisy wheel consists of a wheel with a set of spokes. Each spoke contains a raised character at its tip. The entire wheel rotates. When the desired character is in place, it is struck by a hammer to imprint the character on the paper.

Daisy wheel printers can print up to 70 characters per second. Different typefaces can be obtained by changing the wheel.

IF–THEN Statements

1. Enter and **RUN** this program (see Example 1 on pages 258–259). Use these input values: 95, 1, 68, 1, 70, 0.

```
10 PRINT "ENTER THE STUDENT'S TEST SCORE."
20 INPUT G
30 IF G >= 70 THEN 60
40 PRINT "FAIL"
50 GOTO 70
60 PRINT "PASS"
70 PRINT "ANY MORE STUDENTS (1=YES,0=NO)";
80 INPUT X
90 IF X = 1 THEN 10
100 END
```

2. Modify the program of Example 1 as you indicated in Exercise 8 on page 261. Use the **DATA** listed in Exercise 1 above. **RUN** the revised program. If necessary, make further changes until the program runs correctly.

3. Type **NEW**. Then enter the program of Exercise 1 on page 260. **RUN** the revised program, using the same input as for Exercise 1 above. Is the output the same for both programs?

4. Type **NEW**. Then enter and **RUN** the program of Example 2 on pages 259–260. Use the following input values.

    10,5,6, 1, 8,11,3, 1, 1,2,3, 0.

5. Modify the program of Example 2 as indicated in Exercise 9 on page 261. Use the data listed in Exercise 4 above. **RUN** the revised program. If necessary, make further changes until the program runs correctly.

6. Type **NEW**. Then enter the program of Exercise 2 on page 261. **RUN** the revised program, using the same input as for Exercise 4 above. Is the output the same for both programs?

7. Type **NEW**. Then enter and **RUN** the programs you revised in Exercises 10–11 on pages 261–262. Did you revise the programs correctly?

8. Enter and **RUN** the program you completed in Exercise 12 on page 262. Did you complete it correctly?

5-6 TRACING PROGRAMS

OBJECTIVE:

> **To trace a given program**

EXAMPLE 1 Trace the following program for the data listed in statement 80.

Problem: Given two numbers, subtract the smaller from the larger.

Program
```
10 READ X, Y
20 IF Y > X THEN 50
30 LET D = X - Y
40 GOTO 60
50 LET D = Y - X
60 PRINT "DIFFERENCE = ";D
70 GOTO 10
80 DATA 40,60, 52,35, 20,20
90 END
```

Trace

State-ment Number	Values of Variables			Decision		Output
	X	Y	D	Condition	Yes/ No?	
10	40	60				
20				60 > 40?	Yes	
50			20			
60						**DIFFERENCE = 20**
70				**MORE DATA?**	Yes	
10	52	35				
20				35 > 52?	No	
30			17			
60						**DIFFERENCE = 17**
70				**MORE DATA?**	Yes	
10	20	20				
20				20 > 20?	No	
30			0			
60						**DIFFERENCE = 0**
70				**MORE DATA?**	No	
END						

Here are several important points about the trace of Example 1.

1. For **LET** statements, the trace shows only the value that is computed for the variable on the left of the equality (=) symbol. If necessary, check by computing the value outside of the trace.

2. **40 GOTO 60** does not directly appear in the trace. However, **70 GOTO 10** is shown in the trace. Because statement 10 is **READ X, Y**, this is the only place in the trace to show **BASIC**'s built-in **MORE DATA**? test.

3. A **DATA** statement never directly appears in a trace.

It is important to trace every program you write in order to detect errors in logic. Be sure to choose data values that test all the possibilities of the program.

EXAMPLE 2   **a.** Trace the program below for the values listed in statement **110**.

Problem: Given three numbers, decide how many are equal.

Program
```
10  READ X, Y, Z
20  IF X = Y THEN 60
30  IF X = Z THEN 70
40  PRINT "NONE EQUAL"
50  GOTO 10
60  IF X = Z THEN 90
70  PRINT "TWO EQUAL"
80  GOTO 10
90  PRINT "THREE EQUAL"
100 GOTO 10
110 DATA 4,5,6, 3,3,3, 3,3,2, 2,3,2, 3,2,2
120 END
```

Trace

Statement Number	Values of Variables			Decision		Output
	X	Y	Z	Condition	Yes/No?	
10	4	5	6			
20				4 = 5?	No	
30				4 = 6?	No	
40						NONE EQUAL
50				MORE DATA?	Yes	

State-ment Number	Values of Variables			Decision		Output
	X	Y	Z	Condition	Yes/No?	
10	3	3	3			
20				3 = 3?	Yes	
60				3 = 3?	Yes	
90						THREE EQUAL
100				MORE DATA?	Yes	
10	3	3	2			
20				3 = 3?	Yes	
60				3 = 2?	No	
70						TWO EQUAL
80				MORE DATA?	Yes	
10	2	3	2			
20				2 = 3?	No	
30				2 = 2?	Yes	
70						TWO EQUAL
80				MORE DATA?	Yes	
10	3	2	2			
20				3 = 2?	No	
30				3 = 2?	No	
40						NONE EQUAL ⟵ ERROR
50				MORE DATA?	No	
END						

b. From the trace, identify and correct the error in the program.

The trace shows that the following statement should be added to the program.

```
35 IF Y = Z THEN 70
```

To trace a program completely, you must choose test data so that each possible output is produced at least once. For example, the program in Example 2 required at least the five sets of input values in statement 110 on page 266.

a. One set (3,3,3) where all three numbers are equal

b. One set (4,5,6) where none are equal

c. One set (3,3,2) with only the first and second numbers equal

d. One set (2,3,2) with only the first and third equal

e. One set (3,2,2) with only the second and third equal

These sets could be in the **DATA** list in any order. Only when you have checked that a program handles each possible type of input correctly can you say the program is completely correct.

WRITTEN EXERCISES

Trace the program of Example 1 when statement 80 is replaced by each of the following.

1. 80 DATA 10,15, 12,12, 100,87

2. 80 DATA 11,11, 0,6, 30,27, 15,16

For the programs in Exercises 3 and 4:

a. *Trace each program for the data listed in the program.*

b. *State whether the program produces the same output as the program of Example 1.*

c. *If the program does not produce the same output as the program of Example 1, revise it until it does.*

3.
```
10 READ X, Y
20 IF Y < X THEN 50
30 LET D = Y - X
40 GOTO 60
50 LET D = X - Y
60 PRINT "DIFFERENCE = ";D
70 GOTO 10
80 DATA 60,40, 35,52, 20,20
90 END
```

4.
```
10 READ X, Y
20 IF Y > X THEN 50
30 LET D = X - Y
40 PRINT "DIFFERENCE = ";D
50 LET D = Y - X
60 PRINT "DIFFERENCE = ";D
70 GOTO 10
80 DATA 60,40, 35,52, 20,20
90 END
```

5. Draw a flowchart for the program of Example 1.

Trace the program of Example 2. Add statement 35 near the bottom of page 267. Replace statement 110 with each of the statements in Exercises 6 and 7.

6. 110 DATA 4,4,4, 6,6,5, 9,8,9, 4,7,2, 3,8,8

7. 110 DATA 10,21,21, 16,25,16, 18,18,18, 30,30,20, 30,40,50

For the programs of Exercises 8 and 9:

a. Trace each program for the data listed in the program.

b. State whether the program produces the same output as the program of Example 2 (with statement 35 near the bottom of page 267 added).

c. If the output is not the same, revise the program until it does produce the same output.

8.
```
10 READ X, Y, Z
20 IF X = Y THEN 60
30 IF X = Z THEN 70
40 IF Y = Z THEN 70
50 PRINT "NONE EQUAL"
60 IF X = Z THEN 80
70 PRINT "TWO EQUAL"
80 PRINT "THREE EQUAL"
90 GOTO 10
100 DATA 4,5,6, 3,3,3, 3,3,2
110 DATA 2,3,2, 3,2,2
120 END
```

9.
```
10 READ X, Y, Z
20 IF X = Y THEN 70
30 IF Y = Z THEN 80
40 IF X = Z THEN 80
50 PRINT "NONE EQUAL"
60 GOTO 10
70 IF Y = Z THEN 100
80 PRINT "TWO EQUAL"
90 GOTO 10
100 PRINT "THREE EQUAL"
110 DATA 4,5,6, 3,3,3, 3,3,2
120 DATA 2,3,2, 3,2,2
130 END
```

10. Draw a flowchart for the corrected program in Example 2 (including statement 35 near the bottom of page 267).

The program on the right reads two numbers and decides whether they are equal or which is larger.

Which of the data lists in Exercises 11–13 is a complete set of test data that will check that the program correctly handles each possibility?

If a set is not complete, add numbers to it to make it complete.

```
10 READ A, B
20 IF A = B THEN 80
30 IF A < B THEN 60
40 PRINT A;" LARGER"
50 GOTO 10
60 PRINT B;" LARGER"
70 GOTO 10
80 PRINT "EQUAL"
90 GOTO 10
100 DATA  ?
110 END
```

11. 100 DATA 81,79, 64,78

12. 100 DATA 5,5, 6,7, 4,8

13. 100 DATA 20,10, 16,18, 3,3

For each program in Exercises 14–15, complete the **DATA** *line(s) to include a complete set of data that tests whether the program handles all possibilities correctly.*

14. Problem: Given two numbers, decide whether either of them is zero.

```
10 READ C, D
20 IF C = 0 THEN 60
30 IF D = 0 THEN 60
40 PRINT "NEITHER IS ZERO."
50 GOTO 10
60 PRINT "AT LEAST ONE IS ZERO."
70 GOTO 10
80 DATA  ?
90 END
```

15. Problem: Read two words. Then print whether they have the same first letter.

```
100 READ S$, T$
110 IF LEFT$(S$,1)=LEFT$(T$,1) THEN 140
120 PRINT "NOT THE SAME"
130 GOTO 100
140 PRINT "SAME FIRST LETTER"
150 GOTO 100
160 DATA  ?
170 END
```

16. Trace the program in Exercise 14 for the **DATA** you added to it.

17. Trace the program in Exercise 15 for the **DATA** you added to it.

*Each program in Exercises 18 and 19 has at least one error (**bug**) in it. Choose a complete set of test data and trace each program until you have corrected all the bugs.*

18. Problem: Given three words, decide whether they have the same last letter.

```
100 READ A$, B$, C$
110 LET D$ = RIGHT$(A$,1)
120 LET E$ = RIGHT$(B$,1)
130 IF D$ <> E$ THEN 150
140 LET F$ = RIGHT$(C$,1)
150 IF D$ <> F$ THEN 180
160 PRINT "ALL THE SAME"
170 GOTO 100
180 PRINT "NOT ALL THE SAME"
190 GOTO 100
200 DATA ...
210 END
```

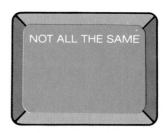

19. Problem: Read three numbers. Then print whether any one of them is the sum of the other two.

```
10 READ U, V, W
20 IF U + V = W THEN 50
30 IF U + W = V THEN 50
40 IF V + W = U THEN 50
50 PRINT "ONE IS SUM OF OTHERS"
60 GOTO 10
70 PRINT "NONE IS SUM OF OTHERS"
80 GOTO 10
90 DATA ...
100 END
```

MORE CHALLENGING EXERCISES

For Exercises 20–25:

a. Write a program.

b. Trace the program for a complete set of test data that you select. For any program that must accept words as input, assume that each word will contain only capital letters. You may use either **READ/DATA** *or* **INPUT** *statements. If your teacher requires it, draw a flowchart for each program first.*

20. Given a word, decide whether it begins with "A".

21. Given three words, decide whether they all have the same first letter.

22. Given two numbers, print whether they are equal.

23. Given two words, decide whether they have the same last letter.

24. Given a word, decide whether it ends in "S" or "T".

25. Given a number, print whether it is positive, negative, or zero.

Did You Know?

A **modem** is a device that allows computers to talk to each other. It allows terminals to talk to computers over telephone lines. For example, a person with a home computer can use a modem to send information to, or receive information from, a mainframe. One modem must be connected to the home computer and another to the mainframe.

COMPUTER LAB ACTIVITIES

Tracing Programs

1. Enter and **RUN** this program (see Example 1 on page 265). Does it produce the output shown in the trace?

2. Replace line 80 with the **DATA** from Exercise 1 on page 268. **RUN** the program again. Does the output agree with what you showed in your trace for Exercise 1 on page 268?

```
10 READ X, Y
20 IF Y > X THEN 50
30 LET D = X - Y
40 GOTO 60
50 LET D = Y - X
60 PRINT "DIFFERENCE = ";D
70 GOTO 10
80 DATA 40,60, 52,35, 20,20
90 END
```

3. Repeat Exercise 2 for the **DATA** from Exercise 2 on page 268.

4. Type **NEW**. Then enter and **RUN** the program of Exercise 3 on page 268. Does it produce the output shown in your trace for Exercise 3? If any answers are not correct, revise the program until it produces correct output.

5. Repeat Exercise 4 for the program of Exercise 4 on page 268.

6. Type **NEW**. Then enter and **RUN** this program (see Example 2 on page 266). Does it produce the output shown in the trace of Example 2 (with the last answer incorrect)?

```
10 READ X, Y, Z
20 IF X = Y THEN 60
30 IF X = Z THEN 70
40 PRINT "NONE EQUAL"
·50 GOTO 10
60 IF X = Z THEN 90
70 PRINT "TWO EQUAL"
80 GOTO 10
90 PRINT "THREE EQUAL"
100 GOTO 10
110 DATA 4,5,6, 3,3,3, 3,3,2, 2,3,2, 3,2,2
120 END
```

7. To the program of Exercise 6 add the statement below. **RUN** the program again. Are all answers now correct?

```
35 IF Y = Z THEN 70
```

8. In the program of Exercise 6 on page 272, replace line 110 with this **DATA** line from Exercise 6 on page 268.

   110 DATA 4,4,4,   6,6,5 9,8,9   4,7,2 3,8,8

   RUN the program again. Does the output agree with what you showed in your trace for Exercise 6 on page 268?

9. Repeat Exercise 8 above for this **DATA**.

   110 DATA 10,21,21,   16,25,16,   18,18,18,   30,30,20,   30,40,50

10. Type **NEW**. Then enter and **RUN** the program of Exercise 8 on page 269. **RUN** the revised program. Does it produce the output shown in your trace for Exercise 8? If any answers are not correct, revise the program until it produces correct output.

11. Repeat Exercise 10 for the program of Exercise 9 on page 269.

12. Type **NEW**. Then enter the program for Exercises 11–13 on page 269. Add the **DATA** line listed for Exercise 11 on page 269 and **RUN** the program. Is every possible outcome of the program produced? If not, add numbers to the data list. Then **RUN** the program again.

EXPLORE: AND, OR

13. Many computers allow the keywords **AND** and **OR** in the **IF** part of an **IF–THEN** statement.

    To see whether your computer accepts these words, enter and **RUN** the program on the right. This program is a revision of the one in Example 2 on page 266.

```
10 READ X, Y, Z
20 IF X=Y AND Y=Z THEN 80
30 IF X=Y OR Y=Z OR X=Z THEN 60
40 PRINT "NONE EQUAL"
50 GOTO 10
60 PRINT "TWO EQUAL"
70 GOTO 10
80 PRINT "THREE EQUAL"
90 GOTO 10
100 DATA 4,5,6,  3,3,3,  3,3,2
110 DATA 2,3,2,  3,2,2
120 END
```

14. How is this program using **AND** and **OR** better than the original program of Example 2?

> *For Exercises 15–17, use **AND** or **OR** to rewrite each program.*
> **RUN** *the revised program. If necessary, make changes until each program runs correctly.*

15. Exercise 14, page 270   16. Exercise 18, page 270   17. Exercise 19, page 271

For Exercises 1–5, complete each statement.

1. In a program, an **IF–THEN** statement should not be followed by a
   __?__ statement.
2. One way of finding a logic error in a flowchart is by __?__ the flowchart.
3. To trace a program completely, test data must be chosen so that
   each possible outcome is produced at least __?__ .
4. The **BASIC** symbol <> means __?__ .
5. The **BASIC** symbol for "less than or equal to" is __?__ .

Write an **IF–THEN** *statement for each decision.*

6. If **A$** equals **B$**, then go to statement 60.
7. If **X$** is not equal to "**X**", jump to statement 110.
8. Go to 250 if **Y** is greater than or equal to **Q**.
9. Trace the flowchart for these input values.

   NEAL, MARGUERITE, DOROTHY

10. Complete the program below so that it
    corresponds to the flowchart on the
    right.

```
10  PRINT "ENTER A NAME."
20  INPUT N$
30  LET L = LEN(N$)
40  IF  ?   THEN   ?
50  PRINT "NOT MORE THAN 5 LETTERS"
60  GOTO   ?
70  PRINT "MORE THAN 5 LETTERS"
80  PRINT "CONTINUE? (1=YES,0=NO)"
90    ?
100 IF Z=1 THEN   ?
110 END
```

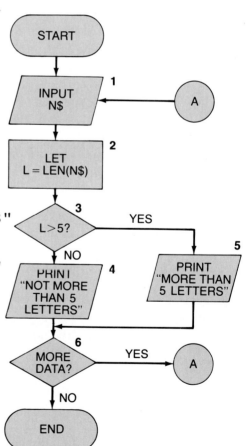

COMPUTERS AND CRIME

Computers are used to solve crimes.

Descriptions given by victims can help police to determine if a criminal has been previously arrested and photographed. The time involved in comparing the 50,000 pictures of criminals that are on file against the description is too great to be practical.

Fortunately, a computer program named **PATREC** ("**PAT**tern **REC**ognition") has been developed to simplify this task. PATREC can analyze a police artist's sketch for such measurements as distance between the temples, the length of nose, and the width of the mouth. With the help of information about height, weight, and the color of the eyes, the number of possibilities can be reduced to a reasonable number.

Robot used by the San Francisco Police Department for removing explosives.

Computers are used to help minimize the effects of crime.

A robot used by the police department of a large city can be used for removing explosives and for other hazardous tasks.

Computer software is protected by copyright laws.

Users of copyright-protected programs should know that these three actions are illegal.

- Copying software programs onto blank disks

- Using a copied "back-up" disk permitted by copyright law for any purpose other than as a back-up

- Loading the same copyright-protected program into many computers, thus allowing several users to work on the program at the same time.

Software "pirates" help to increase the cost of computer software and help to discourage the development of good software.

PROJECTS

1. Find out the annual cost of computer crime to businesses.

2. Find other ways that computers have helped to solve crimes, such as in analyzing and matching fingerprints.

Chapter Summary

Section 5–1   **1.** A flowchart is a step-by-step outline of the procedure to be followed to do a task or to solve a problem.

2. The flowchart symbols are START or END (oblong), INPUT or OUTPUT (parallelogram), PROCESS (rectangle), DECISION (diamond), and CONNECTOR (circle).

Section 5–2   **3.** Before writing a program, a programmer often draws a flow-chart that outlines the essential logic of the program.

4. Flowcharts usually end with a MORE DATA? decision to allow the user to enter as many input values as desired.

Section 5–3   **5.** Flowcharts are most useful for planning programs containing one or more decisions. Decision boxes (other than **MORE DATA?**) may contain the symbols $=$, $<$, $\leq$, $>$, $\geq$, or $\neq$.

Section 5–4   **6.** A flowchart can be checked by a **trace**. To trace a flowchart, you pretend that you are the computer. Then you do exactly what the flowchart tells you to do.

Section 5–5   **7.** In **BASIC**, the statements of the **NO** branch of a decision come right after the **IF–THEN** statement. Therefore, when an **IF–THEN** statement is first written, the programmer often leaves a blank for the statement number behind **THEN**. The statement is filled in after the **NO** branch has been written.

Section 5–6   **8.** Every program you write should be traced to find logic errors. Choose data values that test all the possibilities of the program.

Chapter Review

1. Draw a flowchart that lists the steps you would follow in leaving your home and going to a store to buy a record.

2. Complete the flowchart below.

   Problem: The input is a student's grade, **G**. If **G** is greater than 90, print **PASS WITH HONORS**. If **G** is less than 70, print **FAIL**. Otherwise, print **PASS**.

3. Correct any errors in the flowchart below.

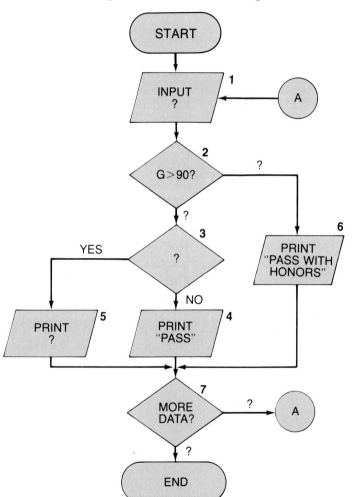

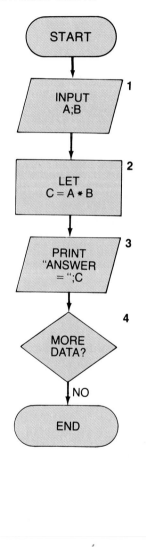

4. Trace the flowchart you completed for Exercise 2.
   Use this data: 85, 91, 68, 90

5. Write a **BASIC** program for the flowchart you completed for Exercise 2.

Chapter Test

For Exercises 1–3, draw the flowchart symbol for each flowchart step.

1. Start   2. Decision   3. Process

4. Write, in correct logical order, the steps for mailing a letter as shown in the box at the right.

> Go to the post office.
> Mail letter.
> Put stamp on envelope.
> Is post office open?
> Wait until post office opens.
> Buy stamps.

5. Draw a flowchart for the procedure of Exercise 4.

6. Complete the flowchart at the right.

   Problem: The input is two numbers, X and Y, and a third number, C.

   If C = 1, multiply X and Y.

   If C = 0, divide X by Y.

   In either case, print the answer.

7. Trace the flowchart you completed for Exercise 6.

   Use this data: 4,2,1 12,3,0 21,10,0

8. Write a program for the flowchart you completed in Exercise 6.

9. Draw a flowchart for this problem.

   Problem: Given a person's first and last names, decide whether the first and last names have the same number of letters.

10. Write a program for the flowchart you drew for Exercise 9.

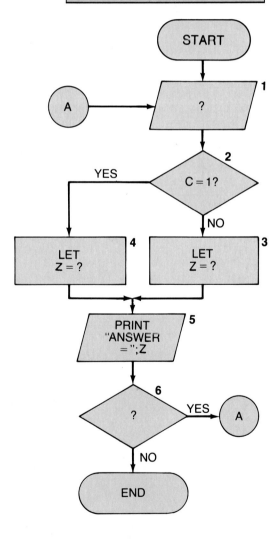

Cumulative Review: Chapters 1–5

Part 1

Choose the correct answer. Choose a, b, c, or d.

1. Which of these persons first used punched cards to program looms?
   a. Charles Babbage   **b.** Blaise Pascal
   c. Herman Hollerith   **d.** Joseph Jacquard

2. Who invented the machines that allowed the Census of 1890 to be completed in record time?
   a. Charles Babbage   **b.** Blaise Pascal
   c. Herman Hollerith   **d.** Joseph Jacquard

3. Which of these persons developed one of the first assembly languages and was also on the original **COBOL** committee?
   a. Herman Hollerith   **b.** Grace Hopper
   c. Howard Aiken   **d.** Ada Lovelace

4. Which of these programming languages was developed first?
   a. Pascal   **b.** LOGO   **c.** BASIC   **d.** COBOL

5. Which command contains a syntax error?
   a. PRINT "HI THERE!"   **b.** PRINT"HI THERE!"
   c. PRINT "HI";" THERE!"   **d.** PRINT "HI THERE"!

6. If **J$ = "JOLISE"**, what is the output of **PRINT "YOUR TURN, ";J$;"."**?
   a. YOUR TURN, JOLISE.   **b.** "YOUR TURN", JOLISE.
   c. "YOUR TURN, JOLISE."   **d.** YOUR TURN, "JOLISE."

7. Which one of the following is a **BASIC** numerical variable?
   a. TO   **b.** 2   **c.** T$ **d.** T

8. What would you type to display only statement 50 of a program in computer memory?
   a. LIST 50   **b.** 50   **c.** LIST   **d.** RUN 50

9. Which of these statements applies to a computer's **ROM**?
   a. It is erased when the computer is turned off.
   b. The user can store programs in it.
   c. The user can change what is stored in it.
   d. It stands for "read-only memory."

10. Which of these devices can store a program outside the computer?
   a. floppy disk   **b.** CRT   **c.** RAM   **d.** keyboard

11. When a program contains a **READ** statement, what other kind of statement must it include?
   a. REM   **b.** IF–THEN   **c.** DATA   **d.** INPUT

12. When a program contains a **GOSUB** statement, what other kind of statement must it include?
   a. READ   **b.** RETURN   **c.** IF–THEN   **d.** INPUT

13. Which of the following is included in the category "software"?
   a. keyboard   **b.** CPU   **c.** printer   **d.** BASIC interpreter

14. Which **IF–THEN** statement is correct and contains no syntax error?
   a. IF X$ = Y THEN 10   **b.** IF X : 1 THEN 100
   c. IF A $>=$ 10 THEN 50   **d.** IFF A$ $<>$ B$ THEN 20

15. Which of the following is the **BASIC** version of the formula $y = x^2$?
   a. LET Y = X$\uparrow$2   **b.** X * X = Y
   c. X $\uparrow$ 2 = Y   **d.** LET X$\uparrow$2 = Y

16. When a program contains a **FOR** statement, what other kind of statement must it include?
   a. REM   **b.** GOSUB   **c.** NEXT   **d.** DATA

17. In graphics mode, what is the name given to the smallest block on the screen a computer can light?
   a. low resolution   **b.** pixel   **c.** high resolution   **d.** home

18. Which of these advises businesses about computer hardware and software?
   a. electrical engineer   **b.** data entry clerk
   c. computer operator   **d.** systems analyst

19. Which statement best describes the first computers?
   a. They weighed about 50 pounds.
   b. They could be easily moved from place to place.
   c. They weighed about 500 pounds.
   d. They filled one or more rooms.

20. Which scientific discovery made microcomputers possible?
   a. integrated circuits   **b.** vacuum tubes
   c. floppy disks   **d.** magnetic tape

Part 2

For Exercises 21–22 write the output of each program.

21.
```
100  FOR I=1 TO 3
110  PRINT "HAPPY"
120  NEXT I
130  PRINT "BIRTHDAY!"
140  END
```

22.
```
10  READ X
20  IF X < 0 THEN 50
30  PRINT "GOOD"
40  GOTO 10
50  PRINT "BAD"
60  GOTO 10
70  DATA 35,0,-3
80  END
```

23. Draw a flowchart for the program in Exercise 22.

For Exercises 24–25, complete each program.

24. Problem: Given a string, print whether it contains more than 8 characters.

```
10   PRINT "WHAT IS THE STRING?"
20   INPUT   ?
30   LET L =  ?  (S$)
40   IF L >  ?  THEN   ?
50   PRINT "8 CHARACTERS OR LESS"
60   GOTO  ?
70    ?   "MORE THAN 8 CHARACTERS"
80   PRINT "CONTINUE? (1=YES)"
90    ?  Z
100  IF Z = 1 THEN   ?
110  END
```

25. Problem: Print rows of 5 asterisks. Print as many rows as the user wishes. Double space the rows of asterisks.

```
100  PRINT "HOW MANY ROWS?"
110   ?   R
120  FOR T=1 TO   ?
130  PRINT "*****"
140   ?
150  NEXT   ?
160  END
```

For Exercises 26–27, correct the errors in each program.

26.
```
200  PRINT "TYPE A CHARACTER."
210  INPUT C
220  FOR I FROM 1 TO 10
230  PRINT C
240  NEXT C
250  PRINT "AGAIN?" (Y=YES,N=NO)
260  INPUT $A
270  IF $A = Y THEN 200
280  END
```

27.
```
10  PRINT
20  PRINT "HOURS, PAY"
30  PRINT -----, -----
40  READ H
50  LET P = 3.50H
60  PRINT H, P
70  GOTO 10
80  END
```

Suppose that **L\$ = "TEXAS"** *and* **M\$ = "FLORIDA".**
Write the result of each of the following.

28. L\$ + " AND " + M\$ **29.** LEFT\$(L\$,3)   **30.** RIGHT\$(M\$,5)

Computer Lab Projects

STRING PROCESSING APPLICATIONS

1. Given a letter of the alphabet, decide whether it is a vowel. Print either IS A VOWEL or IS NOT A VOWEL. (NOTE: Do not count Y as a vowel.)

2. Given two words, print the word that contains the greater number of letters. If the words contain the same number of letters, print that they are equal in length.

3. The **DATA** consists of a list of names of people and their ages. Read each person's name and age. Print only the names and ages of those people who are over 65.

4. Revise the program of Exercise 3 so that the user first enters the "target age." For example, if the user types 18, print the names and ages of all people in the list who are over 18.

5. **READ** from **DATA** a list of names. Print only those that begin with **C**.

6. Revise the program of Exercise 5 so that the user first enters the starting letter. For example, if the user types **B**, print any names in the **DATA** that begin with **B**.

7. **READ** from **DATA** a list of names. Print only those that contain exactly five letters.

8. Revise the program of Exercise 7 so that it prints those names that contain five or more letters.

9. Revise the program of Exercise 7 so that the user first enters the number of letters in a name. For example, if the user types 3, print those names in the **DATA** that contain exactly three letters.

10. **READ** from **DATA** a person's first and last names. If the total length of the two names together, including the space between them, is more than 10 characters, print the first and last names. For example, for **JOHN,SMITH** do <u>not</u> print **JOHN SMITH**. However, for **PETER SMITH**, print **PETER SMITH**.

GENERAL APPLICATIONS

11. Given three numbers **A**, **B**, and **C**, print whether $A - B > C$.

12. Given two numbers, print whether their sum is greater than 180.

13. **READ** from **DATA** a list of numbers, two at a time. Print only those pairs of numbers whose sum is greater than 10. For example, for **DATA 4,3, 6,5, 7,3** print **6 5** only.

14. Revise the program of Exercise 13 so that the user may enter the "target number." For example, if the user types 20, print any pair of numbers in the **DATA** list whose sum is greater than 20.

15. Given a number, print whether it is **GREATER THAN 100, EQUAL TO 100**, or **LESS THAN 100**.

16. Revise the program of Exercise 15 so that the user may enter the "target number." For example, if the user types 25, print whether each number that is **INPUT** or **READ** is greater than, equal to, or less than 25.

17. **READ** from **DATA** a list of numbers. Print only those that are greater than 50.

18. Revise the program of Exercise 17 so that the user may enter the "target value." For example, if the user types 75, print any numbers in the **DATA** that are greater than 75.

19. Given three numbers **A**, **B**, and **C**, print whether $A*B = C$.

20. Revise the program of Exercise 19 to print whether the product of any two of the numbers equals the third.

CONSUMER APPLICATIONS

21. The Rocket Bus Company sells tickets as follows. If you buy fewer than five tickets, they cost $1 each. If you buy five or more, they cost $0.75 each. Given the number of tickets a person wants to buy, print the total cost (without tax) of the tickets.

22. Calculate the sales tax on the purchase of a car. If the price of the car is less than $8,000, the tax is 10% of the price. If the price is greater than or equal to $8,000, the tax is 15% of the price. Given the price of a car, print the amount of tax.

23. Revise the program of Exercise 22 as follows. If the price is more than $8000 but less than $10,000, the tax is 15% of the price. If the net price is $10,000 or more, the tax is $500.

24. Suppose that the amount of mileage on a used car determines its value. If the mileage is less than 10,000, the car costs $6500. If the mileage is greater than or equal to 10,000, the cost is $5500. Given the mileage on a used car, print its cost.

25. Revise the program of Exercise 24 as follows. If the mileage is between 10,000 and 20,000 miles, the cost is $5500. If the mileage is 20,000 miles or more, the cost is $4500.

26. Workers at a plant have the choice of putting 5% of their weekly salary into a savings account. Given the weekly salary of an employee, ask whether the employee wishes to put money into the savings account.

    If so, print the amount put into savings and the net amount (weekly salary minus the amount for savings) the worker will take home. If not, print the complete salary as the "take-home pay."

27. Revise the problem of Exercise 26 so that the savings rate is no longer fixed at 5%. If the worker decides to put money into savings, ask what percent of the weekly salary is to be set aside.

28. Suppose that you have $25 to go shopping. Given the amounts of three purchases you would like to make, determine whether you will have enough money to make all three purchases.

MORE CHALLENGING COMPUTER LAB PROJECTS

STRING PROCESSING

29. Given a person's first and last names, ask how the person wants the name printed: first name followed by last name or last name followed by the first name. If the user enters an F, print the first name followed by the last name. If the user enters an L, print the last name followed by the first.

30. Given a word, decide whether the word contains more than five letters. If it does not, print the entire word. If it does, print only the first five letters.

31. Given three names of unequal lengths, print the one that contains the greatest number of letters.

32. Revise the program of Exercise 31 to print the name with the least number of letters.

GENERAL APPLICATIONS

33. Given three numbers, decide whether the numbers are in increasing order. For example, 5, 6, 8 are in increasing order but 7, 8, 8 and 9, 2, 7 are not.

34. Expand the program of Exercise 33 so that, if the numbers are not in increasing order, the program tests whether they are in decreasing order. 8, 4, 1 are in decreasing order but 12, 12, 3 are not.

35. Given three numbers, print them in decreasing order. For example, given 9, 2, 7, print 9, 7, 2. Given 8, 5, 8, print 8, 8, 5.

36. Revise the program of Exercise 35 so that it prints the numbers in increasing order.

37. Given two numbers X and Y, divide the larger by the smaller and print the result. If the smaller number is zero, print **CANNOT DIVIDE**.

CONSUMER APPLICATIONS

38. Assume that the cost, not including tax, for sending a telegram from Minneapolis to Miami is $4.50 for the first 15 words or less, plus $0.20 for each additional word beyond 15. Given the number of words in a telegram, print its cost.

39. A company's pension plan for its retired workers follows this rule. A worker receives $100 a week if the person is over 65 years of age and an additional $30 per week if over 70. Given the age of a retired worker, print that worker's weekly pension amount.

40. Employees of the Sunshine Power Company are given raises as follows: Sales personnel: 12%; managers: 15%. Given an employee's current weekly salary and a code letter (S or M) indicating the job category of the worker, print the amount of the employee's raise.

41. Revise the program of Exercise 40 to add: Production workers (P) with raises of 8%.

42. Suppose that the cost of a telephone call is computed as follows. On Saturday and Sunday, the cost is $1.25 per minute. On other days, the cost is $1.75 per minute. Given the number of minutes of a call and a code letter (S or W) indicating whether it was made on Saturday or Sunday or during the week, print the cost.

ALGEBRA APPLICATIONS

Exercise 43–47 require a background in first-year algebra.

43. Given a positive number N, print the largest positive integer whose square is less than or equal to N. For example, if N = 55, print 7 since $7^2 = 49$ and $8^2 = 64$. (Hint: Use a FOR–NEXT loop.)

44. Revise Exercise 44 to print the largest positive integer whose cube is less than or equal to N.

45. Given a number, multiply it by 5 add 10; multiply by $\frac{3}{5}$; and divide by 3. Then subtract the number you started with. Check that the result is always two.

46. Given a number, add eight to it; multiply by six; subtract nine; divide by three; subtract 13; divide by two. Test that the result always equals the starting number.

APPLICATIONS OF COMPUTERS

LESSONS

FEATURES

Graphics Tablet

MICR

Computers and E-Mail

Database Management Programs

6-1 COMPUTER APPLICATIONS: THE HOME

OBJECTIVE: To write programs for home applications

More and more families are buying computers to use in their homes. While many families enjoy the games they can play on the computer, they also profit from its ability to perform many other routine tasks.

Home computers can be used to monitor a family's bank account. With a word processing program, a computer can help to write the family correspondence. With a filing program, a computer can store recipes, addresses, important dates, and other kinds of information.

EXAMPLE **a.** Write a program to monitor a family's bank account for a week. Have the user enter the amount in the account at the beginning of the week, then each deposit or withdrawal. (Lines 10–70 below explain the system that will be used.)

Program

```
10  PRINT "THIS PROGRAM KEEPS A FAMILY'S"
20  PRINT "WEEKLY BANK ACCOUNT UP-TO-DATE."
30  PRINT "FOR A DEPOSIT, ENTER C (CREDIT)"
40  PRINT "AND THEN THE AMOUNT.  FOR AN"
50  PRINT "EXPENDITURE, ENTER D (DEBIT) AND"
60  PRINT "THE AMOUNT.  TO END THE PROGRAM"
70  PRINT "ENTER E,0."
80  PRINT
90  PRINT "WHAT IS THE BALANCE AT THE"
100  PRINT "BEGINNING OF THE WEEK";
110  INPUT B
120  PRINT "ENTER CREDITS/DEBITS."
130  INPUT X$, A
140  IF X$ = "E" THEN 230
150  IF X$ = "C" THEN 190
160  IF X$ = "D" THEN 210
170  PRINT "BAD ENTRY.  TRY AGAIN."
180  GOTO 130
```

If the computer reaches line 170, the user did not enter "C", "D", or "E".

```
190 LET B = B + A          ←——— X$ was "C"; add A to B.
200 GOTO 130
210 LET B = B - A          ←——— X$ was "D"; subtract A from B.
220 GOTO 130
230 PRINT                  ←——— X$ was "E"; print the final balance.
240 PRINT "NEW BALANCE = $";B
250 END
```

b. Write the output from a sample **RUN** of the program.

Output
```
THIS PROGRAM KEEPS A FAMILY'S
WEEKLY BANK ACCOUNT UP-TO-DATE.
FOR A DEPOSIT, ENTER C (CREDIT)
AND THEN THE AMOUNT.  FOR AN
EXPENDITURE, ENTER D (DEBIT) AND
THE AMOUNT.  TO END THE PROGRAM
ENTER E,0.

WHAT IS THE BALANCE AT THE
BEGINNING OF THE WEEK? 450.15
ENTER CREDITS/DEBITS.
? C,101.75
? D,33.14
? D,17.08
? D,54.23
? C,82.05
? E,0

NEW BALANCE = $ 529.5
```

A computer can be helpful in the home in many other ways.

Suppose that a family decides to paint a room. A computer could calculate the amount of paint that will be needed.

INPUT VARIABLES

1. Length of the room
2. Width of the room
3. Height of the room
4. Number of square feet per gallon

VARIABLES TO BE CALCULATED

1. Total area to be painted
2. Number of gallons needed

In Exercise 7 on page 290, you are asked to develop a method for computing the total area to be painted and the amount of paint needed.

WRITTEN EXERCISES

*What **NEW BALANCE** is printed by the program of the Example for each of the following lists of input values?*

1. 200, D,20, D,10, C,75, C,15, D,25, E,0

2. 525, C,30, C,55, D,27, D,13, C,105, D,84, E,0

In Exercises 3–5, modify the program of the Example as indicated.

3. Instead of having the user enter a C or D to indicate a credit or debit, simply accept a number each time. If the number is positive, consider it a credit. If it is negative, it is a debit.

4. Tell the user when the balance equals or goes below $0.

5. Read all the input from **DATA** statements. Print a record of each credit or debit as well as the final balance. For the sample input used in the Example the output should look like this.

```
        BEGINNING BALANCE = $ 450.15


            CREDITS        DEBITS
            101.75
                           33.14
                           17.08
                           54.23
             82.05


        NEW BALANCE = $ 529.5
```

MORE CHALLENGING EXERCISES

6. Draw a flowchart for the program of the Example.

7. Write a program for the problem outlined at the end of the lesson on page 289. That is, write a program to compute how much paint will be needed to paint a room.

8. Draw a flowchart for the program of Exercise 6 above.

*Write a **BASIC** program for each problem.*

9. Read from **DATA** statements the information for a mailing list. Print the addresses neatly. For example, for **DATA** statements 1000 and 1010, print the addresses that follow. Notice that the city and the state are listed as separate items in the **DATA**.

1000 DATA CARL BLOUIN, 2600 LONDON AVENUE, NEW ORLEANS,LA,70122

1010 DATA RUTH SCHICKEL, 143 MILAN STREET, PITTSBURGH,PA,13437

```
CARL  BLOUIN
2600  LONDON  AVENUE
NEW  ORLEANS,  LA.      70122

RUTH  SCHICKEL
143  MILAN  STREET
PITTSBURGH,  PA.      13427
```

10. Calculate a family's expenses for a month for these four items: utilities, food, recreation, and transportation. For each expense, have the user first enter a code letter (U, F, R, or T) to indicate the type of expense, followed by the amount. When E,0 is entered, print the total spent in each of the four areas as well as the total of all four areas.

11. Expand the program of Exercise 10 to include other types of expenses.

COMPUTER LAB ACTIVITIES

Home Applications

1. Enter and **RUN** the program of the Example on page 288. Use this data.

200, D,20, D,10, C,75, C,15, D,25, E,0

Is the **NEW BALANCE** you calculated for Exercise 1 on page 290 actually printed?

2. RUN the program of the Example again. Use this data.

525, C,30, C,55, D,27, D,13, C,105, D,84, E,0

Is the **NEW BALANCE** you calculated for Exercise 2 on page 290 actually printed?

3. If you did any of Exercises 3–5 on page 290, make the changes you indicated for each exercise. **RUN** the program each time. If necessary, debug each modified program until it produces the required output.

6-2 COMPUTER APPLICATIONS IN BUSINESS: BANKING

OBJECTIVE: To write programs that calculate simple or compound interest

One use of computers in banking is in calculating compound interest. Simple interest is different from compound interest. Suppose a principal of $100 is invested at a 6% yearly **simple interest** rate. After one year, the investment earns .06 × $100 or $6 interest. The $6 in interest is <u>not</u> added to the principal to calculate the interest for the second year. Thus, the interest for the second year is also $6.00. If no more money is invested, the principal remains $100.

If the $100 is invested at 6% **compound interest**, the $6 in interest after the first year <u>is added to</u> the $100. Thus, for the second year, the principal is ($100 + $6), or $106. The second year's interest is .06 × $106 or $6.36. Therefore the principal for the third year is ($106 + $6.36), or **$112.36**.

EXAMPLE **a.** Write a program to calculate the value of an investment after five years at 6% yearly interest. Allow the user to enter the amount invested and to select one of these plans.

Simple interest

Interest compounded yearly

Interest compounded semi-annually (twice a year)

Interest compounded quarterly (four times a year)

Program
```
10 PRINT "THIS PROGRAM CALCULATES THE VALUE"
20 PRINT "OF AN INVESTMENT AFTER 5 YEARS AT"
30 PRINT "AN INTEREST RATE OF 6%."
40 PRINT
50 LET R = .06
60 PRINT "WHAT IS THE AMOUNT INVESTED";
70 INPUT P
80 PRINT "WHICH INTEREST PLAN DO YOU WANT:"
```

```
90  PRINT "        1.  SIMPLE  INTEREST"
100 PRINT "          2.  ANNUAL  COMPOUND  INTEREST"
110 PRINT "          3.  SEMI-ANNUAL  COMPOUND  INTEREST"
120 PRINT "          4.  QUARTERLY  COMPOUND  INTEREST"
130 INPUT C
140 ON C GOTO 150, 190, 250, 310
150 REM   SIMPLE  INTEREST
160 LET I = P * R * 5    ◄───── Interest = Principal × Rate × Time
170 LET P = P + I
180 GOTO 360
190 REM   ANNUAL  COMPOUND  INTEREST
200 FOR Y = 1 TO 5
210 LET I = P * R    ◄───── Compute the interest, I.
220 LET P = P + I    ◄───── Add the interest to the principal.
230 NEXT Y
240 GOTO 360
250 REM   SEMI-ANNUAL  COMPOUND  INTEREST
260 FOR Y = 1 TO 10 ◄───── There are 10 half-years in 5 years.
270 LET I = P * R/2 ◄───── Since R is a yearly interest rate, multiply
280 LET P = P + I             by R/2 for semi-annual interest.
290 NEXT Y
300 GOTO 360
310 REM   QUARTERLY  COMPOUND  INTEREST
320 FOR Y = 1 TO 20 ◄───── There are 20 quarters in 5 years.
330 LET I = P * R/4 ◄───── When interest is compounded four times
340 LET P = P + I             each year, multiply by R/4.
350 NEXT Y
360 PRINT "AMOUNT AFTER 5 YEARS = $";P
370 END
```

b. Write the output from a sample **RUN** of the program.

Output

```
THIS  PROGRAM  CALCULATES  THE  VALUE
OF  AN  INVESTMENT  AFTER  5  YEARS  AT
AN  INTEREST  RATE  OF  6%.

WHAT  IS  THE  AMOUNT  INVESTED?  100
WHICH  INTEREST  PLAN  DO  YOU  WANT:
        1.  SIMPLE  INTEREST
        2.  ANNUAL  COMPOUND  INTEREST
        3.  SEMI-ANNUAL  COMPOUND  INTEREST
        4.  QUARTERLY  COMPOUND  INTEREST
?  4
AMOUNT  AFTER  5  YEARS  =  $  134.686   ◄─── Amount =
                                              Principal + Interest
```

In the program of the Example, statements 80–120 present a menu. A **menu** is a list of choices the computer shows you before it continues a program. Line 140 is an **ON–GOTO** statement that is useful for deciding which plan the user selects. **BASIC's ON–GOTO** statement works as follows. If the variable after **ON** equals 1, the computer jumps to the statement with the first number after **GOTO**. If the expression equals 2, **BASIC** goes to the statement having the second number, and so on. Thus, statement 140 in the program on page 293 works like this.

$$140 \text{ ON C GOTO } 150, \ 190, \ 250, \ 310$$

$$\qquad\qquad\qquad\quad C = 1 \quad\ \ 2 \quad\ \ 3 \quad\ \ 4$$

WRITTEN EXERCISES

1. What is a menu in computer programming?

2. Use an example to explain the difference between simple interest and compound interest.

    For Exercises 3–6, consider the statement below.

    ```
    100 ON A GOTO 200, 220, 240, 260
    ```

    Which statement will the computer jump to if A has these values?

3. 3   **4.** 2   **5.** 1   **6.** 4

7. Write an **ON–GOTO** statement that tells the computer to jump to statement 350 if $X = 1$, to statement 410 if $X = 2$, and to statement 520 if $X = 3$.

    In Exercises 8–10, modify the program of the Example as indicated.

8. After printing the amount after five years (statement 360), ask the user if another calculation is desired.

9. Instead of fixing the interest rate at 6%, allow the user to enter the interest rate.

10. Instead of calculating the interest for five years, allow the user to enter the number of years.

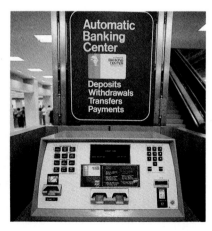

MORE CHALLENGING EXERCISES

For Exercises 11–13, write a **BASIC** *program for each problem.*

11. Given the amount invested, the interest rate, and the number of years of the investment, print the amount of simple interest.

12. Revise the program of Exercise 11 to print the amount of compound interest where the interest is compounded once a year.

13. Suppose that $1000 is to be invested with the interest compounded yearly. Given the interest rate, calculate and print the number of years it will take for the principal to double (equal or exceed $2000).

Banking By Machine

14. Write a **BASIC** program containing an **ON–GOTO** statement for this problem. Allow the user to enter two numbers X and Y. Then display a menu that allows the user to tell the computer to add, subtract (X − Y), multiply, or divide the numbers (X/Y). Print the answer to the calculation that is requested.

15. Expand the program of Exercise 14 so that, if subtraction is selected, the user is asked to specify X − Y or Y − X. Similarly, if division is selected, ask the user to specify X/Y or Y/X.

16. Expand the division section of the program of Exercise 15. If the user selects X/Y and Y = 0, print **DIVISION NOT POSSIBLE**. Similarly, if the user chooses Y/X and X = 0, print **DIVISION NOT POSSIBLE**.

17. Many forms of **BASIC** allow a statement such as the following.

```
ON C GOSUB 300,400,700
```

Rewrite the program of the Example so that the statements computing each type of interest are in a subroutine. After returning to the main program from the appropriate subroutine, print the amount after five years. Then ask the user if another calculation is desired.

Banking

Enter and **RUN** *the program of the Example on pages 292–293. Use the input values listed in each exercise.*

1. $250; simple interest

2. $700; semi-annual compound interest

3. $425; quarterly compound interest

4. $900; annual compound interest

5. **RUN** the program four more times. Each time, enter an investment of $1000 and select each of the four interest plans. Compare the final amounts after five years under each plan.

> *For Exercises 6–8:*
>
> *a. Modify the program of the Example as specified.*
>
> *b.* **RUN** *the program. If necessary, make further changes until it produces the required output.*

6. Exercise 8 on page 294   7. Exercise 9 on page 294   8. Exercise 10 on page 294

EXPLORE: ON–GOTO STATEMENTS

9. Enter and run the program of the Example on pages 292–293. When the menu of interest choices is displayed, type 5. What happens?

10. **RUN** the program again. Type 0 for the interest plan. What does the computer do?

11. To the program of the Example on pages 292–293, add these statements.

```
143 PRINT "ENTER 1, 2, 3, OR 4, PLEASE."
146 GOTO 130
```

RUN the program again. Type 0 for the interest plan. What does the computer do?

Did You Know?

A **graphics tablet** is a kind of electronic drawing board. When the user presses down on the tablet with a special electronic pen, the computer lights up corresponding points on the screen. The computer can also store the drawing in its memory or on a disk.

COMPUTERS AND E-MAIL

With the increased use of microcomputers in homes and offices, electronic mail or **E-mail** is becoming very popular. E-mail uses computers to transmit memos, letters, or manuscripts from a sender to an **electronic mailbox** where they can be accessed by the addressee. Thousands of home computer users and businesses are using this modern delivery service to send personal letters and corporate correspondence thousands of miles in mere seconds. E-mail also makes it easy to send the same letter to several people at the same time.

Large companies are using in-house E-mail systems to send interoffice memos from one executive's desk to another. Executives receive messages without the errors that are sometimes caused by relaying messages from one person to another. While on business trips in distant cities, executives with portable computers can dial into their corporate computer systems and receive their E-mail.

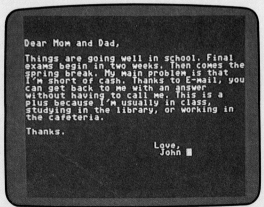

However, there are some problems with E-mail delivery systems. For example, a letter placed inside an envelope gives more privacy than one in a national or corporate computer system. Electronic mailboxes can be opened by the wrong people if they have the right code. Another drawback is that, to be completely efficient, both the receiver and the sender of E-mail must have access to the computer network that will carry the message.

PROJECTS

1. List some advantages and disadvantages of E-mail.

2. Contact a business in your area that uses E-mail. Report your findings to the class.

6-3 COMPUTER APPLICATIONS: SCIENCE

OBJECTIVES:

> To write a program that converts Celsius temperatures to Fahrenheit temperatures
>
> To write as decimals numbers expressed in BASIC's E-form

CELSIUS/FAHRENHEIT TEMPERATURES

Many well-known applications of computers are in science. Without computers, the United States could not have put men on the Moon in 1969. Computers have contributed to many advances in medicine.

EXAMPLE **a.** Write a program to print a table for converting Celsius temperatures to Fahrenheit temperatures. Include Celsius temperatures of 0, 5, 10, . . . , 100.

Program

```
100 PRINT "THIS PROGRAM CONVERTS CELSIUS"
110 PRINT "TEMPERATURES TO FAHRENHEIT."
120 PRINT
130 PRINT "CELSIUS","FAHRENHEIT"
140 PRINT
150 FOR C = 0 TO 100 STEP 5
160 LET F = 9/5 * C + 32
170 PRINT C, F
180 NEXT C
190 PRINT
200 END
```

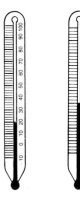

b. Write the output from a **RUN** of a program.

Output

CELSIUS	FAHRENHEIT	CELSIUS	FAHRENHEIT
0	32	55	131
5	41	60	140
10	50	65	149
15	59	70	158
20	68	75	167
25	77	80	176
30	86	85	185
35	95	90	194
40	104	95	203
45	113	100	212
50	122		

The formula in statement 70 of Example 1 involves three operations, division (/), multiplication, (*), and addition, (+). As will be explained in the next lesson, a computer automatically does division or multiplication before addition. To change this order, parentheses must be used. Since there are no parentheses in statement 70, the formula will be evaluated in this way.

$$160 \ \text{LET} \ F \ = \ 9/5 \ * \ C \ + \ 32$$

$$\uparrow \quad \uparrow \quad \uparrow$$
$$1 \quad 2 \quad 3$$

E–FORM

In science and in mathematics, very large and very small numbers are often written in a special form called **exponential form**. For example, in exponential form,

14.358   is written as $\mathbf{1.4358 \times 10^1}$,

and   **.00891**   is written as $\mathbf{8.91 \times 10^{-3}}$.

In **BASIC**, the computer prints very large or very small numerical output in its own exponential form, called **E–form**. Thus, in **BASIC**,

$\mathbf{1.4358 \times 10^1}$ is written as   **1.4358E+1**,

and $\mathbf{8.91 \times 10^{-3}}$ is written as   **8.91E−3**.

In E–form, the E stands for "exponent." It refers to the exponent of 10 that follows the E.

EXAMPLES OF BASIC E–FORM

BASIC E–FORM	Exponential Form	Decimal Form
9.8712E+3	9.8712×10^3	9871.2
1.034E−1	1.034×10^{-1}	0.1034
7.15863E+2	7.15863×10^2	715.863

When a computer prints an answer in E–form, you have to convert it to decimal form.

RULE	To write a number expressed in **BASIC's** E–form as a decimal:

1. When the exponent of 10 is *positive,* move the decimal point to the *right* the number of places equal to the exponent.

2. When the exponent of 10 is *negative,* move the decimal point to the *left* the number of places equal to the exponent without the negative symbol.

EXAMPLE 2   Write each number in decimal form.

      a. $4.00716E + 4$ **b.** $7.48761E - 3$

Solutions   **a.** Since E = +4, move the decimal point 4 places to the right.

           $4.00716E + 4 = 40071.6$

      b. Since E = −3, move the decimal point 3 places to the left.

           $7.48761E - 3 = .00748761$

WRITTEN EXERCISES

In Exercises 1–4, modify the program of the Example as indicated.

1. Center the two columns of output on your screen or printer.

2. Change the list of Celsius temperatures to 50, 40, 30, 20, 10, 0, and −10.

3. Begin by asking the user to enter the starting and ending values for the Celsius temperatures, as well as the amount of increase or decrease between temperatures.

4. Read from **DATA** statements the starting and ending Celsius temperatures as well as the amount of increase or decrease between temperatures.

Meteorologists use computers to predict temperatures and weather patterns.

For Exercises 5–12, write each number expressed in **BASIC**'s *E–form as a decimal.*

5. $1.35462E+1$ **6.** $7.98143E+3$ **7.** $5.40831E-2$ **8.** $9.11283E-4$

9. $8.10327E+6$ **10.** $1.97602E-3$ **11.** $2.18876E-9$ **12.** $6.99724E+20$

13. Which of these numbers written in **BASIC**'s E–form has the largest value?

$$8.76123E+2 \qquad 7.54542E+1 \qquad 1.08764E+7$$

14. Which of these numbers written in **BASIC**'s E–form has the smallest value?

$$9.30879E-6 \qquad 4.52133E-4 \qquad 1.00812E-2$$

MORE CHALLENGING EXERCISES

15. Write a program that prints a table for converting Fahrenheit temperatures to Celsius temperatures. Include Fahrenheit temperatures of 0, 5, 10, . . . , 100. Use this formula:
$$C = 5/9*(F-32)$$

16. Modify the program of Exercise 15 so that the user may enter the beginning and ending Fahrenheit temperatures, as well as the amount of increase or decrease between temperatures.

17. Galileo developed the formula $s = 16t^2$ to calculate the distance, s, that an object falls in t seconds (where s is measured in feet).
Write a program that prints a table of values for t and s where $t = 1, 2, 3, 4, . . . , 10$.

18. Modify the program of Exercise 17 so that the user may enter the beginning and ending values of t as well as the amount of increase between successive values of t.

19. Write a program to find density, **D**, mass, **M**, or volume, **V**, where **D = M/V**. Have the user enter three values, typing a 0 for the unknown quantity. For example, an input of 50,0,250, means that mass is not known and must be computed from the given density, 50, and the given volume, 250.

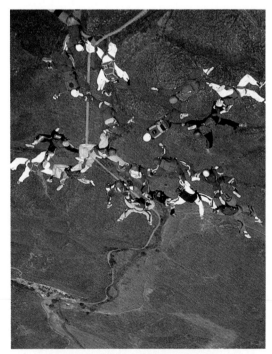

Skydivers fall freely at speeds of more than 160 kilometers per hour.

Science

1. Enter and **RUN** this program. Is the output the same as the output shown in the Example on page 298?

```
100 PRINT "THIS PROGRAM CONVERTS CELSIUS"
110 PRINT "TEMPERATURES TO FAHRENHEIT."
120 PRINT
130 PRINT "CELSIUS","FAHRENHEIT"
140 PRINT
150 FOR C = 0 TO 100 STEP 5
160 LET F = 9/5 * C + 32
170 PRINT C, F
180 NEXT C
190 PRINT
200 END
```

For Exercises 2–5:

a. *Modify the program of the Example as indicated in each exercise.*

b. **RUN** *the program. If necessary, make further changes in the program until it produces the desired output.*

2. Exercise 1, page 300

3. Exercise 2, page 300

4. Exercise 3, page 300

5. Exercise 4, page 300

For Exercises 6–13, enter each direct command. Write the output.

6. PRINT $2\uparrow4$

7. PRINT $2\uparrow6$

8. PRINT $2\uparrow8$

9. PRINT $2\uparrow10$

10. PRINT $2\uparrow15$

11. PRINT $2\uparrow20$

12. PRINT $2\uparrow30$

13. PRINT $2\uparrow50$

14. For which commands in Exercise 6–13 did the computer print the output in E–form?

15. Enter and **RUN** the program on the right. Note the output. For which values of I did the computer print answers in E–form?

```
10 FOR I = 10 TO 30
20 PRINT "2↑";I;" = ";2↑I
30 NEXT I
40 END
```

16. If you have access to more than one type of computer, **RUN** the program of Exercise 15 on as many as you can. Compare results.

17. In the program of Exercise 15, change statement 10 as shown. **RUN** the program. Does the computer print an answer for every value of I or does it print a message about **OVERFLOW?** Overflow means that the program generated a number too large for the computer's memory to hold.

```
10 FOR I = 10 TO 50
```

6-4 COMPUTER APPLICATIONS: MATHEMATICS

OBJECTIVE:

> ### To evaluate BASIC formulas

Suppose that you type this direct command into a computer.

$$PRINT\ 2 + 3 * 5$$

Will the output be 25 or 17? The output will be 17 because the computer follows the usual mathematical rule that multiplication or division is done before addition or subtraction. Thus far in this text, arithmetic formulas have involved only one operation. However, in **BASIC** and in mathematics, two or more operations often appear in the same formula.

EXAMPLE 1 Write each formula in **BASIC**.

a. $20 - 3 \times 6$ **b.** $5^2 (4 + 2)$

Solutions   **a.** $20 - 3 * 6$ **b.** $5 \uparrow 2 * (4 + 2)$

In **BASIC**, the multiplication symbol, *, must always be shown. Thus, $3(8 + 4)$ is entered into a computer as $3 * (8 + 4)$. Note that the blank spaces in a **BASIC** formula are optional. Thus, $3 * (8 + 4)$ may be typed into a computer as $3*(8 + 4)$ or as $3*(8+4)$ or as $3 *(8 + 4)$, and so on.

When two or more operations appear in a **BASIC** expression or formula, the computer follows the order of operations listed below.

Order of Operations Followed by Computers

1. Raising to a power is done first.
2. Multiplications and divisions are done in order from left to right.
3. Additions and subtractions are done next in order from left to right.
4. Parentheses are used to change the order listed in 1, 2, and 3. Operations in parentheses are done first, from the innermost parentheses outward.

The computer will evaluate (find the value of) a formula if you type it into the computer as a direct command.

EXAMPLE 2 Write the output from each command.

    a. PRINT 20 − 3 * 6   **b.** PRINT 5 ↑ 2 * (4 + 2) ←——— 5 ↑ 2 *means* 5^2.

Solutions

    a. 20 − 3 * 6   **b.** 5 ↑ 2 * (4 + 2)
         20 −   18   5 ↑ 2 *   6   ←——— 5^2 *means* 5 × 5.
            2   25 * 6
                           150

In **BASIC** programs, formulas usually appear in **LET** statements. **LET** statements may include one or more variables.

EXAMPLE 3 Write each formula as a **BASIC LET** statement.

    a. $y = 2(l + w)$ **b.** $a = \dfrac{x + y}{2}$

Solutions **a.** LET Y = 2 * (L + W)   **b.** LET A = (X + Y)/2

To evaluate a formula such as **LET Y = 2 * (L + W)**, the computer substitutes the current values of L and W and performs the calculations based on the rules for order of operations listed on page 303.

EXAMPLE 4 What value is assigned to **Z** by each **LET** statement if X = 12 and Y = 4?

    a. LET Z = (X + Y) ↑ 2   **b.** LET Z = 2 * Y / X

Solutions **a.** LET Z = (X + Y) ↑ 2   **b.** LET Z = 2 * Y / X
               = (12 + 4) ↑ 2   = 2 * 4 / 12
               = 16 ↑ 2 ←——— 16^2 = 8 / 12
               = 256   = .75

       Z is assigned **256**.   Z is assigned **.75**.

WRITTEN EXERCISES

For Exercises 1–18, write each formula in **BASIC**. *Use parentheses only where necessary.*

1. $45 - 6 \times 7$

2. $\dfrac{18}{3} + 5$

3. $10 \times 20 \div 5$

4. $3^2 + 4^2$

5. $(3 + 4)^2$

6. $8 \times 9 + 4$

7. $6 - \dfrac{9}{4}$

8. $14 \div 7 \times 3$

9. $17 - 9 + 6$

10. $4(4 + 5)$

11. $(8 - 2)6$

12. $40 - 8 \times 5$

13. $12 \div (3 + 3)$

14. $\dfrac{5 + 6}{2}$

15. $9 - 5^2$

16. $(10 - 4)^2$

17. $\dfrac{5}{9 - 7}$

18. $\dfrac{18}{5 \times 2}$

19. Evaluate (find the value of) each **BASIC** formula you wrote for Exercises 1–18.

For Exercises 20–38, write the output from each command.

20. PRINT 4 + 5

21. PRINT 2 * 8 + 3

22. PRINT 3*(9 − 4)

23. PRINT 30 − 5 * 6

24. PRINT 5*11/2

25. PRINT 40/2*3

26. PRINT (14 + 7)/3

27. PRINT 14/(9 − 5)

28. PRINT 50/5*2

29. PRINT 50/(5*2)

30. PRINT 6 ↑ 2

31. PRINT (8 − 1) ↑ 2

32. PRINT 100 − 4↑2

33. PRINT 2 ↑ 3

34. PRINT (7 + 5)*9

35. PRINT 2 * 3 ↑ 2

36. PRINT 2 * 3 + 5 * 4 − 4 ↑ 2

37. PRINT (2 * 3) ↑ 2

38. PRINT 5 ↑ 2 − 4 ↑ 2 + 3 * 5

39. What is the difference in output between these two commands?

PRINT "6−4"   and   PRINT 6−4

For Exercises 40–48, write each formula as a **BASIC LET** *statement. Use parentheses only where necessary.*

40. $c = 2ab$

41. $y = mx + b$

42. $k = n(n - 1)$

43. $s = \dfrac{.5t}{w}$

44. $v = \dfrac{b + h}{3}$

45. $c = a^2 - 20$

46. $d = (90 - e)^2$

47. $r = 3.14s^2$

48. $z = 25v + 500$

For Exercises 49–54, determine the value assigned to Y by each **LET** statement.

Use the values **U** = 20 and **V** = 5.

49. LET Y = 10 * U + 15

50. LET Y = V ↑ 2 − U

51. LET Y = (U − V) ↑ 2

52. LET Y = 180 − (U + V)

53. LET Y = U / V * 3

54. LET Y = U * V / 4

MORE CHALLENGING EXERCISES

For Exercises 55–62, determine what value is assigned to D by each **LET** statement.

Use the values A = 3, B = 4, and C − 2.

55. LET D = A + B * C

56. LET D = A * B + C

57. LET D = A + B/C

58. LET D = (A + B)/C

59. LET D = A + C ↑ 2

60. LET D = (A + C) ↑ 2

61. LET D = A*(B + C)

62. LET D = (A + B)*(B − C)

For Exercises 63–71, write each formula as a **BASIC LET** statement.

63. $y = x^2 - 2x$

64. $w = \frac{1}{2}bh$

65. $t = r^2 + s^2$

66. $k = x + \frac{y^2}{7}$

67. $m = \frac{a - b}{c - d}$

68. $k = \frac{r - s}{4}$

69. $f = (2a - 10)^2$

70. $n = 2j - 3(k - 1)$

71. $u = (2x - y)(x + 3y)$

A computer keyboard has no symbol for square root ($\sqrt{}$). However, **BASIC** uses the letters **SQR** to indicate square root.

For Exercises 72–74, evaluate each computer formula.

72. SQR(16)

73. SQR(16 + 9)

74. 15/SQR(16 − 7)

For Exercises 75–77, write each formula in **BASIC**.

75. $\sqrt{45}$

76. $\sqrt{24 + 12}$

77. $\sqrt{5^2 + 12^2}$

COMPUTER LAB ACTIVITIES

Order of Operations

1. Type the direct command at the right into the computer. What is the output? Which operation did the computer perform first, addition or multiplication?

   `PRINT 2 + 3 * 5`

2. Type this direct command into the computer. Is the output the same as the output of Exercise 1? Do blank spaces in a formula make any difference in the way the computer evaluates the formula?

   `PRINT 2+3*5`

3. Enter the commands of Example 2 on page 304 into the computer. Is the output the same as the output shown in the Example?

4. To check the answers to Example 4a on page 304, enter and **RUN** the program shown at the right. Does the computer print 256 for Z?

   ```
   10 LET X = 12
   20 LET Y = 4
   30 LET Z = (X + Y)↑2
   40 PRINT Z
   50 END
   ```

5. To check the answer to Example 4b, change statement 30 of the program of Exercise 4 to that shown at the right. **RUN** the program. Is the output .75?

   ```
   30 LET Z = 2 * Y / X
   ```

6. On your computer, enter each command of Exercises 20–38 on page 305. Did you predict each output correctly?

EXPLORE: SQR FUNCTION

For Exercises 7–10, enter each direct command into your computer. Write the output each time.

7. PRINT SQR(3 + 4)

8. PRINT SQR(3) + SQR(4)

9. PRINT SQR(25 − 9)

10. PRINT SQR(25) − SQR(9)

For Exercises 11–14, refer to your answers for Exercises 7–10 to answer each question.

11. Does $\sqrt{3 + 4} = \sqrt{3} + \sqrt{4}$?

12. Does $\sqrt{25 - 9} = \sqrt{25} - \sqrt{9}$?

13. In general, does $\sqrt{a + b} = \sqrt{a} + \sqrt{b}$?

14. In general, does $\sqrt{a - b} = \sqrt{a} - \sqrt{b}$?

DATABASE MANAGEMENT PROGRAMS

A **database** (also called **data bank**) is an electronic filing system. Instead of filing information on cards or in folders, a database management program stores records on diskettes or a hard disk. Many of these programs allow the user to set up a data file, make changes in the file, and obtain information from it.

There are many kinds of computer databases. Here are some examples.

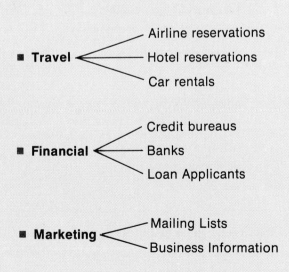

- **Travel**
  - Airline reservations
  - Hotel reservations
  - Car rentals

- **Financial**
  - Credit bureaus
  - Banks
  - Loan Applicants

- **Marketing**
  - Mailing Lists
  - Business Information

Suppose that a person wishes to set up a file of birthdays of relatives and friends. In the file, the key unit of data, the **record,** will correspond to a person. Each record can be subdivided into **fields,** such as name and birthday. The birthday field can be broken down into **subfields,** such as month and day. This allows the user to ask the computer for a list of persons with birthdays in a particular month. Here is a design of the record.

Field	Maximum Number of Characters	Sample Value
Name	20	Aunt Lucille
Birthday	4	
Subfield: Month	2	06
Subfield: Day	2	21
Number/Street	20	731 Woodfield Avenue
City/State	20	Knoxville, TN
Zip Code	9	43561

To create a file, the user loads the **Database Management** program and selects the **Create File** option from the opening menu. Then the user enters the number of fields, the name of each field, the size of each field (number of characters), and the subfields. Next, prompted by the program, the user enters the data for each record. The file is now ready for use. After exiting to the main menu, the user can select the **Search File** option and obtain a listing on the screen of relatives and friends who have birthdays in a particular month. The **Print File** option allows the user to obtain a printout of the listings.

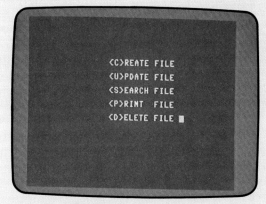

```
<C>REATE FILE
<U>PDATE FILE
<S>EARCH FILE
<P>RINT FILE
<D>ELETE FILE █
```

Typical Opening Menu

The **Update File** option allows the user to add records to the file, to delete records, and to change records.

PROJECTS

1. List three databases that would be useful to you.

2. List three ways in which a business could use a database management system.

3. List three fields of each record in a file that could contain an entry for each book in a person's home library.

Chapter Summary

Section 6–1   **1.** A computer can help a family with such tasks as keeping its bank account up–to–date or computing how much paint will be needed to paint a room.

Section 6–2   **2.** One common use of computers in banking is the calculation of simple and compound interest.

3. A **menu** is a list of choices a program gives the user. An **ON-GOTO** statement is useful for sending the computer to the section of the program that corresponds to the user's menu selection.

Section 6–3   **4.** Programs are useful in problems related to science, such as in converting Celsius temperatures to Fahrenheit temperatures.

5. When numerical output in **BASIC** consists of either very large or very small numbers, the computer prints the numbers in exponential form. Here is an example.

$$1.27536E + 2 \text{ means } 1.27536 \times 10^2$$

Section 6–4   **6.** **BASIC** follows the usual order of operations of mathematics. That is, raising to a power ($\uparrow$) is done first. Then multiplication and division are done (in order from left to right) before addition and subtraction. When a mathematical expression contains parentheses, the operations inside the parentheses are done first.

Chapter Review

1. Write a program that helps a family plan its budget. Given the total amount of income and the percents to be budgeted for savings, entertainment, utilities, food, clothing, and medical, print the amount that can be spent in each category. For example, if the total income is $20,000 and 3% is to be spent on entertainment, then .03 × 20,000 or $600 is budgeted for entertainment.

Computers link the home investor to the stock exchange

2. Given the amount of an investment, the yearly interest rate, and the number of years, write a program that calculates the value of the investment after that number of years. Assume that the interest is compounded twice yearly.

3. Given a Celsius temperature, write a program that prints the corresponding Fahrenheit temperature.

For Exercises 4–6, write each number in decimal form.

4. $9.01326E+3$

5. $4.82034E-2$

6. $6.71385E-1$

Write the output.

7. PRINT 2 * 8 − 3

8. PRINT 4 * (7 + 1)

9. PRINT 5*4/2

10. PRINT 23 / (9 − 1)

11. PRINT (9 + 1) ↑ 2

12. PRINT 12/2*3

*Write each formula as a **BASIC** formula. Use parentheses only where necessary.*

13. $y = 2 - 3x$

14. $e = mc^2$

15. $x = \dfrac{2z + 6}{z - 2}$

16. $w = 14(x - 4)$

*If X = 10 and Y = 8, what value is assigned to Z by each of these **LET** statements?*

17. LET Z = 3 * X + Y

18. LET Z = X*(Y + 1)

19. LET Z = (X + Y)/2

20. LET Z = 36/(X + Y)

21. LET Z = (X − Y)/(X + Y)

22. LET Z = X ↑ 2 − Y ↑ 2

Chapter Test

For Exercises 1–4, refer to the statement below.

```
50 ON X GOTO 90, 130, 70, 150
```

Which statement will the computer jump to if **X** *has the given values?*

1. 3   **2.** 1   **3.** 4   **4.** 2

For Exercises 5–7, write each number as a decimal.

5. $8.10346E-4$ **6.** $7.89113E+2$ **7.** $9.91543E+3$

For Exercises 8–10, write each formula in **BASIC**.

8. $w = 4x + 7$ **9.** $d = c^2 - 12$ **10.** $y = \dfrac{7 - 2r}{10 + r}$

If F = 12 and G = 6, what value is assigned to H by each of these **LET** *statements?*

11. LET H = F * 2 + G   **12.** LET H = (F + G)/9   **13.** LET H = F↑2 − 3*G

14. Given the amount to be invested, the interest rate, and the number of years the money will be invested write a program that calculates the total value of the investment after the given number of years. Assume that the interest will be compounded four times a year.

Cumulative Review: Chapters

Part 1

Choose the correct answer. Choose a, b, c, or d.

1. If K has the value of 3 in the following statement, to what statement number will the computer jump?

```
ON K GOTO 250,270,290,310
```

    a. 250   **b.** 270   **c.** 290   **d.** 310

2. What is the decimal form of $3.28764E-3$?

    a. 328.764   **b.** 3287.64   **c.** .00328764   **d.** .000328764

3. What is the output for **PRINT 10/5*2**?

    a. 4   **b.** 1   **c.** 2   **d.** 5

4. Which of the following is an example of software?

    a. CPU   **b.** RAM   **c.** DOS   **d.** ROM

5. Name the first electronic digital computer.

    a. UNIVAC I   **b.** MARK I   **c.** Analytical engine   **d.** ENIAC

6. Which of the following is another name for a personal computer?

    a. microcomputer   **b.** minicomputer   **c.** mainframe   **d.** time-sharing

7. Which of the following is not a direct command?

    a. RUN   **b.** 60 END   **c.** PRINT "HERE IT IS"   **d.** NEW

8. Which of the following is correct and contains no syntax errors?

    a. PRINT "THIS IS MINE"   **b.** 20 LET X\$ + Y\$ = Z\$

    c. 40 PRINT READY?   **d.** INPUT LEN(K\$)

9. What is loading a computer's operating system called?

    a. listing   **b.** booting   **c.** DOS   **d.** translating

10. Which of the following languages was created first?

    a. BASIC   **b.** FORTRAN   **c.** COBOL   **d.** Pascal

11. What is the output for this program?

    a. 25   **b.** 6

    c. 150   **d.** 35

```
10 LET R = 30
20 LET T = 5
30 LET S = R * T
40 PRINT S
50 END
```

12. Suppose that 8 is entered for G in this program. What is the output?

    a. 8   **b.** 6

    c. 4   **d.** 2

```
10 INPUT G
20 LET M = G/4
30 PRINT M
40 END
```

13. If A\$ = "KALAATU", what is the value of LEFT\$(A\$,4)?

    a. KALA   **b.** AATU   **c.** LAAT   **d.** ALAK

14. If B\$ = "I AM HERE", what is the value of LEN(B\$)?

    a. 1   **b.** 3   **c.** 7   **d.** 9

15. Which of these is the flowchart symbol for a decision?

a.

b.

c.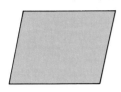

d.

16. What is the **BASIC** command that puts a character directly into a memory location?

    a. PEEK   **b.** PUT   **c.** POP   **d.** POKE

17. Which of the following is an application of graphics?

    a. digital watch   **b.** video games   **c.** microwave oven   **d.** food processor

18. If $A = 10$ and $B = 50$, what value is assigned to C by this statement.

$$\text{LET } C = B/A\uparrow 2$$

    a. 2   **b.** 2.5   **c.** .5   **d.** 25

19. How is "A greater than or equal to 6" written in BASIC?

    a. $A>6$ **b.** $A<6$ **c.** $A<=6$ **d.** $A>=6$

Part 2

20. Complete this program.

Problem: Print the odd whole numbers from 51 through 75.

```
10   ?   PRINT ODD NUMBERS 51 TO 75
20 FOR C =  ?   TO   ?   STEP   ?
30 PRINT   ?
40 NEXT   ?
50 END
```

21. Write the output after the computer does the given steps.

```
LET A = 40
LET B = 800/A
PRINT B
```

22. Write the missing statement.
```
10 REM   TAKE A FOURTH OF IT
20 PRINT "PLEASE TYPE A NUMBER."
30   ?
40 LET F = N/4
50 PRINT "A FOURTH IS ";  ?
60 END
```

23. Correct any errors in the following program.
```
10 PRINT "WHAT IS THE NAME OF A FISH"
20 INPUT F
30 LET LEN(F&) = C
40 PRINT F$;HAS;C;"CHARACTERS IN IT."
50 DONE
```

24. If J$ = "JEAN", write the instruction involving J$ that will produce the output below.

JEAN IS NINE

25. On your microcomputer, what command is needed to clear the screen?

26. Write the output for the program below.
```
100 FOR G=100 TO 10 STEP -10
110 PRINT G
120 NEXT G
130 END
```

27. Draw a flowchart for this problem.

Problem: Given a word, print whether the last letter of the word is "G".

28. Write a program for the flowchart you drew for Exercise 27.

Did You Know?

MICR stands for **Magnetic Ink Character Reading.** In this system which was developed for use in banking, specially-shaped digits and other symbols are printed on each check and deposit slip a bank issues. When a bank receives a check, machines read the magnetized ink symbols and store the code numbers on magnetic tape. The tape is then read by a computer which updates the customer's account.

PAY TO THE
ORDER OF _____

_____

NORTH
BANK

North Bank, N.A.
Lake Road
Orlando, Florida

FOR
⑈123⑈029⑈120⑈

Computer Lab Projects

General Instructions

The Exercises in the **Computer Lab Projects** *are intended to be used for individual student assignment.*

1. Write a program for each exercise. Unless otherwise directed, programs may use either **INPUT** or **READ/DATA** statements.

2. **RUN** each program. Check whether it produces the required output. If it does not, revise it until it does.

STRING PROCESSING APPLICATIONS

1. Convert a list of numerical grades to letter grades as shown at the right.

94–100:	**A**
85–93:	**B**
77–84:	**C**
70–76:	**D**
Below 70:	**F**

2. Expand the program of Exercise 1 as follows. In addition to converting the numerical grades to letters, count and print the number of A's, the number of B's, and so on.

3. Have the user enter a string. Then **READ** from **DATA** a list of strings. Print whether the user's string is in the **DATA** list.

4. Given a person's name and address, print the name and address, centering horizontally and vertically on the screen or printer page.

5. Given a two–digit whole number, print the number with the digits interchanged. For example, given 37, print 73. (HINT: Input the number as a string.)

6. Revise the program of Exercise 5 using three-digit whole numbers. For example, given 397, print 793.

GENERAL APPLICATIONS

7. Given each player's name on a basketball team, the total points scored, and the number of games played, calculate each player's average points–per–game. Print the output in four labeled columns as shown.

PLAYER, GAMES, POINTS, POINTS/GAME

8. Start with your year of birth. Multiply this number by five; add 25; multiply by 20; add your age; add 365; subtract 865. The first four digits of the number that results should be the year you were born. The last two digits tell your age.

CONSUMER APPLICATIONS

9. Given the amount of an investment and the interest rate, calculate the value of the investment after one year. Assume that the interest is compounded daily for 365 days.

10. A person wants to invest some money, part of it at one interest rate and part at another rate.

Given the two simple interest rates and the amount to be invested at each rate, calculate the total value of the investment each year for ten years. Print the output in four labeled columns as follows.

YEAR, FIRST AMOUNT, SECOND AMOUNT, TOTAL AMOUNT

11. Given a person's present age, calculate how much the person must save each year in order to have $100,000 by age 50.

12. Print an interest table for an investment of $1000 at simple interest rates of 5%, 6%, and 7%. Print the amount of interest for 1, 2, 3, . . . , 10 years. The output should be in the form shown.

YEAR	5%	6%	7%
1	50	60	70
2	100	120	140
.	...	...	...
10	500	600	700

13. Revise the program of Exercise 12 so that the interest is compounded yearly.

14. Revise the program of Exercise 12 so that the interest is compounded quarterly.

15. Read from **DATA** the sales total for each of the ten sales agents of a company. Print how many of the agents sold more than $500.

GRAPHICS APPLICATIONS

16. Pick any point on the screen. Light the point and then draw lines radiating out from it.

17. Draw a picture of your computer on the screen or printer.

18. If your computer's **BASIC** has a command for drawing a circle, draw a picture of a soccer field.

19. Print a block of asterisks A positions wide, B positions deep, and C positions from the left margin. Have the user enter values for A, B, and C.

20. Print your computer's name in large letters.

21. Draw a square on the screen. Then draw the same size square moved over (but overlapping the first square). Continue in this way until the screen is filled with copies of the square. If you have a color system, make the squares different colors.

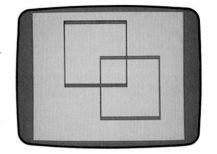

22. Draw a castle on the screen or printer.

23. Draw a face on the screen or printer.

24. Draw a picture of a house on your computer's screen or printer.

MORE CHALLENGING COMPUTER LAB PROJECTS

STRING PROCESSING APPLICATIONS

25. Translate whole numbers into words. Use numbers from 1 to 99. For example, given 87, print **EIGHTY-SEVEN**.

26. Change a date from the form 05/10/68 to the form May 10, 1968.

27. Convert a telephone number from letters and numbers to all numbers. On a telephone dial, the letters A, B, and C correspond to the number 2, DEF correspond to 3, GHI correspond to 4, JKL correspond to 5, MNO correspond to 6, PRS correspond to 7, TUV correspond to 8, and WXY correspond to 9.

28. Change any given English word into Pig Latin. To do this, take the first letter, place it at the end of the word, then add **AY**. For example, **COMPUTER** becomes **OMPUTERCAY**.

GENERAL APPLICATIONS

29. Given the day of the week on which the first day of a month falls and the number of days in the month, print the calendar for the month.

30. Program the computer to tell a story with appropriate text and graphics.

CONSUMER APPLICATIONS

31. Given the amount of an investment and the interest rate, calculate how many years it will take for the investment to be worth a thousand dollars. Have the interest compounded four times a year.

32. Write a foreign currency exchange program.

Assume that the user has some U.S. money that is to be traded for foreign money.

Offer a menu of at least three countries.

Depending on which country is selected, the program uses the current exchange rate to print the equivalent amount in the foreign currency. (Research is suggested to determine the current exchange rates.)

33. Help the Reliable Robot Rental Company calculate a customer's charge for renting one of its robots. The rate is $50 for the first hour and $25 for each additional hour. Given the number of hours the robot was rented, print the total charge.

34. **READ** from **DATA** the amount sold by a company for each of the 12 months of a year. Print the average monthly amount sold by the company.

GRAPHICS APPLICATIONS

35. Simulate fireworks exploding on the screen.

36. Draw an object, such as a flying saucer, on the screen. Make it move across or up and down the screen.

37. Make a point bounce between two "walls."

38. Revise the program of Exercise 37 so that the point bounces inside a square.

39. Revise the program of Exercise 38 so that the point leaves a "trail" as it bounces between the walls.

ALGEBRA APPLICATIONS

Exercises 40–43 require a background in first-year algebra.

40. Input two real numbers. Without actually multiplying the numbers, determine whether their product is positive, negative, or zero.

41. Given the coordinates of a point in the *xy*-plane, decide the number of the quadrant in which the point lies. Assume that the point does not lie on an axis.

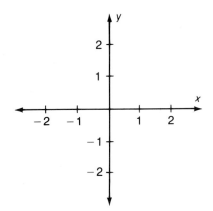

42. Expand the program of Exercise 41 to cover points that are on either axis or both.

43. Given a number X and a whole number N, calculate X^N without using the ↑ operator of **BASIC** (or its equivalent on your keyboard).

APPENDIX:

WORD PROCESSING

This Appendix provides an introduction in a *self–study format* to two popular word processing programs—the **Bank Street Writer** and **SCRIPSIT**®.

This Appendix may be studied independently of the text. However, it is suggested that the Appendix be used after covering the two-page optional lesson on *Word Processing* on pages 86–87 of the student text.

Appendix A: Bank Street Writer

A–1   **Entering and Saving Text**

A–2   **Retrieving and Editing Text**

A–3   **Centering, Printing, and Erasing**

A–4   **Moving and Indenting Text**

Introduction

These lessons are for the Apple II+ and IIe versions of the Bank Street Writer. Most procedures are the same for the versions of the program for other computers. It is assumed here that you are familiar with the Apple keyboard and with the steps for booting the machine and loading a program from a disk.

First Step

Obtain a Bank Street Writer disk from your teacher. You will also need a data disk to save what you write. Put the *Bank Street Writer* disk in drive 1 and turn on the computer. Read the title screen and the first screen after the title. With an empty "text box" on the screen, you are in **Write Mode**.

WORD PROCESSING ACTIVITIES

1. What symbol is showing as the cursor?

2. Type your name. All letters will be small letters. Now press the left arrow key (◄—). What happens?

3. Use the left arrow key to erase your name.

4. **a.** If you are using an Apple II+, press the ∧ symbol (shift N). Then type the first letter of your name. What happens?

   b. If you are using an Apple IIe, hold down either **SHIFT** key and type the first letter of your first name. What happens?

5. Finish typing your complete name. Capitalize the first letter of each name. Then continue typing this sentence

   "(Your name) is now learning how to use the Bank Street Writer."

   If you make a mistake, use the left arrow key to move the cursor back and then type over the error. When you reach the end of a line on the screen, do **not** press the **RETURN** key. Instead just keep typing. What does the program do when you reach the end of a line on the screen?

6. Use the left arrow key to erase the sentence you typed. Then type the following paragraph. The width of the lines on the screen will not match the width below. If you make a mistake, use the left arrow key to move the cursor back to the error and retype. When you have typed the paragraph, press **Return** (after the word "printer").

> Any computer must perform four functions: storage, input, processing, and output. Main storage is usually called memory. The most common form of input for microcomputers is a keyboard. Processing is done by a microprocessor. Output goes either to a CRT screen or to a printer.

7. Press the **Escape** key. This puts you into **Edit Mode**. Read the new prompts at the top of the screen.

8. Press the **Escape** key again. This returns you to **Write Mode**. Then go back to **Edit Mode**.

9. Save the paragraph you have written. Follow these steps.

   a. Place the computer in **Edit Mode**. Look at the choices at the top of the screen. You want the **TRANSFER MENU**.

   b. The choice **ERASE** is highlighted. On the Apple II+, press the left arrow key. On the Apple IIe, press the "open apple" key just to the left of the space bar. Either way, the words **TRANSFER MENU** should now be highlighted. Press the **Return** key.

   c. A new menu appears at the top of the screen. **RETRIEVE** is highlighted. Press the space bar. Now **SAVE** should be highlighted.

   d. Take the *Bank Street Writer* disk out of drive 1 and replace it with a data disk. If the data disk has been **initialized** (prepared to accept data), go on to **f** below.

   e. If the data disk has not been initialized, press the right arrow key (on the Apple II+) or the "solid apple" key just to the right of the spacebar (on the Apple IIe). Now the choice **INIT** (initialize) should be highlighted. Press **Return**, and answer **Y** to the question asked. Then type **GO**. The computer will now initialize the disk. When it is finished, press left arrow (on the Apple II+) or open apple (on the Apple IIe) to highlight **SAVE**.

   f. With **SAVE** highlighted, press **Return**. Answer **Y** to **SAVE ENTIRE FILE?** . To the question   **DO YOU WANT A CATALOG?** , type **N**. Then type a name for the file in the spaces provided at the top of the screen. It is suggested you use your first or last name. When asked for a password, just press **Return**. The drive should start and, after a short pause, **FILE SAVED** should appear at the top of the screen.

10. After another pause, the menu with **RETRIEVE** highlighted reappears. Press the right arrow (on the Apple II +) or the closed apple (on the Apple IIc) key three times to highlight **QUIT**. Press **Return**. To the question   **ARE YOU SURE YOU WANT TO QUIT NOW (Y/N)?**   , press **Y**. The computer will now leave the *Bank Street Writer* program. The screen is cleared and a] appears in its upper left. Remove your data disk from the drive.

SUMMARY

A. When the *Bank Street Writer* is loaded, it begins in **Write Mode**. In this mode, you can enter or correct text.

B. Whatever you type in **Write Mode** goes into memory and on the screen. The cursor (__) marks your place on the screen.

C. When entering text when you reach the end of a line, you *need not* press **Return**. The program automatically *wraps around* the text. That is, a word started at the end of one line is moved to the beginning of the next line.

D. The left arrow key (◄—) moves the cursor back and erases any character in its path.

E. On the Apple II +, you type a capital letter by first pressing ∧ (Shift N) and then typing the letter. On the Apple IIe, hold down either **Shift** key to type a capital.

F. In **Write Mode**, pressing the **Escape** key converts to **Edit Mode**. In **Edit Mode**, pressing the **Escape** key converts to **Write Mode**.

G. To save what you have written onto a disk, place the computer in **Edit Mode**. Select the **TRANSFER MENU**, then **SAVE**. Type a name for the disk file.

H. You can initialize a disk by selecting the **TRANSFER MENU** and then **INIT**.

I. To end a session, select the **TRANSFER MENU** and then **QUIT**.

PROJECT

Load the *Bank Street Writer*. Type at least two paragraphs summarizing what you have learned thus far in your Computer Literacy course. Then save what you write onto a data disk. Do not use the same file name you used for Exercise 9 on page 323.

A-2 RETRIEVING AND EDITING TEXT

WORD PROCESSING ACTIVITIES

1. Load the *Bank Street Writer* program. Then remove the *Bank Street* disk and replace it in drive 1 with the data disk containing the file you saved in Section A–1.

2. Press **Escape** to enter **Edit Mode**. Select **TRANSFER MENU** and then **RETRIEVE**. If you wish, you may have a **CATALOG** of files on the disk printed. Then type the name you used to save the file. (The computer loads the file into memory. It will soon appear on the screen.)

3. Press **Escape** twice to return to **Write Mode**. The cursor should be at the beginning of the paragraph.

4. In **Edit Mode** press the **B** key. What happens?

5. Press the **E** key. What happens?

6. **a.** On the Apple II +, press the **J** key several times. What happens?

   b. On the Apple IIe, press the left arrow key several times. How does the result differ from what happens when you press that key in **Write Mode**?

7. **a.** On the Apple II +, press the **I** key several times. What happens?

   b. On the Apple IIe, press the up arrow key several times. What happens?

8. **a.** On the Apple II +, press the **K** key several times. What happens?

   b. On the Apple IIe, press the right arrow key several times. What happens?

9. **a.** On the Apple II +, press the **M** key several times. What happens?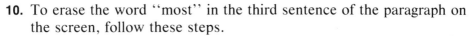

   b. On the Apple IIe, press the down arrow key several times. What happens?

10. To erase the word "most" in the third sentence of the paragraph on the screen, follow these steps.

    a. In **Edit Mode**, move the cursor until it is under the **"m"** of "most."

    b. Press **Escape** and return to **Write Mode**.

    c. Press the right arrow key five times. What happens on the screen when you press the right arrow key the fifth time?

11. To add a sentence between the second and third sentences of the paragraph, follow these steps.

   a. Press **Escape** and go to **Edit Mode**.

   b. Move the cursor so that it is under the **"T"** at the beginning of the third sentence of the paragraph.

   c. Press **Escape** and return to **Write Mode**.

   d. Type this sentence.

   Disks are used for secondary storage.

   (Be sure to press the spacebar twice after the period.) Describe what happens on the screen as you type the new sentence.

12. To change "**CRT**" in the last sentence to "tv", follow these steps.

   a. Press **Escape** and go to **Edit Mode**. What happens to the paragraph on the screen when you do this?

   b. Press **E** to jump to the end of the text.

   c. Move the cursor under the "**C**" of "**CRT**".

   d. Press **Escape** to return to **Write Mode**.

   e. Type "**tv**" (without the quotation marks).

   f. Erase "**CRT**" by pressing the right arrow three times.

13. The paragraph on the screen should now read as follows. If it does not, try to change it until it does.

   Any computer must perform four
   functions: storage, input,
   processing, and output. Main storage
   is usually called memory. Disks are
   used for secondary storage. The
   common form of input for
   microcomputers is a keyboard.
   Processing is done by a
   microprocessor. Output goes either to
   a tv screen or to a printer.

14. Follow the steps in Exercises 9–10 on pages 323–324 to save the file. Use the same name you gave the file in those exercises.

SUMMARY

A. To load a text file from a disk, select the **TRANSFER MENU** on the **Edit Mode** menu and press **Return**. Then select **RETRIEVE** by pressing **Return**. When the program asks for the file name, type it.

B. In **Write Mode**, pressing the **Escape** key converts to **Edit Mode**. In **Edit Mode**, pressing the **Escape** key converts to **Write Mode**.

C. It is important to remember these characteristics of **Edit Mode**.

    a. Pressing **B** moves the cursor to the beginning of the text.

    b. Pressing **E** moves the cursor to the end of the text.

    c. On the Apple II+, pressing the **I**, **J**, **K**, or **M** keys moves the cursor **up**, **left**, **right**, or **down** respectively, without erasing any characters in its path.

    d. On the Apple IIe, pressing any of the four arrow keys on the bottom right of the keyboard moves the cursor in the indicated direction without erasing any characters in its path.

D. To insert one or more characters within the text, go to **Edit Mode**. Move the cursor to the position where the addition is to start. Return to **Write Mode** and type the new text.

E. To erase characters within the text, go to **Edit Mode**. Move the cursor to the place to the left of where the erasure is to start. Press the right arrow key once for each character to be erased.

PROJECT

Load the *Bank Street Writer.* Then **RETRIEVE** the disk file containing the paragraphs on your Computer Literacy course that you wrote and saved for the Project on page 324. Make changes in what you wrote by erasing words, changing words, and adding words and sentences.

Save the paragraphs again. Use the file name you used on page 324.

A-3 CENTERING, PRINTING, AND ERASING Bank Street Writer

WORD PROCESSING ACTIVITIES

1. Load the *Bank Street Writer* program. Then remove the *Bank Street* disk and replace it in drive 1 with the data disk containing the file you saved in Exercise 14 on page 326.

2. Follow the steps in Exercises 2–3 on page 325 to **RETRIEVE** the file you saved at the end of the lesson and to enter **Write Mode**.

3. To type a centered title for the paragraph, first press the **Control** and **C** keys simultaneously. Describe what happens on the screen.

4. Immediately after the **CENTER** arrow, type this title.

Components of Any Computer

Then press **Return** twice.

5. The title will not be centered on the screen. However, it will be centered when you print the file. The **CENTER** arrow applies to all text typed until **Return** is pressed.

6. Go to **Edit Mode** and move the cursor to the end of the text. Then return to **Write Mode**.

7. Press **Return** twice. Then add the following paragraph to the text. Remember to press **Return** only at the end of the entire paragraph.

   Computers come in three sizes. Very large computers,
   called mainframes, usually fill an entire room.
   Computers about the size of a desk are called
   minicomputers. And a microcomputer can sit on a desk.
   But each type of computer can perform the four
   functions listed in the first paragraph.

8. To obtain a printout of the text, follow these steps.

   a. Go to **Edit Mode**, select the **TRANSFER MENU**, and press **Return**. Then move the cursor to select **PRINT–FINAL** and press **Return**.

   b. For each question printed at the top of the screen, press **Return**. Before pressing **Return** after the prompt **WHEN PRINTER IS READY PRESS RETURN**, be sure the printer is turned on and has paper loaded.

9. Is the title centered on the printed copy?

10. Go to **Edit Mode** and select the **ERASE** option. Follow what the program tells you at the top of the screen to erase the last paragraph that you typed in Exercise 7.

    How does the program mark on the screen the text to be erased?

11. With the **Edit Mode** menu back on the screen, select the **UNERASE** option. What happens on the screen? To restore the paragraph to the text, answer **Y** to the question asked.

12. **Save** the complete text using the same file name you used in Exercise 14 on page 326. Then **QUIT** the program.

PROJECT

Load the file you saved on page 327. Add a centered title to the text. Print the file. Then practice erasing and unerasing parts of the text. Finally, save the file with the title. Use the same file name.

A–4 MOVING AND INDENTING TEXT   Bank Street Writer

WORD PROCESSING ACTIVITIES

1. Load the *Bank Street Writer.* Then remove the program disk and replace it with the data disk containing the file you saved in Exercise 12 on page 328.

2. **RETRIEVE** the file you saved in Exercise 12 on page 328.

3. In **Edit Mode**, move the cursor to the end of the text. Then go to **Write Mode** and add the following paragraph to the text. What happens when the screen box is filled with text?

   > The first generation of computers used vacuum tubes. The second generation used transistors. Integrated circuits filled the third generation. The current microcomputers are the fourth generation of computers.

4. To move the third paragraph of the text ahead of the second, go to **Edit Mode**. Select **MOVE** and press **Return**. Then follow the directions the program gives. How does the program mark the block of text to be moved?

5. After the third paragraph has been moved ahead of the second and if no changes were made in the third paragraph, you may go to **Edit Mode** and select **MOVEBACK**. Put the paragraph back where it was.

6. To **INDENT** the third paragraph, go to **Edit Mode**. Place the cursor at the beginning of the third paragraph. Then in **Write Mode**, press the **Control** and **I** keys at the same time. What happens on the screen?

7. To see what the text now looks like, obtain a printout of it. Follow the steps of Exercise 8 on page 328. How is the third paragraph printed?

8. Return to **Write Mode**. Press the **Control** and **S** keys at the same time. What do you see on the screen?

9. Save the text onto the data disk. Use the same file name you have been using. Then **QUIT** the program.

SUMMARY

A. To move a block of text from one position to another in a document, go to **Edit Mode**. Then select **MOVE**, press **Return**, and follow the directions the program gives.

B. Text can be returned to an original position if the return move is made immediately after the first move. Select the **MOVEBACK** option in **Edit Mode**.

C. In **Write Mode**, you can find out how much room remains in memory for more text by pressing the **Control** and **S** keys at the same time.

PROJECTS

1. Load the file you saved for the Project on page 329. Practice moving blocks of text from one point in the document to another. Immediately after moving a block, move it back to its original position.

2. Obtain a *Bank Street Writer* manual. From the manual, find out how to use the **FIND**, **REPLACE**, **DELETE**, **RENAME**, and **PRINT–DRAFT** features.